Mexican A
A Brief History

Mexican Americans in Texas: A Brief History

Third Edition

Arnoldo De León
ANGELO STATE UNIVERSITY

HARLAN DAVIDSON, INC.
WHEELING, ILLINOIS 60090-6000

Copyright © 1993, 1999, 2009
Harlan Davidson, Inc.
All Rights Reserved.

Library of Congress Cataloging-in-Publication Data

De León, Arnoldo, 1945-
  Mexican Americans in Texas : a brief history / Arnoldo De León. — 3rd ed.
    p. cm.
  Includes bibliographical references and index.
  ISBN 978-0-88295-268-0
  1. Mexican Americans—Texas—History. 2. Texas—History. 3. Texas—Ethnic
relations. I. Title.
  F395.M5D37 2009
  976.4'0046872--dc22
                                                    2008040503
                                                    CIP

Front cover photo: Unidentified woman holding a parasol with a U.S. flag used as
a backdrop. Attributed to a studio photographer in Beeville, Texas, ca. 1910s. The
UT Institute of Texan Cultures at San Antonio, No. 81-149. Back cover photo:
ASU Photo of Arnoldo De León by Danny Meyer.

13 12 11 10 09 1 2 3 4 5 VP

Contents

Preface

Serious scholarly study of Mexican Americans in Texas dates back only to the early 1970s. It is true that before that decade historians wrote on the Spanish colonial era (circa 1519 to 1821) and even touched on some aspects of Texas-Mexican life during Mexico's rule of the province (1821–36). But their interests stopped there, for they assumed that Tejano society collapsed when Anglo Texans established an American rule following the 1836 war for Texas independence against Mexico. A smattering of theses, dissertations, and academic articles on Mexican Americans did appear before 1970, but by and large historians mistakenly believed that Tejanos lacked a distinct history worthy of scholarly attention.

In the late 1960s, however, there appeared in Mexican-American communities throughout the United States what is termed the "Chicano Movement," an ethnic-charged explosion of cultural pride that called for fundamental changes in society. Among other things, activists in colleges and high schools throughout different parts of the nation—supported by faculty members, community leaders, parents, journalists, bureaucrats, and others—demanded the dismissal of racist educators, the alteration of a curriculum they viewed as ethnocentric, the recruitment of more Mexican-American teachers and administrators, and the development of classes in Mexican-American history. Inside academe, scholars heeded the cry by concentrating their research on what came to be known as

"Chicano Studies," a scholarly inquiry that utilized revisionist approaches to meet several objectives: to wit, determine the origins and degree of the subordination of Mexican Americans throughout the United States, chronicle the Mexican-American participation in the historical process, and ultimately attempt to integrate the Mexican-American experience into United States history.[1] Some historians chose to narrow their field of inquiry to the history of Mexican people in the state of Texas; their efforts during the last four decades have yielded a rich harvest of scholarly work. This survey acknowledges that literature.

In writing Chicano history, many scholars follow an unwritten assumption that the history of Mexican Americans in the United States began when citizens of Mexico became American citizens. The year 1848 would, therefore, be the logical starting point, for it was then that the United States, victorious in the War with Mexico (1846–48), acquired the modern-day states of California, New Mexico, Arizona, Colorado, and parts of Utah and Nevada. The Treaty of Guadalupe Hidalgo, which ended the war, gave U.S. citizenship to the Mexican residents of those territories. In comparison, Mexicans living in Texas became citizens of the Texas Republic when Anglo Americans acquired Texas's independence from Mexico. Though Mexican people in Texas were not technically U.S. citizens until 1845, when Texas became a state in the Union, historians recognized 1836 as the year in which Texas Mexicans became an ethnic group, since for all intents and purposes Anglo citizens of the Republic of Texas were ideologically and culturally Americans.[2]

More recently, another group of historians has questioned the year 1848 (or 1836 in the case of Texas) as the inception of Mexican-American history. In the considered judgment of this school, the history realistically begins in the last decades of the nineteenth century or the first decade of the twentieth. Before then, the Mexican-American population amounted to only a few thousand people and immigration from Mexico did not significantly modify the culture of pre-existing Mexican-American communities—nor for that matter did it spark waves of xenophobia across the nation. Mexican Americans, moreover, were players in an essentially rural economy, so that those inter-racial conflicts that did occur typically involved competition over land, business (such as freighting and the cattle trade), and natural resources. A deeply ingrained racism governed social relations in that age.

This second group of scholars argue that with the close of the frontier and the turn of the twentieth century, Mexican-American history took a dramatic turn that marked its distinctiveness and therefore its beginning. The economic structure of the United States changed considerably during this period. American multinational corporations operating in Mexico caused great upheaval there, forcing rural villagers to search for work elsewhere, many times in the United States. The mass trek of immigrants into the United States overwhelmed older settlements of native-born Mexican Americans, unmooring their cultural bearings. New tensions surfaced, not necessarily linked to old, rural-based controversies but to heavy immigration and its impact on Mexican-American communities and the nation. Earlier racial views now fused with class interests to pit a large and exploitable workforce of Mexican-American laborers against white workers and the interests of an increasingly corporate (and often callous) America.[3]

A third school of historical thought disagrees with both of the above frameworks. To advocates of this view, Chicano history extends all the way back to the colonial era, when Spaniards first explored New Spain's Far North and made contact with its indigenous peoples. These scholars remind us that in the case of Texas, Spanish Mexicans were the first people to transplant European civilization to the region, people who contributed strongly to Texas's material culture, named numerous places and rivers, and were the predecessors of today's Mexican-American Texans. Spanish-Mexican pioneers carried forth into the American epoch their cultural accouterments, institutions, survival mechanisms, sentimental attachment to the land of their birth or upbringing, approach toward land usage, agricultural work rhythms, family and gender relations, and numerous other aspects of community living.

Stressing continuity, such scholars note that Tejano society did not face exhaustion in 1836 but crossed nationhoods without much disruption. This line of analysis seems imperative to correct the pre-1970s scholarship that minimized the historical role in Texas of people of Mexican descent by implying that Tejano civilization became inert at the moment American rule supplanted Spanish-Mexican rule. Thus the first two chapters of this book attempt to bridge the history of Spaniards and Mexicans who lived in the land we now know as Texas as well as that of Mexican Americans who maintained an uninterrupted residence in the state as Texian and then American citizens.[4]

During the last forty years, in part because of the influence of the Chicano Movement, historians have written Tejano history from approaches that stress the mistreatment of Tejanos by whites, Tejano resistance to that victimization, but also the strides Mexican Americans voluntarily took in order to meld with the mainstream society.[5] In these pages I recognize those themes, but I also consider the process of acculturation, the class status *within* the Tejano population itself, and the diversity that separates Tejanos living in the various geographic regions of the state. I am particularly interested in portraying Texas Mexicans as subjects in the ongoing Texas story and not merely as objects in another people's history.

Another consideration in the writing of Chicano history is terminology. Throughout the book, I use different words to identify people of Spanish-Mexican descent. The term "Tejanos" refers to persons of Mexican origin, regardless of nativity, who resided or reside within the modern boundaries of Texas from the early eighteenth century to the present. I use the term "Texas Mexicans" to describe Mexicans in Texas after 1821, at which time settlers severed their ties with the Spanish empire and became citizens of a new sovereignty, namely the independent country of Mexico. Though the government of the Republic of Texas gave Tejanos a new citizenship after 1836, Tejanos continued to refer to themselves as "Mexicans," and, in any event, Anglo Americans called them by that name, albeit disparagingly. I also use the word "Mexicans" broadly to include both native- and foreign-born Texans of Mexican descent. I use "Mexican American" synonymously with the above terminology, but only in discussing the period after 1845, the year in which people of Mexican ancestry in Texas became citizens of the United States, for "Mexican American" implies U.S. citizenship, whether by birth or naturalization. The term "Chicano" was not used in public discourse until the 1960s, so it does not appear herein until Chapter Nine, where it is placed in proper historical context: in that era the word came to symbolize a particular political ideology and a cultural emphasis on Mexico's heritage, including its pre-Columbian past. I reserve the use of the terms "Hispanic" and "Latino" for the post–1976 era, when they became part of the popular lexicon, again to identify individuals of Spanish-Mexican descent. Folks who migrate from Mexico are referred to as "immigrants."

In writing this book, I also have tried to keep a particular student audience in mind. *Mexican Americans in Texas* may be used as a core text for classes that deal specifically with the history of Mexican Americans in Texas (Tejanos) or as a useful reader to supplement courses in Mexican-American, Texas, and United States history.

The second edition of *Mexican Americans in Texas* appeared ten years ago. Our purpose in reissuing this popular classroom text is to bring the student readership up to date on the ongoing Tejano chronicle as reflected in the ever-expanding body of scholarship that constitutes Tejano historiography. Certainly, not every new contribution to the field of Mexican-American history in Texas has been incorporated into this third edition: some of the studies are too specialized or too narrowly focused; other recent works are significant but elaborate on events and issues already a part of the second edition. I acknowledged the value of these works in the appropriate endnotes. However, new works that alter or modify our previous knowledge of Tejano history, add fresh perspectives to our understanding, or unearth valuable new information prompted me to revise what I had presented earlier. Some of these important books and articles are cited in the text; all of them are referenced in the endnotes, which for the serious student of Tejano history will, I hope, serve as a thorough and current bibliography.

In addition to having incorporated the pertinent new literature, I attempted to add a more human dimension to the Tejano story by opening each chapter with a brief vignette that captures the tenor of the age. Some of these stories tell of harrowing fates that befell individuals, others relate accounts of common courage, while still others document the drama of high achievement. The passage of ten years since the publication of the second edition of *Mexican Americans in Texas: A Brief History* necessitated some coverage of more contemporary times, and I have done so by adding a new chapter that encompasses the first few years of the twenty-first century. Many have been the strides made by Tejanos during the last decade. These achievements may be attributed to the decline of obstacles faced by earlier Mexican Americans, but they are also the product of individual and community resourcefulness as well as specific actions taken by Tejano office holders who have increasingly come to serve at the city, county, and state levels. In Chapter 11, I have sought to capture a moment in time approximately two decades before Mexican-Americans will comprise, according to some predictions, the majority population in the Lone Star State.

Happily, Tejano history has thrived in recent decades, and this third edition of *Mexican Americans in Texas* is richer for the effort. The future remains bright for a field that has now won broad recognition within mainstream Texas history.

I wish to thank Thomas H. Kreneck, Special Collections Librarian/ Archivist at Texas A&M University—Corpus Christi Bell Library, for his help in acquiring a number of photographs that appear in this book. I also owe a debt of gratitude to numerous scholars who made suggestions for revisions of my original manuscript, but the remarks of three readers were especially helpful. My special thanks go to Jesús F. de la Teja of Texas State University-San Marcos, Richard Griswold del Castillo of San Diego State University, and Emilio Zamora, Jr., of the University of Texas. Dr. Zamora's insightful commentary proved particularly valuable and led me to rethink some of the book's earlier themes.

Arnoldo De León
Angelo State University

CHAPTER ONE

Texas: A Spanish Outpost, 1716–1790s

The town consists of fifty-nine houses of stone and mud and seventy-nine of wood, but all poorly built, without any preconceived plan, so that the whole resembles more a poor village than a *villa,* the capital of so pleasing a province.[1]

Fray Agustín Morfi, 1778

Father Morfi, writing about San Antonio de Béxar in 1778, was misleading in his observation that the town had been built "without any preconceived plan." Actually, local *presidio* Captain Juan Antonio de Almazán had followed a strict blueprint when he platted the Villa of San Fernando (today's San Antonio) in 1731 after fifty-six immigrants from the Canary Islands arrived there as the municipality's first settlers. He complied with royal decrees that had historically mandated the manner in which towns were to be laid out in Spain's New World empire. Captain Almazán thus located the new community in the proximity of a water source (the San Antonio River), close to a presidio (that of San Antonio de Béxar), and on a slight elevation for protection. Methodically, Almazán mapped out the streets of the would-be settlement, denoted the place for the plaza, chose sites for the church and administrative buildings, and assigned lots to the citizens.[2]

By the 1770s, the descendents of the Canary Islanders (no longer of "pure" European blood, as they had been drawn into the process of racial mixing so common on frontiers) were living a hardscrabble existence—one considerably different than that they had visualized for themselves as a once-privileged European group. Like fellow settlers on the hinterlands, they found it difficult to improve on the lodgings such as the ones described by Morfi.

Iberian and Indian Roots

Mexican Americans in Texas descend from people whose ancestry is Spanish and Mexican Indian. After the Spanish conquest of present-day Mexico in the early sixteenth century, Iberian males intermixed with Indian women. Cultures also blended, and those people of a fused heritage and culture moved northward from Mexico and laid the foundation for what would become Mexican-American communities in the United States. Since that time to this day, immigrants to Texas from Mexico continue to bring aspects of a common past with them. The history of Mexican Americans, then, may be traced to the Iberian Peninsula.

People from Spain themselves owe their heritage to several civilizations. Like other Europeans, Spaniards became indebted to the Greeks, borrowing much concerning laws and traditions. Rome contributed extensively to Spanish life as well, imposing on Iberia its political institutions, language, and religion. Germanic groups, namely the Visigoths, dominated Spain from the fifth century to the eighth, but the invaders ended up melding their own way of life with that of the cultures they vanquished. When the Muslims conquered Spain around A.D. 711, they preserved native customs and institutions but implanted the best traditions of their native North African civilization.[3]

The Muslim conquest opened a new chapter in Spanish history. During the next seven centuries, the Spaniards waged a war to repel the Moorish invaders and regain control (both politically and religiously) of their nation—the campaign called the *reconquista* (reconquest). Not until the year 1492 did the king's *conquistadores* (conquerors) overwhelm the last of the Moors and succeed in extricating them from their last line of defense in Granada, a city in southernmost Spain. With matters at home finally settled, the powerful Spanish crown was eager to explore the known world in hopes of increasing its wealth. Coincidentally, one Christopher Columbus, sailing under the flag of Spain, departed from Europe in a westerly course with the objective of finding a shorter route to the Indies. Instead, he unexpectedly encountered a new world with new peoples when he landed in the islands now known as the Bahamas on October 12, 1492.

The Madrid government now took up the task of assembling an overseas empire by subduing the "New World" peoples and their lands. Leading the advance into the mainland of modern-day Latin America were conquistadores whose mission and spirit resembled that of those who had regained the Iberian Peninsula from the Muslims. One such conquistador, Hernán Cortés, directed the attempt in 1519 to establish Spanish domination of present-day Mexico. As his armed entourage marched west from the Gulf Coast towards the interior, it encountered resistance from indigenous tribes, whom they defeated with superior European weapons and, inadvertently, by spreading deadly diseases to the tribespeople. Convinced that Cortés's apparent invincibility on the battlefield marked the Spaniard as Quetzalcoatl, the legendary god prophesied to return from the eastern seas to reclaim his lost lands, the Aztec emperor Montezuma dispatched envoys to show the foreigners into the beautiful capital city of Tenochtitlán, built on an island in Lake Texcoco. At Tenochtitlán (today's Mexico City), the Aztecs presented the Spaniards with gold, slaves, and other presents. After a time, however, the foreigners wore out their welcome. In June of 1520, the Aztecs massed to evict the invaders. The Spaniards attempted an escape from the island city over a causeway, on which the Aztecs surrounded and killed many of the would-be escapees, destroying more than forty of their horses and forcing the surviving Spaniards to scuttle their treasure in the bottom of the lake. That evening became known in Spanish history as *la noche triste* (the sad night).

By April of 1521, however, the Europeans were back in Tenochtitlán, this time better prepared. For three months the Aztecs withstood a Spanish siege of their city, but finally the invaders took the town block by block. Cuauhtémoc, the nephew of the slain Montezuma, surrendered Tenochtitlán in August 1521, thereby paving the way for the ruthless Spanish domination of the indigenous Indian population throughout the rest of the region.[4]

The Spanish Colonial Era in Texas

EXPLORATION

Now the Spaniards wanted to find and conquer more new lands, hopefully ones with riches as valuable as those they found in Tenochtitlán. The reports of one Álvar Núñez Cabeza de Vaca whetted their appetites. Cabeza de Vaca and three others had been shipwrecked in 1528 on an island near present-day Galveston. After six years of coexisting with local

Indian tribes, Cabeza de Vaca and company traversed today's southern and western Texas, finally reaching New Spain—as the modern-day country of Mexico was called until the 1810s—in 1536. Upon arriving in Mexico City, the castaway reported tales of great riches that lay to the north of the lands he had roamed.[5]

Hurriedly, the royal government ordered two expeditions into the unexplored lands of the northern *frontera* (frontier). In 1540, Francisco Vásquez de Coronado directed one of these probes, but failing to find anything of substance in what would become New Mexico, he headed eastwardly into the present-day Texas Panhandle. The conquistador encountered nothing to substantiate Cabeza de Vaca's claims, so his expedition retreated to the interior of New Spain without having fulfilled its mission of conquering valuable territories.[6] Follow-up efforts to discover wealth in New Spain's Far North (the region that belonged to Mexico until 1848 and today constitutes the Southwestern United States) met similar defeat.

In subsequent decades, the crown pressed beyond the lands of the early conquests, colonizing the lands of New Spain and South America. Not until the early eighteenth century, however, did the Spaniards see fit to settle Texas permanently, though exploration and Catholic missionizing among the Indians had persisted intermittently. In 1716, in response to French activity along the Texas coast, the government in Mexico City dispatched Domingo Ramón to present-day East Texas. Behind Ramón marched an entourage of some twenty-six soldiers, about twelve missionaries, and several families. Ramón's party colonized a site that eventually became Nacogdoches. Two years later, Martín de Alarcón also headed northward with instructions to plant a colony that would serve as a midway point between outposts in New Spain's interior and the forts and missionary sites in the eastern part of the province. This expedition founded the presidio of San Antonio de Béxar and the mission of San Antonio de Valero along the San Antonio River.[7] In 1731, fifty-six immigrants from the Canary Islands (most of them of common stock—fishermen, farmers, and ordinary laborers) arrived there. Other efforts to protect the coast and Christianize surrounding indigenous tribes explain the origins of La Bahía (Goliad), where the Crown had erected a presidio and mission in 1721. In 1749, Spanish officials relocated the site westward along the San Antonio River in anticipation of the establishment of two civilian communities.[8]

Authorities delayed colonization along the Rio Grande until the 1740s and 1750s, but then executed some of the most successful settlement projects in New Spain's Far North. That success may be attributed to the commitment and foresight of José de Escandón, who colonized regions on both banks of the river, among them Laredo (though the belt of land between the Rio Grande and the Nueces River belonged to the state of Tamaulipas until 1848).[9]

POBLADORES

No more than a few thousand souls inhabited the land north of the Nueces River throughout the colonial era. As of the early 1730s, these *pobladores* (settlers) numbered about 500.[10] A census taken in 1777 counted 3,103 people in the territory: some 2,060 of these lived in the San Antonio complex of the town proper, one presidio, and five missions; 696 made their home in La Bahía; and 347 resided in Nacogdoches. By the 1780s, some 700 people inhabited the river community of Laredo. Although some of them earned their livelihood from urban vocations, the majority did so as ranchers or ranch hands.[11] In the eyes of these Spanish frontierspeople, it was their responsibility to hold the province for the crown and ward off foreign interlopers.

In the earliest stages of colonization in Texas, the imperial government had recruited settlers from among those conditioned to frontier living, but eventually populating the colonies depended on a voluntary migration. Though movement northward never intensified, people arrived in Texas from New Spain villages in the colonial provinces of Coahuila and Nuevo León, others from places as far away as central New Spain.[12] A variety of forces urged migrants to head toward the frontier. Oppressive conditions on the *haciendas* (large rural estates owned by Spanish families and worked by laborers bound to the institution by debt peonage) or in colonial towns, for instance, motivated the more intrepid to search out new surroundings. Talk of better working conditions and improved pay in northern mines or ranches also enticed many into braving the trek north into the unknown. The prospect of finding legal or extralegal employment on the frontier as a merchant, a peddler of contraband goods, or even as an outlaw also lured folks away from the land of their upbringing and thrust them into a migratory wave. Natural disasters such as droughts and severe downturns in New Spain's economy further induced pioneers to strike out for the borderlands.[13]

Still, the reasons why people from New Spain did not migrate to imperial outposts in great numbers are not difficult to ascertain. Fatal diseases frequently afflicted the population, thereby blunting pressures of

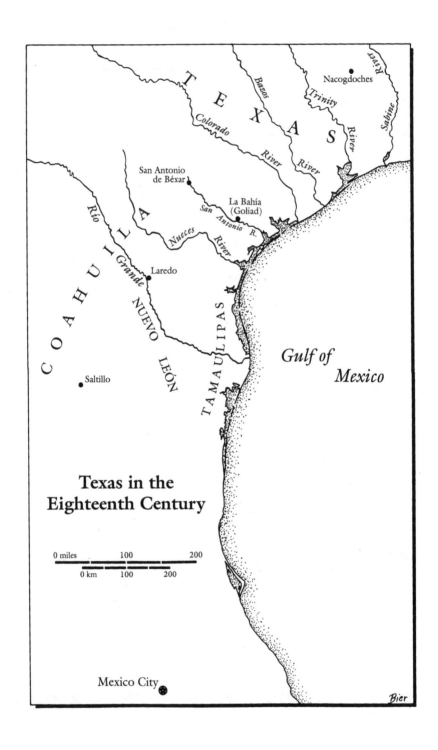

TEXAS

Nacogdoches

Brazos
Trinity
River
Sabine River

Colorado

River

River

San Antonio
de Béxar

La Bahía
(Goliad)

San Antonio R.

COAHUILA

Nueces

River

Río
Grande

Laredo

NUEVO LEÓN

TAMAULIPAS

Gulf of
Mexico

Saltillo

Texas in the
Eighteenth Century

0 miles   100   200

0 km   100   200

Mexico City

Bier

overpopulation that frequently have compelled people to relocate. Facing labor shortages, hacienda owners deterred the mobility of the rural masses, sometimes using brute force to prevent the escape of those wanting to flee the grim living and working conditions on the big ranches. Finally, towards the latter decades of the eighteenth century, the crown faced less external threats from foreign competitors and thus pursued a more relaxed colonization policy.[14]

THE FRONTIER ADVANCE

One can associate New Spain's advancement toward the frontier country with four well-known institutions. These mainstays of Spanish colonization had their genesis during the reconquista but developed further in Spain's New World empire. On New Spain's northern frontier and elsewhere, the crown counted on these institutions to claim and colonize unsettled territories and stimulate the pioneer economy. Around them community life converged and cultural life flowered. They gave pobladores a needed feeling of familiarity in a region starkly detached from major centers of population.[15]

The Mission As a pioneer institution, the mission served to bring new lands under the king's dominion, expand the empire, and execute imperial designs. Primarily, however, it sought to save the Indians' souls and covert Native Americans into Catholics and, not incidentally, loyal Spanish subjects. Apart from their immediate tasks of converting Indians, the missionaries ministered to civilian settlers, government officials, and soldier-settlers by performing a variety of spiritual services such as administering the sacraments at birth, marriage, and death. Recent research by Robert E. Wright, however, argues that diocesan (secular) clergy actually ministered to most civilian communities in Texas by the latter half of the eighteenth century. From them, and the missionaries, all family members learned the Church's beliefs or had them reaffirmed. Still, the missions served functions other than religious ones. Foremost, they became magnets for unofficial settlements. Pobladores gravitated towards the mission compounds, which generated economic activity and socialization. Missions continued their good work of propagating the Catholic faith until well into the eighteenth century.[16]

The Presidio The *presidio* (military garrison) served to defend the frontier. Strategically placed to guard conquered territories and, hopefully, to help lay claim to new ones, presidios quartered soldiers charged with protecting civilians and mission friars from attack by hostile Indians and policing the missions to ensure that the converted Indian neophytes continued their religious training and work in the mission fields, gardens, and groves.[17]

The presidio's presence, furthermore, stimulated demographic and economic growth. Not infrequently, soldiers traveled to their frontier posts accompanied by their entire families. The presidio also enticed local recruits attracted by the military pay, privileges, and uniform. Presidio soldiers often married women from nearby communities, and older soldiers sometimes chose to remain in Texas at the end of their military careers, further augmenting the size of the colonial population. Finally, the presidios became commercial centers in which farmers sold their agricultural goods, ranchers exchanged livestock products, townsfolk conducted mercantile transactions, and tailors, smiths, and other artisans plied their trade.[18]

The Rancho The Spaniards introduced the *rancho* (ranch) into the borderlands as still another agent of colonization. Although its primary function was to sustain civilian life, over time the institution served a multitude of purposes: it helped to safeguard remote sections of the empire from foreign threats; it contributed to the work of the missionaries by producing foods needed to nourish the padres and the neophytes; it furnished civil communities with beef, wool, hides, and tallow; and it supported the task of the presidios by supplying the soldiers with oxen for plowing, mules for hauling, and horses for cavalry.[19]

Stock for ranch operations in Texas derived from the abundance of horses, cattle, sheep, and hogs that had been left in Texas by the pre-eighteenth-century military expeditions (due to unfitness, stampedes or other accidents, or for the intended purpose of propagation). Expeditions undertaken after the 1710s also brought fresh animals to the region. The earliest stockmen in Texas were actually the missionaries, for the Crown had given the Church the first grants of land. Recent scholarly studies find mission lands in the 1760s overrun with semiwild stock. The padres claimed these *mesteños* (ownerless stock) as their own, but settlers took from the herds in desperate efforts at frontier survival.[20]

During the middle eighteenth century, ranching entered a flourishing era, primarily in Central Texas in the land between the San Antonio and the Guadalupe rivers, considered by the historian Jack Jackson as the cradle of Texas ranching.[21] In San Antonio, industrious stockmen produced meat, soap, and candles for nearby markets and the local presidio, made tallow and hides for export, and manufactured protective leather gear for the soldiers from cattle by-products. In the distant Piney Woods of East Texas, landowners raised fine horses, especially around the Nacogdoches area. In modern-day South Texas, in the expanse between the Rio Grande and the Nueces River, another pastureland thrived, containing unnumbered heads of cattle, sheep, and horses.[22]

By the 1770s, Tejanos had established commercial relations with French Louisiana and Nuevo León and Coahuila in northern New Spain. Tejanos conducted a good amount of trade in cattle and horses for manufactured goods and tobacco from east of the Sabine River, even as royal decrees discouraged such trade as contraband.[23] Additionally, Texas cattlemen drove herds southward below the Rio Grande during the 1770s and 1780s. Yearly, ranchers and merchants journeyed to Saltillo (in the state of Coahuila), where north met south for a fair each fall. At the Saltillo fair, Tejanos could pick from merchandise such as spices and salt, clothes and boots, cosmetics, tableware, or liquor either imported from Europe or manufactured in the interior of New Spain, buying such goods or acquiring them in exchange for their own Texan wares, among them cowhides, dried meat, sheepskins, tallow, and other ranch commodities.[24]

The Farms While the frontierspeople planted some crops, few pursued farming on any large scale. Several factors underlay this phenomenon. First, the pioneers banked on a ranching future tied to their illicit trade with Louisiana. Second, poor roads inhibited travel—and thereby the shipping of crops to markets—cutting into profit margins. Third, farming demanded field hands but labor was always in short supply on the frontier. Finally, frontierspeople preferred to ranch, for, unlike standing crops, livestock could be moved to evade raids by hungry Indians.[25]

Farms, therefore, amounted to little more than hardscrabble ventures. In San Antonio and its vicinity, townsfolk, soldiers and their family members, and Hispanicized Indians worked small vegetable garden plots with oxen and farm implements as could be improvised on the frontier, relying on the waters of the San Antonio River and San Pedro Springs for irrigation. In the town of Nacogdoches, frontierspeople raised corn and wheat on residential lots or on surrounding land parcels to supplement their food supplies. Since Tejanos found farming neither a simple undertaking nor a profitable enterprise, foodstuff shortages, primarily corn, were common during the eighteenth century.[26]

The Towns To secure dominion over new lands and defend them, the crown depended on still another frontier institution—the civilian settlement. Four urban sites existed in Texas during the colonial period: Nacogdoches and Goliad were dependent outcroppings of their local presidios, missions, and ranches; San Antonio and Laredo had been founded according to royal ordinances regulating the creation of towns. Within urban spaces, colonists earned a living in various ways. Some worked as government bureaucrats, while craftsmen—including merchants, housebuilders, cobblers, tailors, blacksmiths, and barbers—rendered valuable services to the presidios and missions. Unskilled workers turned to unspecialized tasks, and Hispanicized Indians eked out a living as servants. Finally, an assortment of individuals such as jobless migrants or transient peddlers found ways to survive on the urban scene. Others used the settlements as bases for commuting to their place of work. These included clergymen (ordained and secular) opting for city living, *rancheros* (ranchers) overseeing their stock operations in absentia, *vaqueros* (cowhands or range hands) working seasonally on the range, and *arrieros* (freighters) transporting foodstuffs, supplies, and building materials between different points in Texas.[27]

In municipalities pobladores faced living conditions not much better than those in remote rural areas. But like their counterparts on the ranchos, city dwellers undertook initiatives to improve their quality of life. Communities launched efforts to establish schools, a difficult undertaking due to lackluster support from the Crown. The building of homes amounted to an enormous task considering the isolation in which the settlers lived, but they tapped the flora around them, gathering stones, mesquite wood, and coarse grass to construct *jacales* (huts) and mud (which they mixed with grass) to make *adobes* (mud-walled homes).[28]

Furthermore, the urbanites contended with many other adversities. With practically no sewage system on the frontier and water often fouled by human and animal waste or rotting carcasses, townspeople faced the constant outbreak of epidemic diseases such as smallpox and cholera. Health care was often nonexistent, as medical personnel preferred the security afforded by the larger cities in the interior of New Spain. Drifters, malcontents, and social misfits the towns attracted only added to the daily concerns of the permanent residents. As if all of this was not bad enough, the fear of attack by hostile Indians hung over the heads of everyone.[29]

FRONTIER COMMUNITY

Isolation, the need for mutual protection, and the shared desire to maintain a degree of political independence from the crown induced diverse elements of frontier society to come together to form a community. In time, even the Canary Islanders abandoned their inclination to remain aloof and formed a bond with the other residents of Béxar. Ultimately there evolved in Texas a unique frontier identity based on shared circumstances, family ties, and friendships that united folks from different social strata and racial ancestry, as well as those from the ranches, farms, presidios, missions, and towns.[30]

In frontier communities settlers accepted their purpose for being in the Far North, respected those royal decrees that they deemed appropriate for maintaining an orderly society, and abided by common-law practices adaptable to the new lands.[31] Culturally, whole communities had common familial arrangements, architecture, foods, religious beliefs, and language. In San Antonio, for example, Bexareños carried on numerous traditions customary to the frontier, several of which were practiced during December. In that month, they celebrated their perseverance in the province by holding festivities, which included the observance of the days of the Immaculate Conception and the Virgin of Guadalupe, as well as bullfights, games, and dances. In between the fall harvest and the spring livestock branding and planting, the tradition of rejoicing in December persisted until the time of the Texas war for independence in 1836.[32] Yet Tejano culture was not solely the product of the frontier communities; some of the prominent families of Béxar partook in the lifestyle of the prosperous city dwellers of Saltillo by vacationing or maintaining houses there, or by sending their children to the schools of that important city.[33]

Living on the periphery of the empire, Tejanos determined their affairs according to immediate needs and concerns. Local interests came before imperial policy, and Tejanos rejected the crown's efforts to dictate life on the frontier.[34] Thus, they defied forced compliance with rules of civilized behavior prescribed by the Church and the crown. Instead settlers practiced a lifestyle that sought relief from an often dull and dreary life. They organized *fandangos* (festive dancing events) in their own homes wherein those attending took to drinking, carousing, and, from the point of the view of the crown, unruly comportment. Even though officials frowned upon the sport of horseracing—because organizers generally held them on holy days and observers were inclined to gamble and commit other transgressions—the contests went on. Soldiers themselves violated royal regulations that prohibited their intermingling with the local women; many soldiers courted women from nearby civilian settlements, wed them, and started families.[35]

Social Divisions Even though life on the frontier tended to blur social distinctions, colonial Texas society was not without them. Bureaucrats from New Spain's core, presidio officers assigned to the province, rancheros with large herds of livestock, and town merchants selling large quantities of goods to the missions, presidios, and ranches constituted an entrepreneurial sector. As a socioeconomic group, they owned the better homes, worked the more productive ranch lands, and earned the better incomes. They were the ones most creative in developing interstate trade in livestock and goods produced on the frontier. That said, they did not command deference from the less affluent or deserve special privileges. In reality, they were no different from the rest of the population in their upbringing, amount of schooling, manner of dress, or racial origin. Their status hinged almost solely on their material accumulation. The above description applies to the standing of the Canary Islanders, who over time relinquished their elite status through intermarriage with the local Bexareños. Some descendants of the original Canary Islanders did, however, manage to perpetuate a degree of relative affluence.[36]

Underneath the top-level stratum lived the majority of Tejanos, most of them ranch hands, weavers, cobblers, and day laborers. This group also included some Indian converts who lived marginally in the missions, the presidios, and the ranches. People did not belong to the lower class due to their ethnic background but because of financial misfortune or disadvantage.[37]

Mixed Bloods Demographers who study the size of Texas communities in the colonial era note high birth rates but a slow population growth. In remote societies such as those in the Far North, many factors inhibited natural reproduction, including a high rate of infant mortality and the high toll of hazardous frontier living on the adolescent and adult populations. Furthermore, people on the frontier had poor diets and faced recurrent shortages of agricultural products, improper medical attention, and extremely poor sanitary conditions. While the news of Indian attacks in the province continued to discourage immigration from New Spain's interior, demographic expansion still resulted principally from in-migration.[38]

Most Tejano pioneers during the colonial era were the product of *mestizaje* (the unions of European Spaniards and African slaves with the native Indian peoples). By the seventeenth century, much of the population of New Spain were *mestizos* (a label applied to the offspring of Spanish males and Indian women). Though this element composed the majority population in Texas, various other racial categories existed, including Christianized Indians, mulattoes, and Spaniards, all of whom further amalgamated the province racially.[39]

Censuses taken in the 1780s actually enumerate more Spaniards than any other classification, but such figures distort actual ancestry. Demographers know that the term "Spanish" did not necessarily identify European, white-skinned Spaniards; instead, it represented a social categorization. In fact, racial makeup could be "upgraded" on the frontier, as one's racial constitution did not bar upward social or economic mobility. Realistically, the term "Spaniard" identified those worthy of a certain status because of accumulated wealth, family connections, military standing, or even distinguished service to the community. European Spaniards, therefore, included but a few government or church appointees. The rest of those labeled Spaniards by the census enumerators were undoubtedly mixed-bloods who "passed" as Spaniards. As noted, the Canary Islanders of San Antonio themselves intermixed with the New Spain–born population; within two generations after their arrival, no "islander" could claim undiluted blood.[40]

Women on the Frontier Most pioneer women in colonial Texas lived ordinary lives similar to those of their counterparts in the other northern provinces of Tamaulipas, Nuevo León, or Nuevo Mexico. As a group, women in Texas possessed privileges denied their Anglo-American counterparts in the thirteen British colonies at the time, among them the right to judicial redress and the right to own property (acquired through land grants, for instance) whatever their marital status. Married women could keep any income earned by the couple and they could assign power of attorney to husbands who could then conduct business on their wife's behalf. Whether single or married, women qualified for land grants, and the record shows several Tejanas (generally of the upper stratum of society) to have been property owners. While some of these women inherited their real estate, others received grants from the Spanish government because of a desire to increase acreage for expanding livestock herds or because (as in the case of widows) they needed a form of livelihood to sustain their family. Among the largest land holders in Texas during the late colonial era were María

Gertrudis de la Garza Falcón, owner (upon her husband's death) of the 300,000-acre Espiritu Santo Grant in contemporary Cameron County, and Rosa María Hinojosa de Ballí, who presided over a successful ranch estate (inherited from her husband and father, the original grantees) that spanned several modern-day South Texas counties. When Doña Rosa died in 1803, she left to her heirs a successful ranching enterprise comprising immense herds of livestock and thousands of dollars in property value.

While women on the frontier escaped the more severe proscriptions imposed on them in the heartland—as the hardships of the Far North acted to temper the roles that differentiated the sexes—male society dictated specific tasks to women, primarily household chores. In the home, wives and mothers were expected to perform many services for their husbands and families; these included cooking the meals, raising and passing on cultural values to the children, tending the garden plot, making household necessities such as soap, spinning material for cloth, and nurturing family members during stressful times.

Furthermore, women lived with slim expectations for improved conditions. Colonial society deemphasized literacy, for reading and writing commanded little value on the frontier. Professional occupations, always limited to a minority of the population, were invariably closed to women. Some aspects of the legal system were also discriminatory. Ending a marriage through divorce, for example, amounted to a major feat, and society tended to ostracize divorcees. As a political bloc, moreover, women mustered little power.[41]

THE LATE EIGHTEENTH CENTURY

Toward the last decades of the eighteenth century, historical circumstances altered New Spain's relations with the mother country and incidentally the crown's continued domination of Tejanos. First, the Enlightenment's emphasis on equality and the rights of Man undermined the thoughts by which the imperial government ruled its possessions throughout Latin America. The example set in 1783 by the North Americans' successful break from England, furthermore, inspired Spain's New World colonists to reconsider their subject state. Finally, in the last decades of the eighteenth century, Spain proved inept at dealing with international affairs, embroiling itself in hostilities with France and England. To Latin Americans these costly conflicts seemed senseless. Colonists were pressed with increased taxation and forced donations to help Spain finance and prosecute its wars. Widespread resentment within Spain's colonies ensued.[42]

Other events unraveling in Texas further enfeebled the precarious imperial presence in the province. The missions, long fixtures of life on the frontier, declined as centers of Christianization. Enlightenment thinkers back in Spain condemned the Church, the Crown sought ways to cut expenditures, threats by foreign powers from east of the Sabine River had dissipated, mission Indians persisted in their dissatisfaction with efforts at their conversion to Catholicism, and Tejano ranchers, coveting the mission herds, called upon royal officials to cease government support of the missions. In the 1790s, the government ordered the closing of all Texas missions (a policy known as "secularization").[43]

Also by this period, economic fortunes in Texas began to decline. While ranching had gone through cycles of birth and development up to midcentury, it experienced a decline in the 1790s due, ironically, to the excessive number of cattle that had been driven east to Louisiana and south into provinces below the Rio Grande, as well as to the widespread slaughtering of cattle that roamed public lands. In the face of the downturn, influential families in San Antonio struggling to stay solvent became even more resentful of royal authority and its taxation decrees.[44]

And generally, throughout most of New Spain, job openings and prospects for a better lot in life decreased during the final years of the colonial period, producing broad discontent among commoners and growing criminality and banditry. In San Antonio, for instance, opportunity for upward mobility lessened.[45]

In this mood, political dissatisfaction heightened. In the last decades of the 1700s, the crown assigned officials to the province of Texas who were more dedicated than their predecessors had been to the serious enforcement of royal decrees, such as those dealing with the cattle industry. Accustomed to a certain amount of autonomy, Tejanos resisted the new encroachment upon their affairs and protested what they perceived as unjustified and meddlesome supervision.[46]

CHAPTER TWO

Under Three Nations:
Spain, Mexico, and the Texas Republic,
1790s–1836

It was the morning of March 6, 1836, and the eight-year-old lad, along with his father, mother, and four siblings, had already endured some thirteen days of grapeshot designed to take down the walls of the Alamo at San Antonio de Béxar. The army of Antonio López de Santa Anna intended to starve out the defenders sworn to die for the cause of Texas liberty. The siege had taken its toll on the men whom the boy had come to know by sight if not personally: most were tired, hungry, cold, and sleep deprived.

Suddenly, around 5:30 that morning, he awoke to his mother's sharp warning that "the soldiers have jumped the wall"! Thunderous discharges from lethal weapons both inside and outside the Alamo gripped him, the gunfire turning darkness into daylight. The men guarding the top of the Alamo walls, exposed in order to fire back at the attacking columns, dropped to the ground, dead or mortally wounded. The boy could hear the frantic sounds of the attackers attempting to climb the Alamo walls, as well as their shrieks of fright or agonizing in death as the Texians shot at them point blank. He could imagine both the valiant stand being taken by the defenders but also the enemy soldiers' dogged determination to claw their way past the volunteers. From his place of refuge, he grasped the exact moment when Santa Anna's troops opened the gates from the inside, letting more attackers pour in for the final strike.

He heard cannon fire, this time obliterating nearby doors, for the enemy had now turned the Alamo's heavy guns on the Texians and their supporters taking cover inside the Alamo compound. Man-to-man combat became evident, made unmistakable by the steely clashes of swords, bayonets, and muskets, as well as the grunts of men driven by adrenalin. Suddenly, the noises stopped, signaling an end to the carnage. The Mexican troops informed the boy and his family that they would not be harmed. Thus did Enrique Esparza, son of the Alamo defender Gregorio Esparza, live to tell the ghastly tale of the fall of the Alamo.[1]

Identity in the Far North

As Spain's presence in the Far North approached an end in the waning years of the eighteenth century, the core government estimated that 5,000 people inhabited the region that constitutes Texas today. About one-half of these resided in San Antonio de Béxar and its surrounding missions (among them the Alamo). Another 1,200 pobladores made La Bahía their home, and approximately 500 persons lived in Nacogdoches. The river settlement of Laredo (still a part of New Spain's state of Tamaulipas) was home to some 1,400 people according to the last census taken by Spanish authorities in 1819.[2]

By this time, the people of Texas and other parts of the Far North practiced a variation of the culture found in New Spain below the Rio Grande. Royal institutions such as the church, the bureaucracy, and the military had not greatly influenced the pobladores. Instead, argues the noted historian David J. Weber, the immediate environment and local circumstances had played more powerful roles in socializing the frontierspeople. Remoteness from the center of imperial power had conferred upon them a social space, and through time they had developed modes of conduct appropriate to their frontier existence. Given the situation, borderland society was inclined to be more receptive to new thoughts, sentiments, and patterns of living.[3]

Residence in the Far North molded a culture with discernible traits. In the wilderness expanse, the pobladores strove to implant Spanish civilization and protect the region even as the royal government in Mexico City neglected them. This experience, according to Weber and other students of the Far North, fomented a particular regional identity that was a variant of New Spain's culture. Isolation engendered egalitarianism, a sense of duty, and a respect for physical prowess and gallantry in the face of adversity.[4] Those living in Texas accepted a similar ethos, adapting a familiar ranching culture to the new land, enduring the rigors that accompanied life on the range, devising means of wringing a profit from contraband trade (primarily with Louisiana), and taking political stands expressing regional desires. In such a surrounding, there developed an ethic for self-reliance and the feeling that local needs held priority over the expectations of the crown.[5]

By the last years of colonial Texas, several influential families still lived in the province. Concentrated primarily in San Antonio, their concerns also centered less on imperial goals and more on their immediate problems. Citizens did not look kindly on soldiers and crown officials who arrived in the early 1800s to reinforce the province against westering citizens from the United States. The new military presence taxed the capacities of the local economy, and a streamlined and more efficient administration produced unwanted royal decrees regulating political and economic life.[6] The solidification of frontier-minded individuals in the north plus the rise of a prominent circle of Bexareños with their own ideas and interests, particularly in local matters, acted by the early nineteenth century to strain relations between the province and the central government in Mexico City.

HIDALGO'S GRITO

In the last decades of the eighteenth century, New Spain began to reassess critically its colonial standing. The Enlightenment and the American Revolution had stirred notions of freedom among many residents of New Spain, and, as mentioned, tighter controls over the colony's administration had bred discord among the privileged classes. The masses by this time had come to associate the Spanish regency with callous misrule. When in 1810 a curate named Miguel Hidalgo y Costilla raised a cry for independence in Dolores, Guanajuato, on the *Diez y Seis de Septiembre* (September 16), folks from different classes rallied to his cause. But the war against bad government quickly took an ominous turn, becoming a social revolution of the lower classes against their Spanish oppressors, both native- and foreign-born.

Within weeks, therefore, of the *"Grito de Dolores"* ("Cry of Dolores") Tejanos faced the dire choice of either joining or renouncing Hidalgo's movement. Like their counterparts in other corners of the Spanish empire, some considered insurrection an act of disloyalty, while others received it heartily. Hence, when a retired presidial officer named Juan Bautista de

Las Casas headed a military uprising in Béxar to remove the few crown officials still there in January 1811, he attracted followers within the local presidio as well as among some of the less fortunate of the town's civilians, though some people of high station in the community also supported him firmly. The rebellion soon widened, as patriots in other Texas settlements took up Hidalgo's struggle against royal authority.[7] Las Casas, however, proceeded to confiscate property and cattle, jail people, and, with sundry other acts, estrange many important citizens, including many who had originally assisted him in his insurgency. Soon he faced a challenge from important rancheros troubled by his rash behavior.[8]

Therefore, on March 1, alarmists from the church, the military, and some of the influential ranching families of San Antonio succeeded in forming a counter-rebellion, ousting Las Casas and taking control of the town. For his impudence, crown officials in Coahuila shot Las Casas in the back on grounds of treason, decapitated him, and forwarded his head to Béxar so that citizens could witness firsthand the punishment for taking up arms against royal power. Later that month, Father Hidalgo, the major leader of the insurrectionary forces against the crown, met defeat on the battlefield near the city of Guadalajara and suffered the same fate as Las Casas.[9]

Not all the distinguished families in San Antonio had supported the restoration of royalist influence in reaction to Las Casas. In August 1812, as a matter of fact, another group of Béxar leaders and ranchers welcomed one Bernardo Gutiérrez de Lara, who, claiming to be carrying on Hidalgo's dream of an independent Mexico (as New Spain was now called), entered Texas from Louisiana and seized Nacogdoches. From there, Gutiérrez de Lara and his Republican Army of the North (whose ranks included both Mexican and Anglo filibusters), marched toward Béxar and La Bahía, subduing both communities and raising their independence flag over the province in the spring of 1813.

Select families in Béxar endorsed Gutiérrez when he appointed a junta.[10] Ill-advised deeds, however, swiftly put off many in the town, as Gutiérrez committed atrocities in the region, including the execution of the royalist governor. Nonetheless, to regain command of the province, crown representatives in the interior of Mexico directed Commandant General José Joaquín Arredondo to march into Texas to break the republican movement. In August 1813, Arredondo accomplished his mission and expelled the rebels. Through incarceration, the sequestering of private properties, and the arbitrary execution of suspected conspirators, the Spaniards had reasserted crown governance but further aggrieved the province's citizens.[11]

Several of the oldest rancho families of the province made their way to Louisiana to escape Arrendondo's wrath. There, José Antonio Navarro, one of the Tejano ranchers turned refugee, and some of his peers survived as common workers near Opelousas, Attakapas, and Bayou Pierre. The wealthy ranchero Erasmo Seguín, who was accused of treason and had his property confiscated, suffered similarly in Louisiana. Others took to the wilderness. José Francisco Ruíz, for example, remained with Texas Indian tribes for several years. Many other influential Tejanos who did not succeed in reaching sanctuary met their death at the hands of Arredondo's military men.[12]

Following Arredondo's purge, crown representatives lorded over Tejanos, eking out a survival from whatever abandoned fields and ranches could produce, by force of arms. Opportunistic individuals in the province made use of the chaos to confiscate property adjoining their own or to take a neighbor's belongings. Raids by hostile Indians increased, adding to the turmoil and forcing landowners to practically abandon stock raising.[13] By 1821, when Mexico got its independence from Spain, the number of inhabitants in Texas had declined to about one-third of what it had been before Hidalgo's "Cry of Dolores." In East Texas, the nearly depopulated settlement of Nacogdoches struggled to remain in existence.[14]

La Independencia: Texas Under Mexico's Rule

On September 27, 1821, triumphant armies marched into Mexico City, marking the winning of Mexico's independence from Spain. For Tejanos, the change of sovereignties caused little disruption in daily life or behaviors. The people of Texas passed into the new age with their identity intact and confident of their ability to affiliate themselves with the political and economic structure now before them.

Among cultural trappings surviving into the 1820s intact were many associated with rancho work. Riding gear that the Spaniards had fashioned after that of the Moors was still employed on Texas ranches, as were methods of handling stock: annual roundups that determined ownership of wild animals; the branding of cattle and horses; and, naturally, range terminology. The manner of working sheep similarly persisted, so that *pastores* (sheep herders) abided by customs practiced since their forefathers arrived in Texas in the first expeditions of the 1710s.[15]

Aspects of the Iberian legal tradition also endured, such as those pertaining to women. In Mexican Texas (1821–36), a woman retained the title to property she held at the time of matrimony. (In the United States during the same era, the newlywed surrendered any such possession to her husband.) Wives, moreover, laid equal claim to assets earned while married, gains made during the marital state became the community property of the couple, and the husband could not dispose of said property without his spouse's consent. Society respected a woman's power to negotiate contracts and a widow's or unmarried daughter's right to handle the affairs of her own estate.

Customs protecting debtors similarly persevered. The Spaniards had followed the tradition holding that working persons in debt could not, by demand of the creditor, be dispossessed of the means by which they earned their livelihood; thus work animals, as well as necessary gear and other implements, could not be confiscated except to indemnify the king or an overlord. Similarly, laws during the Mexican period in Texas acknowledged a common man's right to retain his tools, field animals, and even his land despite his degree of indebtedness.

This cultural baggage passed not only from Spanish to Mexican rule, but to American domination of the province, as Anglo Texans absorbed many aspects of the land's Spanish heritage after 1836. To this day Texas ranch terminology preserves terms such as "lariat" (*la reata*), "lasso" (*lazo*), "stampede" (*estampida*), "buckaroo" (*vaquero*), "cinch" (*cincha*), and common loan words like mesquite, burro, and corral. The highly competitive American sport of rodeo traces its beginnings to the Iberian custom of performing an annual cattle roundup to clarify ownership. The Spanish legacy to post-1836 Texas is also apparent in the work methods and vocabulary of modern-day sheep and goat raisers.[16]

TOWN LIVING

During the years of Mexico's rule over Texas, Tejanos continued to live in the old localities of central and southern Texas, surviving on their agrarian skills. Others, however, preferred to reside in the three urban communities that had been established in the 1710s and 1720s: San Antonio, Goliad, and Nacogdoches. According to one census count, about 2,500 souls lived in the province in 1821.[17] Their numbers soon increased. Juan Almonte, who toured Texas in 1834 on a fact-finding mission on behalf of the government in Mexico City, reckoned that San Antonio (and its rural environs) was home to about 2,400 Tejanos, Goliad for 700, and

Nacogdoches for 500. Victoria, a new settlement founded by the ranchero Martin de León in 1824, had a population of 300 that year. To the south of these Central Texas towns lay the tenacious settlement of Laredo, home to about 2,000 people in 1835.[18]

The towns were home to small groups of skilled tradesmen and merchants, though by no means were these professions avenues to a life of ease. The former still found it difficult to find stable employment in a predominantly pastoral economy, while the latter, primarily in San Antonio, engaged chiefly in buying merchandise in Mexico—bedding, footwear, and dry goods—and reselling it locally. Merchants generally descended from those having land, livestock, political power, and social prestige.[19]

Townfolk generally assumed efforts (through donations, for example) to provide schooling for their children when neither the government nor the church (which under both Spain and Mexico had a prerogative over such matters) could fulfill their commitment to education. When and where they existed, schools relied on the Lancastrian system of education, a method that utilized advanced students to teach those in lower grades. Young charges learned the fundamentals of arithmetic, reading and writing, Catholic doctrine, and civics. But in a frontier society, the provision and maintenance of a sound educational system did not hold priority over matters of survival. Therefore most children in Texas went unschooled.[20]

Throughout the 1820s and 1830s, the church, confronted with political and other assorted problems in the interior, struggled to serve the spiritual needs of those in the province. Still, it managed to give basic ecclesiastical care to pobladores. During the late colonial period, bishops in the Far North had successfully ordained men from the region, and it was this clergy (assisted by lay church members) that assumed diocesan responsibilities in Texas when during the 1820s the Church finally terminated its connection to the missions. Texas priests ministered not solely to urban believers, but they also rode across the countryside spreading the Catholic word to isolated ranchsteads. Common folks, meanwhile, expressed their devotion to Catholicism in more personal ways. Many built home altars while those living out in the hinterland erected private chapels. Mothers led their families in home prayer or the recitation of the rosary. Parish communities often came together to celebrate the *día de la Virgen de Guadalupe* (Our Lady of Guadalupe, on December 12) or Holy Week, or to start off a secular holiday (such as the *Diez y Seis*) with a mass celebration.[21]

RANCHING AND FARMING

Wild horses and cattle continued to wander freely throughout Central and South Texas at this time. Neglect, violent storms, and Indian raids had dispersed many a herd. As had their ancestors during the colonial period, rancheros around San Antonio tracked down mesteños as a source of livelihood, but now the government intervened by enacting decrees that regulated the capturing, branding, marketing, and butchering of the wild animals.[22] To an extent, government regulation got in the way of the ranching industry's expansion, but Bexareños devised ways to make unreported beef sales to the local soldiers and families and even to covertly export herds to Louisiana and Mexico south to the Rio Grande.[23]

In the trans-Nueces region there roamed additional cattle and horse stock, some of it tamed, much of it wild, but almost wholly available to men of enterprise. Since the late eighteenth century, grantees had struggled to found the ranching industry there: frequently by entrusting local cowhands to manage their affairs as they retreated to the safety of the river communities, sojourning back to inspect their ranching concerns as the occasions arose. Constant Indian attacks forced the area's pioneers to abandon their homes periodically, but their invariable return bore an increasingly successful claim to the region by the late 1820s. Town dwellers in Laredo during the same period similarly ventured into neighboring rural properties to establish ranches; these undertakings created new occupations for commoners and increased the landowners' benefits.[24]

Farming in Mexican Texas still remained as unappealing to Tejanos (for reasons previously given) as it had during the colonial years. What little of it existed amounted to subsistence horticulture. In San Antonio, Bexareños worked family-owned tracts, while more fortunate property owners cultivated vegetables, grains, fruits, and even cotton in irrigated fields. Any surplus agricultural products went to local markets. Rarely did the farms in Texas yield enough for exchange outside the province.[25]

SOCIETY

As it had been before 1821, socioeconomic condition and not race primarily distinguished classes in Mexican Texas. Government position, membership in a prominent family, business achievement, and land ownership might make one eligible for elite status. On the other hand, *peones* (commoners) who performed unskilled labor and were of a mixed-blood or Indian stock constituted the lower stratum, though being a peon did not preclude one's rising in class; wealth, if acquired, could elevate the peasants to a higher social category.[26]

The elite, whose wealth by outside standards was not immense, tended to be literate, and they enjoyed certain privileges. They tried to provide for their children's education, sometimes sending them to private institutions in Coahuila or hiring local tutors. They held their own dances to which attendance by the poor was discouraged. During special occasions, the affluent led ceremonial processions down the main streets or gave speeches at important events; such roles magnified their status as members of the upper class. Politically, it was the better established that expressed opinions. Plain folks either voiced sentiments resembling those of their providers or remained detached from the realm of politics.[27]

WOMEN

Men's attitudes toward women and gender roles passed sovereignties without modification. Tejanas continued to suffer from old restrictions. The male-oriented culture of the Tejanos discouraged political activism among women by barring them from holding office or voting. Cultural dictates still subordinated women to men and attempted to confine women to the home. Societal norms also imposed a double standard of moral behavior: husbands could be unfaithful and escape censure, but an unfaithful woman incurred ostracism from frontier society and even the wrath of the law, which permitted confiscation of an adulteress's property. Marriages were not easily dissolved; indeed, the law could compel wives to stay in an unhappy union. Similar to other Western cultures of the era, women in Mexican Texas attended first to their husbands at meal time, then withdrew to eat apart.[28]

In this frontier atmosphere, women still rendered a valuable service to society. As wives and mothers, they sought to maintain family stability and acted as guardians of Spanish-Mexican values and morality. Some volunteered for religious work, becoming spiritual mentors to parishioners or the organizers and coordinators of religious functions. Tejanas similarly engaged in promoting civic festivities, such as during patriotic holidays. To women, of course, fell the duty of midwifery, and many Tejanas earned well-deserved local recognition for their abilities in tending to women in childbirth.

Women of the wealthier class fulfilled frontier tasks as capably as did ordinary Tejanas, but given their financial means they also saw to the education of their children and to ensuring they received the proper religious upbringing. For the purpose of having church doctrine readily available, they donated funds to have church buildings constructed locally. Wives of the well-to-do also became efficient at managing ranches in the absence of their spouses. Responsibilities included supervising the servants, giving orders to the working crews, transacting livestock business, and handling the ranch's finances.

Among Tejanas who excelled at such multitasking was Señora Patricia de la Garza de León. In 1824, she arrived in Central Texas with her husband Martín (to found the town of Victoria), and until her husband's death in 1834 worked zealously to see that their colony evolved into a successful venture. She seriously concerned herself with religious, civic, and educational matters in Victoria in an effort to create a proper place where her family—and those of others who had colonized the town with them—could prosper. Though left with a large family when her husband died, she rose to the task of running her ranch property to the extent that by the 1830s, the de León family ranked among the wealthiest in Texas.[29]

Different than Doña Patricia but equally successful with land enterprises was Ana María del Carmen Calvillo. Doña Patricia had been able to take up public leadership roles because of her status as a widow; María Calvillo could not display open determination, as Spanish Mexican society frowned on single women. María had broken up with her husband, and was thereafter independent. Nonetheless, Calvillo resisted male-dictated strictures, and through the force of self-determination and resolve she made a going concern of ranch property she inherited from her father in 1814. At its peak of success, the ranch featured a fair-sized labor force, an irrigation network, a granary, and of course a large livestock herd. María Calvillo died in 1856, having been in her lifetime a citizen of Spain, Mexico, the Republic of Texas, and the United States.[30]

ANGLO AMERICANS ARRIVE IN TEXAS

Mexico not only inherited Spain's heritage but the old country's problems in the Far North. Texas, particularly, faced the menacing encroachment of Anglo Americans from the east who seemingly edged closer to the Sabine River with each passing year. Mexico was quite concerned about the Anglos' westward tide, but as of 1821 demographic forces in the Mexican interior still were not pressuring citizens to migrate north. After weighing different plans to augment the Tejano population, the new government

in Mexico City finally opted to encourage European and American immigrants to settle in the northern province in order to counteract threats
posed by other national powers and hostile Indians.

In so doing, Mexican leaders had continued an immigration policy
begun in early 1821 when the Spanish crown granted to Moses Austin, a
Missouri entrepreneur, a contract to settle three hundred Catholic families
in Texas. When Austin died that summer, his son Stephen accepted the
agreement and founded a settlement on the Brazos River.[31]

SETTLEMENT AND REACTION

Tejano property holders had long dreamed of seeing their part of the Far
North prosper. They saw excellent promise in the immigration program
adopted by the state of Coahuila and Texas—when Mexico established a
new government after achieving independence from Spain, Texas became
a section of the state of Coahuila—in 1825, which invited settlers from
the United States. Tejano leaders greeted Anglo arrivals warmly, for they
hoped that large numbers of immigrants would offer protection from the
region's roving Indian tribes and recovery from the general devastation
created by the turmoil of the 1810s: the rancho economy would be resurrected, new lands turned into productive cotton fields, and commercial
activity would be stimulated. For industrious Texas Mexicans, the new
order would mean unbounded trade spreading to regions beyond the Rio
Grande, to Coahuila, and even to Nuevo México and the westernmost parts
of the United States. Understandably, therefore, Bexareño entrepreneurs
backed efforts to persuade the Mexican government to exempt the new
arrivals from payment of such taxes as custom duties and tariffs. They
also helped the new Anglo settlers, many of whom were slaveholders, to
stave off abolitionist efforts.[32]

By the late 1820s, the Mexican immigration policies had, in the
view of the national government, worked much too well, for the Anglo
settlers had designs other than discharging their responsibility to act
as good Mexican citizens and protect the province from interlopers. In
the eastern section of the province they had implanted their own way of
life, broken agreements such as their promise to practice Catholicism (a
condition upon which they had become Mexican citizens), and engaged
in private land speculation and smuggling.[33]

In what may have been Mexico's first gesture to reverse a policy gone
awry, President Vicente Guerrero in 1829 issued directives freeing all slaves

throughout the country. But influential Tejanos teamed up with leading Anglo spokesmen such as Stephen F. Austin to win a temporary respite; after hearing the case for needed labor, the government decided not to apply the manumission decree to the province. The next year, however, Mexico turned to a more decisive course, passing the Law of April 6, 1830, to slow immigration from the United States by prohibiting the importation into the province of African American slaves or indentures.[34]

Though a government receptive to both Tejano and Anglo Texan needs came to office in Mexico City in 1833, it lasted only until 1835, when Antonio López de Santa Anna assumed power in the capital. By then, some 35,000 Anglo Americans had streamed into the eastern areas of Texas, creating increased concerns in Mexico over the possibility of a separatist revolt in that area.[35]

THE ANGLO TEXAN REBELLION 1835–1836

Anglos, however, had always objected to stricter regulations regarding commerce in the Gulf ports, collection of tariffs, abolitionist talk, and efforts to strengthen military forces in the province. In 1835, therefore, they joined the resistance movement emerging throughout Mexico against Santa Anna's regime. Texan troops clashed with Mexico's forces at San Antonio de Béxar from November through December. More than sixty Tejanos assisted the Anglo Texans in taking Béxar from Mexican troops on December 11. Among Tejanos leading units in the assault was Captain Juan N. Seguín. Many of the families who had participated in the Mexican independence movement of the 1810s again aligned themselves with the concerns of the Texas region. On the other hand, numerous Tejanos, even among the social elite, sided with Mexico against the Anglo Texans. The majority of Tejanos, however, took a neutral stand on the hostilities.[36]

Determined to smother the Texas rebellion in the same manner as he had one in Zacatecas, Santa Anna (duly authorized by the Mexican congress) headed for Texas with a force of 6,000 soldiers. Not all of Santa Anna's soldiers qualified as professionals, however. His army comprised many untrained conscripts, political prisoners, and Mayan Indians who had been impressed into the military even though they lacked a command of the Spanish language.[37] The firearms with which Texas would be conquered, moreover, hardly ranked with the latest in weaponry. Cavalry units carried smoothbore muskets that had been acquired from the British after the English army had condemned them as obsolete; they had a range of some seventy-five yards. The operation also was devoid of medical staff; the army included no trained physicians and only a minimum of essential medical supplies.[38]

On February 23, 1836, the Mexican army arrived in Béxar. Santa Anna then laid siege to the Alamo, one of the town's old missions, in which Texan and Tejano volunteers led by William Barret Travis had taken refuge. While Santa Anna prepared for the assault, the volunteers inside the Alamo planned their defense. Finally, after thirteen days, Santa Anna ordered 1,100 of the 2,600 men with him at the Alamo to attack and give no quarter. But the attackers found the Alamo a difficult fortification to crush. Like other strongholds that the Spaniards had constructed, the mission's purpose was defense—indeed, its designers had positioned it on elevated ground so as to permit defenders a good view of would-be attackers rushing toward its eight- to nine-foot walls. Moreover, those inside the Alamo had already fortified it with twenty-one artillery pieces, making it the best-equipped military installation between New Orleans and Monterrey, Mexico. Furthermore, the defenders (numbering between 240 to 260) enjoyed an advantage in small weapons, possessing knives, handguns, and, most significantly, Kentucky long rifles, which many inside the compound used expertly.

As the Mexicans charged, the Alamo defenders greeted them with deadly fire. Downed immediately were those carrying ladders; consequently, the officers and the experienced soldiers in this first wave found it impossible to scale the high stonewalls of the fortress. For the moment, the attack appeared to be on the verge of fizzling out. Refusing to lose territory to the foreigners, Santa Anna called upon 400 men in his reserve units to uphold the nation's integrity. As this wave attacked, however, it accidentally shot those amassed at the base of the walls. Eventually, however, the remaining attack force managed to place the ladders and scramble up and into the Alamo. After more than an hour of combat the bloodshed ended: all of the Alamo's defenders were dead and Santa Anna had suffered about 400 casualties, among them 200 deaths.[39] The lives of only a few of the people inside the Alamo were spared. These included several family members of the nine Tejanos (among them Gregorio Esparza's) who had elected to side with the Texians, two Anglo Americans (Susannah Dickinson and her small child), and one African American (a slave owned by the slain Travis).[40]

Four days prior to the fall of the Alamo, Anglo colonists had already decided upon a complete break with Mexico. At Washington-on-the-Brazos on March 2, 1836, three Mexican-descent persons were among the signers of the Declaration of Independence. One of the Texas signatories was Lorenzo de Zavala, a prominent liberal from Yucatán who had arrived in Texas to manage his real estate holdings there and escape the wrath of Santa Anna. José Antonio Navarro and José Francisco Ruíz of Texas also signed the declaration. These two men had been among the Mexican oligarchs committed to fulfilling regional objectives through Anglo immigration. Swollen streams deterred another Tejano representative, Juan Antonio Padilla, from participating in the momentous gathering.[41]

Following his costly victory at Béxar, Santa Anna headed for East Texas to battle Sam Houston, in command of the main Texan army. At San Jacinto, Santa Anna's army, which now numbered about 1,300, engaged Houston's force of 1,000, though from a position that ceded the Texians an advantage: Santa Anna was enclosed on all sides, having Houston at his front, swamp terrain behind him, and part of the San Jacinto River to his right. At 4:30 P.M., Houston's units (which included a small company of Texas Mexicans led by Juan N. Seguín) launched a surprise maneuver that the Mexicans could not repulse. Many of Santa Anna's men retreated in the confusion, unable to regroup since so many of the experienced veterans and lower officers who might have been able to rally their subordinates had died at the Alamo. After only eighteen minutes, therefore, Houston's army had secured command of the Mexican camp. The Anglos, however, continued the onslaught into nightfall, slaying Mexicans attempting to flee into the prairie, the swamp, or the San Jacinto River. Santa Anna's army suffered some 650 deaths and 208 injuries. Only eight or nine Texans died, and seventeen to thirty were wounded.[42]

Three weeks following the Battle of San Jacinto, the Anglo Texans negotiated with Santa Anna the Treaties of Velasco, wherein the defeated general conceded Texas independence and agreed to remove his army to Mexico beyond the Rio Grande. The congress in Mexico City disavowed the agreement, but Texas independence proved to be a fait accompli, since Mexico's army subsequently proved unable to retake the lost province.[43]

VIVA MEXICO, VIVA TEXAS

The war for Texas independence placed Texas Mexicans in a quandary. Initially, some Tejanos had contributed to the siege of Béxar in November and December of 1835, but that had been in consequence of cruel treatment before the hands of the local commander of Mexico's forces, Martín Perfecto de Cós, who compelled many men to perform menial tasks such as sweeping the streets and made the women bake tortillas for his troops.

Additionally, he had impressed draft animals, wagons, and drivers and had destroyed people's homes on the outskirts of Béxar in order to get a clearer view of any attacking Texan forces.

But the withdrawal of the Mexican troops from San Antonio hardly improved the Tejano lot, as the triumphant Anglos now occupying the town insisted that the local populace share their livestock, corn, beans, and other provisions. When Bexareños resisted, the Texans forced them to cooperate. Further, the Anglo soldiers eyed the Tejano citizens with suspicion, considering them potential spies, as the town residents had not been unanimous in backing the Texan army during the siege.

In Goliad, where an Anglo-Texan army had taken over the presidio in October 1835, Mexicans faced a similar predicament. The servicemen forced Texas Mexicans to barricade the plaza in Goliad and help them with sundry manual tasks. Lacking critical supplies, they commandeered Tejanos' property, including livestock, food, weapons, and tools. Many Texas-Mexican rancheros were stripped of their possessions in this way.

Also posing a dilemma to Tejanos, and explaining their vacillation toward supporting the war for Texas independence, was the changing stand taken by the Anglo Texans. Initially the Anglos had talked only of maintaining certain rights and liberties, but then they declared for complete independence. While Tejanos supported the struggle for a democratic Mexico (as citizens had in other Mexican states such as Zacatecas and Coahuila), a complete break with the mother country was another matter. Additionally, Tejanos had misgivings about their status in the new republic, for they would certainly be transformed into a minority population.

The majority of Tejanos, however, had decided not to side with either belligerent. Though some may have sympathized with the Anglo cause and others might have preferred to defend the motherland from the threat of Anglo-American domination, they took to the countryside, opting to ensure the safety of their loved ones. These people assumed a tenuous neutrality throughout the crisis.[44]

MEXICAN AMERICANS

The Texas Constitution of 1836 proclaimed that all people living in Texas had automatically become citizens of the new republic at the moment the delegates at Washington-on-the-Brazos had declared independence. Thus did the subjects of Mexico become citizens of the new republic by the stroke of a pen. (Those absent at the time the document was signed but who later returned and desired citizenship could apply through normal procedures for naturalization.) Then, in 1845, residents of the Lone Star Republic received another new citizenship when the United States annexed Texas into the Union. The recognition of U.S. citizenship applied to Texas Mexicans as well,[45] but by then Tejanos had already realized that the rights and privileges that accompanied citizenship in an Anglo-dominated society did not necessarily extend to them.

CHAPTER THREE

A New Citizenship:
Life in Anglo Texas,
1836–1880

In a span of four years, the fate of Antonio de la Garza and his sister Trinidad turned topsy-turvy. As of 1874, both lived comfortably off their ranch property in South Texas, and from what can be gleaned from the stories they passed on to their descendants, held the respect of neighboring Tejanos and even some Anglos. Their good fortune changed abruptly.

The de la Garza siblings descended from the Manuel Becerra family. The elder Becerra lived on land he claimed had been granted him by the Mexican government in 1832 in what is today Refugio County. Daughter Gertrudis Becerra married Francisco de la Garza, and when Francisco died in 1870, he bequeathed part of the original Becerra concession (about 2,200 acres) to his children Antonio and Trinidad.

Starting around early 1874, de la Garza family descendants told, strange events began occurring at the Alamito Ranch (part of the Becerra grant) of Antonio de la Garza, a married man still in his early twenties. One night in January of that year, his livestock came under gunfire; the perpetrators (almost certainly Anglos, according to family legend) no doubt wishing to send the young Antonio a message, to wit: leave the Alamito Ranch or suffer further livestock killings and possible destruction of his ranchstead. Antonio refused to be intimated until ruffians rode into his property again during the summer of 1875, this time burning down his barns and chasing away his horses, cattle, and sheep. A few days thereafter, family history contends, night riders once more appeared at Rancho Alamito, this time threatening Antonio in no uncertain terms:

leave or be killed. In what became a harrowing experience, Antonio, his wife Ponposa, and their two children in late July 1875 stole away in the night, leaving their beloved land behind forever. They made their way to Goliad, where relatives extended them protection.

Next to leave the Becerra properties was Trinidad, Antonio's sister. She had lost her husband Juan Elías Lozano in an ambush committed in 1877, and she now worked the old Becerra land alongside her six-year-old step-daughter Paula Lozano and two teenage nephews. But the tragedy that had befallen Antonio soon visited Trinidad: in 1878, from what Paula later recounted, strangers in the night killed the family milk cow and some goats and otherwise made their lives in Refugio County untenable. Unprotected, Trinidad and her family, like Antonio before them, departed for Goliad. By July 1878, the land so dear to Manuel Becerra had slipped away from his heirs.[1]

On Three Frontiers

Between 1836 and 1850, the year in which the United States govern-ment took the first federal census in Texas, the Tejano population rose to more than 14,000. During the next thirty years, the Tejano community swelled approximately fivefold; the historian Roberto M. Villarreal esti-mates the number at 71,000 for 1880. Immigration accounted for much of the increase. Migrants from Mexico made up some 40 percent of the population total in 1850, 64 percent in 1860, and 61 percent in both 1870 and 1880.[2]

During the period, Texas Mexicans were clustered in three discernible population nodes. Some Tejanos still lived in the old Central Texas settle-ments, others in the new towns and on ranches that had been founded by Anglo Americans and European immigrants pushing west. After the American Civil War (1861–65), Mexican immigrants and Tejano migrant workers from below the Nueces River filled in for ex-slaves on farmlands adjoining San Antonio to the east, and by the 1870s Tejanos had become daylaborers on farms around Travis County and the Brazos River district. The massive movement of Texas-Mexican farm hands into Central Texas would not occur, however, until the 1890s. In that part of the state, therefore, Texas Mexicans in the nineteenth century occupied a minority status in a predominantly Euro-American populace.[3]

The setting in South Texas differed markedly. There, Mexicans formed a substantial majority. Many had moved into new communities founded by Anglo Americans after the U.S. war with Mexico (1846–48)—among them Brownsville, Rio Grande City, Roma, and Corpus Christi—and into other sites that arose after the Civil War. But Anglos in the trans-Nueces controlled the region's economic and political foundations. Tejanos living in South Texas, therefore, faced a quasi-colonial situation in which they were ruled by a small "foreign" element bent on directing the social life and development of their home region—even though Tejanos and Anglos alike were citizens of the same nation.[4]

West Texas remained much of a hinterland as late as 1880, for American settlers did not start moving into the area west of the 100th meridian en masse until after the Civil War. During the 1870s, native-born Texas Mexicans and recent immigrants from Mexico began entering newer communities such as Fort Davis, Fort Stockton, Alpine, and San Angelo searching for work as shepherds, vaqueros, and farm hands. The El Paso Valley, however, had been home for Mexican-descent people since the 1830s, when the Rio Grande shifted course, putting the Mexican villages of San Elizario, Ysleta, and Socorro on what would become the American side of the river following the signing of the Treaty of Guadalupe Hidalgo, which ended the U.S. war with Mexico. Also, the beginnings of modern-day El Paso had been established in the 1850s when Anglo farmers and merchants appeared as part of the U.S. expansion westward to California (though the population of El Paso as of 1880 stood at about 700). Within the fifteen-year period between 1865 and 1880, however, enough Anglos had pushed into West Texas to make it a section in which each group composed roughly half of the population.[5]

An Unneighborly Country

In these three regions, Central, South, and West Texas, Tejanos coexisted with unneighborly Anglo Texans who regarded them as a people of a lower caste. White society contemptuously thought Mexicans to be undeserving of equality with caucasians, and mechanisms to ensure Anglo supremacy abounded: these included political bossism, co-optation of the elites, a new and often racist police force, and threats and the use of physical violence, both from law enforcement officials and vigilante-style groups.

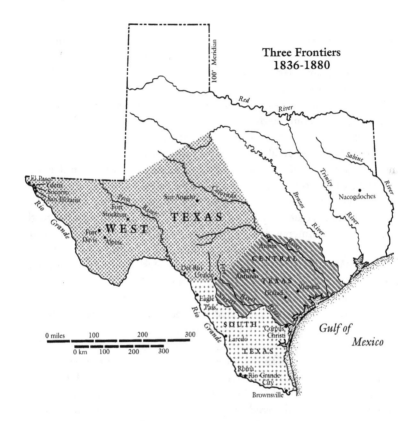

Three Frontiers
1836-1880

VIOLENCE

Violence directed against Mexicans in Texas had boiled over during the struggle for Texas independence and continued after the war. Suspected by Anglos of disloyalty and complicity in Santa Anna's atrocities, many Mexicans after the Battle of San Jacinto faced the choice of finding haven in Mexico, parts of the Republic other than Central Texas (which in the summer of 1836 was still considered a war zone), or Louisiana. When the Tejano exiles returned in the late 1830s, many of them found their land confiscated or their cattle lost to Anglo claimants.[6] The residents of Béxar faced new perils after about 1838, as whites arrived in the old community, turning San Antonio into "an open field for their criminal designs," as Juan N. Seguín, the city's mayor (1841–42), put it.[7]

In the 1850s, flagrant attacks upon Tejanos persisted as xenophobia, politics, and economic rivalries incited racial conflict. Communities in Central Texas, where slavery had existed since before the Texas war for independence, expelled Texas Mexicans whom they suspected of having aided local slaves to escape to Mexico. In the 1850s, racial animosity also emerged out of competition between Tejano arrieros and Anglo freighters who competed to transport goods between settlements in the interior of the state and the gulf ports. In 1857, some of the Anglo freighters launched an all-out attack on the arrieros, waylaying the cart-men, destroying their cargoes, causing thousands of dollars in damages, and even killing some of the drivers. The so-called Cart War finally ended following the intervention of the Mexican minister in Washington, D.C., the American secretary of state, and some Texans who objected to the standstill in commerce and the blatant racist attacks on the Mexicans. Arrieros continued carrying goods to the coast after this episode, though the Civil War and subsequent economic changes after 1865 undermined their earlier monopoly on the transport trade.[8]

Similar clashes between the races spread to the territory below the Nueces River as Anglos penetrated the South Texas frontier for the first time. Anglo arrogance and Texas-Mexican rights became causes for contention. A by-product was the so-called "Cortina War," led by Juan N. Cortina, a scion of the old Tejano land grantees and a well-known local leader in Brownsville. Cortina resented the ways in which the newly arrived Anglos misused the judicial structure to divest Texas Mexicans of their property, challenged the old leaders for political supremacy, and compelled people to submit to new labor authority on their recently ac-quired rangelands—all the while displaying a racist contempt for Tejanos. His embitterment reached a climax on July 13, 1859, at a Brownsville cafe. There he witnessed the city marshal brutalizing a Mexican ranch hand. Cortina intervened on behalf of the Tejano, only to be insulted by the peace officer with an ethnic epithet. Cortina responded by firing on the lawman and injuring him.

Leaving an enraged Anglo population in the town, Cortina retreated to Mexico. In September 1859, he laid siege to Brownsville with a band of followers, threatened "death to the gringos," and killed three whites. He was subsequently persuaded by Mexican authorities from Matamoros to relinquish his hold on the town. Regrouping at Rancho del Carmen, his mother's ranch situated about nine miles west of Brownsville, he issued proclamations denouncing the Anglo presence in South Texas and vowing to seek redress for inflicted wrongs. Several efforts to dislodge him from his stronghold failed, and with every Cortina victory talk increased about expelling Anglos completely from the lower border region. Texas Rangers and federal troops quelled the insurrection early in 1860, however, and chased Cortina deeper into Mexico. Anglo Texans along the border then sought vengeance for Cortina's actions by waging a campaign of violence against suspected sympathizers. The retaliation involved the burning and looting of property as well as the killing of several Texas Mexicans.[9]

Following the American Civil War, lynchings and other barbarities perpetrated against Tejanos at the hands of Anglos accelerated. South Texas during the late 1860s and into the 1870s became an arena of violence in the competition between profiteers from both sides of the border who sought to rustle cattle and mavericks from local ranches and the open South Texas range. Many in the region suffered, but much violence was inflicted on innocent Tejano residents of the area whom Anglos accused of complacency in the cattle raiding from Mexico. Such atrocities were committed so frequently that the Texas Adjutant General mused that few considered it a criminal act to kill Mexicans in South Texas.[10]

Similar outbursts of hate crimes broke out in West Texas in the postbellum era, among them a notorious clash in the El Paso Valley over local salt lakes. For generations, people from both sides of the Rio Grande had communally mined the salt lodes located in the Guadalupe Peak, about one hundred miles east of El Paso. In the fall of 1877, tension over disputed claims to the lakes erupted in a confrontation near San Elizario between border Mexicans (both Tejanos and residents of Mexico) and Charles H. Howard (a local entrepreneur representing the interests of an Austin banker named George B. Zimpelman), resulting in the death of an Anglo spokesman for the Tejanos. Wider violence broke out in December, but troops, Texas Rangers, and volunteer posses from New Mexico arrived to pacify the region. The outsiders suppressed the insurgency (as historian Paul Cool labels it), which came to be known as the "Salt War," by committing indiscriminate killings and other heinous acts. After that, the people of the valley were compelled to pay salt lake fees to Zimpelman (and to subsequent salt lake owners) for access to the salt beds.[11]

INTERETHNIC ACCOMMODATION

Whites also maintained authority over the mass of Texas Mexicans by securing alliances with prominent members of Tejano society. (To what extent this co-opted faction avoided the aforementioned violence is difficult to measure.) As noted in the previous chapter, a social gradation had characterized the Tejano community before the widespread arrival of Anglos, and this delineation withstood changes in nationhood. The fact is that throughout the nineteenth century, a segment of the Texas-Mexican population either retained parts of their old lands or acquired small parcels of real estate. In the towns, furthermore, men and women with business acumen profited by operating successful concerns.[12]

Attracted by such material assets, Anglo men formed connections with these Texas-Mexican elites, at least until about the 1870s, by wooing available young women from prominent families. In San Antonio many succeeded to the extent that between 1837 and 1860, a minimum of one daughter from almost every well-to-do family in the city had become the wife of an Anglo suitor. In South Texas, the newcomers not only acquired valuable ranch property by marrying women from landed families but incidentally acquired esteem and economic and political authority. With time, Anglos could capitalize on Tejano cultural traditions to further their place in the upper stratum. Being a godparent at an infant's baptism, sponsoring a youth at confirmation, or simply being the best man in a marriage made one a *compadre* to a family. Through these ritual practices, the newcomer's political clout among the Texas Mexicans broadened.[13]

MANAGING THE MEXICAN VOTE

Anglos employed clever political mechanisms to control Tejano behavior at the polling booth. No law passed in the nineteenth century disfranchised the Tejano population, but whites took steps to deflect potential threats to their political power base. Intimidation helped to keep Tejanos in check, but beginning as early as the 1850s, political bosses scornful of political procedure increasingly used what is termed the controlled franchise. Under the stratagem used in South Texas, a local *patrón,* or boss, dictated his resolve to Tejano "cross-mark patriots" or to noncitizens, influencing both with free food and alcohol on the day of the vote, then directing them to cast their ballot for a specific issue or individual.[14] Not infrequently, Anglo politicians solicited the assistance of certain Texas Mexicans in their intrigues. Although these lesser bosses were from the Tejano community, they ordinarily belonged to well-off Texas-Mexican families and were motivated by a desire to protect their status and belongings through political collusion.[15]

THE LAW

Also instrumental in assuring Anglo sovereignty over Tejanos were certain law enforcement agencies. In the years following the Battle of San Jacinto, the republic's soldiers had administered law and order, but Anglo lawmen replaced troopers as time passed. (Some Mexican Americans did serve as members of the constabulary, though most of these men were related to one of the landed families.) Peace officers symbolized white authority and often acted as the interpreters of the law. Linkages to other men of power, either locally or at the state house, gave them license to jail Mexicans if they deemed it proper, organize posses to hunt down lawbreaking Mexicans, and even to execute insolent Tejanos (on the pretext of self-defense).[16]

Then, the Texas Rangers in the post–Civil War period came to oversee the frontier, often taking law enforcement into their own hands, applying the *ley de fuga* (law of flight) in their encounters with Texas Mexicans. Though some scholars have recently begun to revise the widely held image of the Texas Rangers as a unit of white American control, noting, for instance, that throughout the nineteenth century several Tejanos served capably alongside Anglo Rangers, Mexican Americans during the nineteenth century still regarded the force as an agent of institutional power and referred to its members derisively as *"los rinches,"* a transliteration of the English word "Rangers."[17]

WORKING THE OLD LANDS

After the war for Texas independence and the U.S. war with Mexico, land grantees experienced formidable problems in retaining claims to their holdings. Rapacious Americans pressured Tejanos to sell their property. In Central Texas, Navarro and some of Seguín's relatives had sold out by midcentury. Seguín himself signed away what remained of his family's real estate in Wilson County in the 1870s, then moved to Mexico to join family members.[18] Also, Tejano landowners wrestled with the vagaries of the new American economy. Part of their dilemma, observes Professor David Montejano, stemmed from their outlook on the rancho. To Mexicans of South Texas, land sustained one's familial well-being and bestowed respect and status upon its owners. Comparatively, Anglo ranchers regarded land purchase as an investment, or as means to turn a quick profit. When a great demand for longhorns outside Texas boomed following the Civil War, the Mexican ranching elite was ill-prepared to compete with the Anglo ranchers. Having neglected to invest in their estates, the rancheros were hard pressed to organize and finance their own cattle drives north. In desperation to supply the buying market, rancheros contracted with Anglo agents who bought their stock from them cheaply and then drove the herds to Kansas or Missouri, where they sold it expensively.

Other forces contributed to the losses Tejano stockmen suffered. Barbed wire had fenced off all of the open range in South and Southwest Texas by the end of the 1870s, yet few Tejano ranchers could muster the capital to buy their own supplies of barbed wire to enclose their lands. Nor did most of them have the cash (or access to loans) to pay taxes, improve their cattle breeds, survive droughts, or expand their grazing lands. Therefore, the financially overextended Tejano rancheros became severely vulnerable to downward spirals in demand for beef or, for that matter, even erratic weather conditions. Montejano's research shows that Mexican land sales to Anglos with available credit increased during economic slumps.[19]

The quality of life for laborers on the ranches of South Texas varied. Despite the Mexicans' acknowledged ranching skills, Anglos considered them a lazy people, ascribing to them a weakness for indolence and revelry, perhaps as a means of justifying their exploitation of Tejano laborers.[20] Such attitudes did not stifle the Tejano cowboys will to work the range the Mexican way. "When Mexicans could no longer ride for themselves," notes the historian Jack Jackson, "they rode for others, passing on their knowledge and customs to subsequent generations of 'buckaroos.'"[21] This range culture, of course, harked all the way back to Spain, but Tejanos applied it to the Anglo border ranches that functioned so successfully under American rule. When sheep ranching grew in the Rio Grande Plain after the Civil War and then spread toward West Texas, Texas Mexicans applied their time-tested practices to that industry as well.[22]

Anglos also presumed themselves the social superiors of Mexicans, but most white ranchers did not work their ranch hands ruthlessly. Actually, Anglo landholders held only tenuous control over their laborers, who could leave the ranch to find better-paying jobs. In a few cases, however, men and women working on Texas ranches continued to look to a patrón for the necessities of life, among them a place to live and a provider of wages (either in cash, or, as was more often the case with the vaqueros, in food, clothing, ammunition, tobacco, or other provisions). Whatever the work relationship between boss and vaquero, a clear understanding existed between the white ranchers and the Mexican-American ranch hands: Mexicans were to be deferential, assent to their social inferiority, and the men were to avoid mixing with white women.[23]

THE BARRIOS

Like most Texans, Texas Mexicans were predominantly rural dwellers. As of 1850, only 16 percent of the total Tejano population resided in municipalities. At no time during the nineteenth century did the number of Texas-Mexican urban denizens exceed 25 percent.[24]

Several general observations may be made regarding the lives of late-nineteenth-century urban Tejanos. First, most of them lived amidst poverty and blight. As Texas urbanized in the last half of the nineteenth century, jobs in trade, transportation, and manufacturing opened up, but Anglos were the primary beneficiaries. Left for Tejanos in the growing towns and small cities were jobs of an unspecialized nature that offered little chance for material advancement.[25] Also, most Mexicans resided in neighborhoods of their own founding, generally because most towns in Texas after 1836 were Anglo developments, built close to some important ranch, a frontier fortification, or another commercial center.

In the *barrios* (Mexican neighborhoods), furthermore, the racial order of the countryside that associated Tejanos with backwardness and inferiority also applied. In Texas cities, the result of the ethnically divided neighborhoods saw the barrio as a district receive a distinct lack of attention from city officials, including from the police, civic leaders, and the common citizenry. But by the same token, the Mexican quarter acted as a focal point for Tejano life. In that setting, political ideologies of various persuasions took form, merchants sold products suited to Mexican tastes and delivered services in ways familiar to their customers, Catholic priests (and some Protestant clergymen) ministered to the faithful, and, overall, Tejanos were free to preserve an in-group culture. In San Antonio, for example, Bexareños after the Texas war for independence retained loyalty to their religious past. According to historian Timothy Matovina, they often found in earlier practices and beliefs reinforcement for their Mexican way of life and solidarity against rising racial oppression. They continued to observe the *día de la Virgen de Guadalupe* (December 12) with demonstrations of religious devotion at the parish of San Fernando as well as with public festivities that included ornate processions down the streets of the city. As San Antonio became increasingly Americanized following the Civil War, however, public expressions of faith diminished, but not the people's commitment to *la virgen*, for parishioners now paid homage to the brown-skinned Guadalupe indoors, with special masses and other worship rites.[26]

Community in American Texas

Like their counterparts in other parts of the United States—especially the northern cities where immigrant groups tended to settle—Tejanos in both the ranching areas and the urban barrios retained components of the culture of their homeland. After all, Mexico-born people constituted a majority of the overall Tejano population as late as 1880. Gradually, however, Tejano culture came to comprise a fusion of Mexican and Anglo ways.

A DUAL CULTURE

Linkages to Mexico in Tejano culture are evident in language, a patriotic loyalty to the old country, an aesthetic appreciation for Mexico's heritage, housing types, foods, folklore, religious beliefs, and modes of entertainment. Thus, Tejanos built their homes in the form of jacales and adobe as they had in both the Mexican and Texan frontiers. They partook of *frijoles, tortillas, tamales, chiles, cabrito* (young goat), and *nopalitos* (leaves of cactus) as they had for generations. Ethnic festivals including commemorations of Mexican national holidays, such as the Diez y Seis de Septiembre and the Cinco de Mayo—the date on which the forces of Mexico repelled a major French invasion in 1862—and maintained patriotic Mexican sentiments. Spanish-language newspapers informed readers of current events in Mexico, educated immigrants about American society, and incidentally preserved use of the native language. Such newspapers first appeared in San Antonio in the 1850s (actually, a hiatus in publication had existed since the 1820s), then in select cities throughout the state after Reconstruction (1865–76). Texas Mexicans also established, during the 1870s, benevolent associations that offered barrio dwellers and their families assistance in times of unemployment, destitution, sickness, or death of a loved one. These societies went by such names as *Club Recíproco* (Reciprocal Club) and *Sociedad Mutualista Benito Juárez* (Benito Juárez Mutualist Society).[27]

The building of the Tejano community in Texas also involved acculturation, however. In everyday affairs, Texas Mexicans had common
interchange with Anglo employers, merchants, policemen, Catholic
and Protestant churches, public organizations, and other agents of the
mainstream white society. Naturally, they came in contact with Anglos in
schools, though several factors interceded to foil any significant degree of
acculturation there, among them the fledgling state of the Texas school
system, a curriculum that disparaged Mexican culture and thereby alien-
ated Tejano students, and an ethnocentric attitude that schooling ought
not to be for Mexicans. Nonetheless, from the school or from necessity,
Tejanos learned the English language, though not necessarily fluently.
Those piqued by politics joined the debate over controversies of the state
and nation. Common men and women incorporated Anglo-American
motifs into popular folklore; *corridos* (folk ballads) made mention of
American personalities such as Ulysses S. Grant, for example. Similarly,
American national holidays, among them George Washington's birthday,
Independence Day, and even the U.S. Centennial in 1876, came to be
observed as part of a group consciousness.[28]

SOCIAL DIVERSITY

Just as the community was ethnically diversified, so it was economically
and socially. Most Tejanos lived as members of the lower stratum, but a
small part of the community fared better. Among them were landowners
who traced their ancestry to the pre-1836 era and still retained portions
of their property. Though the majority of Tejano land grantees had lost
their possessions to Anglos by the time of the Civil War, many others
had managed to keep them—according to recent studies by Ana Carolina
Castillo Crimm and Armando C. Alonzo—losing their ranches only
after the 1880s through the practice of leaving equal portions of their
estates to heirs.

Through resiliency, a number of Tejano stockmen found ways to pay
off their taxes, prove the titles to their lands in court, fight off land-hungry
squatters, or beat the odds in times of depression by commercializing
and acclimating themselves to the new market.[29] A case in point was the
De León family of Victoria, which fended off Anglos who felt entitled
following the war for Texas independence to harass Tejanos and even
appropriate their belongings. To avoid the wrath of vengeful Anglos,
the family, led by the matriarch Doña Patricia de León, had relocated to

Louisiana in 1836, but upon their return to Texas in 1845, they waged numerous court battles and successfully regained titles to their tradition-ally held properties. Along the border region, one also could find several other successful Tejano ranch enterprises, some of them either owned or operated by women who had gained lands through marriage or upon the death of their spouse. Salomé Ballí, already a land owner (and widow) when she married John McAllen in Cameron County in 1861, ranked among the wealthiest Tejanas in South Texas during the mid-nineteenth century. Petra Vela similarly gained land ownership following her marriage in 1854 to the prominent South Texas entrepreneur and rancher Mifflin Kenedy. During the latter 1870s and after, Rafaela Hinojosa worked, along with her husband, on the 19,000-acre ranch the two of them owned in Brooks County.[30] Other Tejano-owned ranches in South Texas of note were the Laguna Seca of Don Macedonio Vela, the Randado of Hipolito García, and Los Ojuelos of Dionisio Guerra, all of which made good in the cattle boom of the 1870s and even expanded after that era.[31] The success of these ranches set their owners (or co-owners) apart from the bulk of South Texas Tejanos who served as ranch hands and day laborers.

Also above the general caste of Tejano *obreros* (laborers) stood a mercantile class that managed upstart business establishments. After the War with Mexico, members of the South Texas elite used already estab-lished economic networks in Texas and across the Rio Grande to their advantage. In the 1850s and after, they reaped profits from the trafficking of industrial goods going into Mexico from the United States as well as from agricultural products coming into Texas from south of the border.[32] Meanwhile, some Mexican immigrants with fortitude found ways to start up modest business ventures and keep them afloat. Additionally, a corps of Tejano professionals, modest in size, evolved as settlements expanded in the post–Civil War years. Teachers, newspaper editors, physicians, druggists, and attorneys, as well as government officials serving as peace officers, sanitary inspectors, or custom collectors in the border areas augmented this Tejano middle class.[33]

As they had under Spain and Mexico, the newly American citizens of the community acknowledged social distinctions. The well-to-do now preferred to remain aloof and thus created their own circle of clubs and sponsored exclusive social affairs. Naturally, they lived commensurate with their status; they owned comfortable and well-kept homes and dressed more fashionably than did most other Tejanos.[34]

POLITICAL ISSUES AND TEJANOS

Ethnic variation and social differentiation in turn influenced the posture that Tejano political activists took on matters of relevance to their lives and the people they represented. Anglos, however, sought to limit Tejano suffrage, life in ranchos and barrios tended to isolate Tejanos from politics, and, as a group, Tejanos suffered from a list of political liabilities: a smaller proportion of Mexicans than Anglos qualified to vote because females in the Tejano population outnumbered males; the average age among Tejanos was lower than that among whites; foreign-born status made many ineligible to vote; and the inability of many to read in English kept them away from the polls.[35]

Nonetheless, Tejanos evinced passion in deliberating the political and socioeconomic topics of the times. As expected, they espoused diverse, even conflicting positions. Some Tejanos joined in the politics of the Republic of Texas as officeholders, though these individuals were primarily the oligarchs from the Béxar region who had previously served in government under Mexico. Among them were José Antonio Navarro and Juan Seguín. The former went on to win local and state office several times, while the latter, a hero of the Battle of San Jacinto, found himself exiled from Texas in the 1840s for allegedly having switched his allegiance to Mexico.[36]

The turmoil of the 1850s, the Civil War (1861–65), and Reconstruction engrossed Tejanos in affairs of immediate pertinence to the community. In 1855–56, Bexareños succeeded in helping defeat the Know-Nothing party, which ran on an anti-immigration, anti-naturalization, and anti-Catholic platform. Though the ideological postures assumed on political issues varied as much within the Tejano community as they did elsewhere in Texas, Tejanos were mostly sympathetic to Democratic party principles. When the party split into two competing factions in the late 1850s over the question of secession, there were Tejanos in both camps. When the Civil War erupted in 1861, oligarchs like Navarro and Santos Benavides of Laredo (who had managed to retain property and political influence) sided with the Confederacy while Cortina, who had taken refuge in Mexico following his defeat by Texan forces in 1860, allied himself with the Union cause. In fact, Cortina waged guerrilla war on Confederate forces and exploited the atmosphere of chaos in an effort to forcibly subvert the presence of those Anglos wanting to encroach on the lands, politics, and economy of South Texas.[37]

Like their elite counterparts, common folks took adversarial sides during the Civil War. Although the mass of Tejanos could not identify with the philosophical underpinnings of the war, approximately 3,400 Tejanos participated in the conflict, according to the historian Jerry D. Thompson. Some 950 Tejanos joined the Union ranks, about 2,500 sided with the Confederate forces. Aside from action in the trans-Nueces (where many preferred to serve in order to watch over the well-being of their families), Tejanos fought in significant engagements in New Mexico, as well as in Tennessee, Virginia, and other states east of the Mississippi.[38] During the time of Reconstruction, political factions clashed on the question of rights for the freedmen, sometimes as heatedly as did their Anglo cohorts who split on the issue along Conservative and Radical lines.

Following the Civil War, Tejano incumbents (most of whom were associated with families having lucrative business and ranching interests) occupied numerous local offices, ranging from county commissioners to collectors, assessors, and treasurers. This was especially the norm along the border, as well as in the El Paso Valley. Tejanos even earned appointments or won election to offices in counties being newly created in West Texas during the 1870s.[39] The commitment of such politicians to advancing the lot of the Mexican-American population varied from indifference to firm commitment.

José Antonio Navarro, perhaps the best-known spokesman of the antebellum era, practiced politics driven by the ambition to see his region (Béxar) prosper economically (as he had during the Mexican era), by a nationalistic passion for the land of his birth (Texas), and by his awareness of white racial intolerance of Tejanos. Since the days of Stephen F. Austin, Navarro had developed linkages with powerful Anglo-American leaders, and between 1836 and 1871, when he died, he had signed the Texas Declaration of Independence, attended and participated in the constitutional conventions of 1836 and 1845, won election and served in the Congress of the Republic of Texas (1838–39), served in the Texas legislature (1846–49), and supported the secessionist movement in Texas and later the South. Simultaneously, however, Navarro did not forsake the cares of Tejanos. A recent study sees him as a lifelong defender of Tejano constitutional rights, an open critic of Anglo mistreatment of Tejanos, and a sensitive chronicler who resented the ways in which Anglos ethnocentrically misinterpreted Tejanos and their actions in historical events.[40]

Analogous is the career of Santos Benavides. A border-region politician who accommodated readily to American institutions following the war with Mexico, Benavides occupied various political offices in Laredo and Webb County in the 1850s, assisted Anglo military forces in suppressing the Juan Cortina disturbance in 1859, then fought on the side of the Confederacy. Serving in the state legislature between 1879 and 1885, Benavides sought to remain nonpartisan in ethnic matters while he worked to modernize the border region. Reputedly, his political comportment earned him high marks among white colleagues in the legislature.[41]

Bolder in affirming political convictions was Cortina, who forcefully resisted the Anglo-American presence on the border. During the Cortina War, he professed to be championing Tejano rights and in his statements issued from Rancho del Carmen inveighed against the Anglos' systematic expropriation of Tejano lands and the mistreatment of Texas Mexicans simply because of their nationality. He had threatened the extermination of the foreigners and had met them courageously on the battlefield. As a *caudillo* (regional strongman) in Tamaulipas during the 1860s and 1870s, Cortina warred against the border Anglos by coordinating cattle raids into South Texas. Force remained his political style, whether to defend fellow Tejanos, uphold his character and rights, or perhaps to advance his personal fortunes.[42]

A MARGINAL PEOPLE

Throughout much of the nineteenth century, Tejanos struggled as a people living in the margin of the dominant society. Government, schools, private institutions, and social agencies neglected them. The Catholic Church and Protestant denominations provided spiritual guidance but launched no efforts to achieve Tejano equality. Agrarian labor leaders dismissed Tejanos during the fledgling unionizing drives of the 1870s. Ranchers and farmers ignored notions about fair wages and treatment for their Mexican hands.

Treated as second-class citizens, Tejanos sought to work out their own survival in poverty-stricken neighborhoods or on ranches. Actually, in some ways many Texas Mexicans may have preferred their own separate sphere, for in segregated areas they were free to enjoy familiar and comforting amenities beyond the distrustful eye of outsiders. Indeed, some Tejanos, like European immigrants of the same era, resisted Americanizing influences. But many other Tejanos rejected their marginal status, seeking a life beyond the confines of the semiautonomous enclaves and displaying a firm resolve to join the mainstream society. Barrio merchants and rancheros pushed to integrate their businesses into the larger economy. Parents enrolled their children in public schools. Newspapers and benefit societies encouraged Tejano community members to stay abreast of local matters. And political leaders tried to find solutions to issues affecting the community. Anglos might have preferred a docile proletariat, but the Tejano will to improve the human condition produced an assertiveness that influenced the course of Texas history.

CHAPTER FOUR

Mexican Americans and Inmigrantes *in a Modernizing Society, 1880–1910*

Sara Estela Ramírez was still a young woman when her mother died in Mexico, a tragedy that would have felled most other youngsters. But Sara Estela persevered, looking out for her father's well being as well as that of her younger sister. In fact, she completed her education in Saltillo, Coahuila, before deciding to strike out to the north toward Texas. She arrived in Laredo in 1898, at the age of seventeen, and found gainful employment as a teacher of Spanish at the Seminario Laredo.

Laredo in 1898 and the early twentieth century was a city undergoing a rapid transformation, due in part to the arrival of the railroad in 1881 that connected it both with the Texas coast and the interior of Mexico. Simultaneously with the railroad came many modern amenities, among them telephone service, an upgrading of the infrastructure and the down-town, and the establishment of the English-language *Laredo Daily Times*. Laredo also became a hotbed of union activity, as labor activists recruited among dissatisfied railroad and mine workers on both sides of the Rio Grande. Finally, revolutionaries disgruntled with Mexico's dictatorial president Porfirio Díaz (1876–1911) used the city as a base in which to intrigue against him. It was with this latter element that Sara Estela, a liberal thinker (who believed, among other things, that women should not be confined to the domestic sphere), allied herself.

In 1904, Ricardo Flores Magón, a radical idealist from Mexico, arrived in Laredo with thoughts of toppling the Díaz administration and supplanting it with his own *Partido Liberal Mexicano* (PLM, or the

Mexican Liberal Party). Harassed endlessly by both Díaz's gunmen and U.S. officials, Flores Magón kept out of the public eye, leaving it to Sara Estela Ramírez to speak out about PLM plans for land reform in Mexico and to advocate for the party's labor ideology, which Tejano working men found appealing. Her involvement with the PLM and outspokenness on such issues as the need to end gender-based discrimination, as well as her career as a poet and a journalist ended early, however, when Ramírez died in Laredo at the age of twenty-nine.[1]

Ramírez's struggles to rouse Tejano workers most certainly entailed a degree of risk, for at the time, an affront to the racial order usually provoked an angry, even violent, response. Injury, death, or insult of a white by a Tejano, for example, brought certain wrath down upon the whole Tejano community. When in June 1901 the farm renter Gregorio Cortéz shot a local sheriff near Kenedy in Karnes County, the Tejano, knowing that he faced summary lynch law, even though he had killed the lawman in self-defense, fled toward Mexico. Before being caught a few days later, he became the target of one of Texas's most massive manhunts; those who had helped Cortéz try to escape suffered threats, imprisonment, and, in one notorious case involving an innocent thirteen-year-old boy, torture.

In the early twentieth century, lynching remained a method of racial control. In November 1910, Anglo vigilantes in Rocksprings went to the local jail, took Antonio Rodríguez (accused of killing a white woman on a ranch near the town), and burned him alive. In a similar case of impulsive action, a white mob in Thorndale beat fourteen-year-old Antonio Gómez to death in 1911 for killing a German Texan in a fight. They then dragged his corpse through the streets of town behind a buggy.

The tense nature of Anglo-Tejano relations also exploded in violent demonstrations. A handful of race riots erupted in the southern and western sections of the state in the 1880s and 1890s in which Tejanos reacted angrily to individual cases of harassment or to some act of injustice perpetrated upon the community. The most frightening riot occurred in Rio Grande City in 1888 when local Mexican residents sought to make amends for the Anglo shooting of newspaper man Catarino Garza, who had been editorializing against local white law enforcement officers suspected of lynching Mexicans in the area. Hysteria gripped Anglo communities throughout the region as Tejanos were seemingly "loose" on the border, though they mainly sought the capture of Garza's assailant, who had taken refuge in a local military post. Not much in the form of property destruction or loss of life actually occurred, and the "rioting" passed after a few days. Garza recovered from his injuries to resume his career as an activist journalist in South Texas.[2]

Other aspects of Anglo-Tejano relations seemed backward in a modernizing age. Political bosses still manipulated Mexican voters, and movements to disfranchise Tejanos culminated in a federal courtroom in 1896 in the case of *In re Ricardo Rodríguez.* In an unsuccessful attempt to deprive Mexican Americans of the vote legally, two lawyers petitioned a San Antonio judge, reasoning Mexicans had descended from Indian blood and were therefore not qualified U.S. citizens.[3] On the landed estates of South Texas, ranch hands earned their keep under labor arrangements that were throwbacks to the Spanish-Mexican era.[4]

Texas Society in Transition

There existed little doubt among all Texans, however, that the period from the 1880s through the 1910s was one of marked transformation. For one thing, commercial farming replaced cattle ranching as the most common rural livelihood. Since the 1860s, Anglo Americans had been moving into new areas of the state—towards the Cross Timbers, West Texas, and the Panhandle—to establish new farms. There followed a general pattern of land transfer from ranches to farms across the state during the 1870s as the age of the cattle kingdom waned. A similar turn away from ranching occurred in South Texas, where the majority of Tejanos resided, as Anglo farmers from other parts of the United States began arriving in the region during the 1890s to supplant the old nineteenth-century ranch society. The farming revolution in the lower Rio Grande Valley did not unfold until the first decade of the twentieth century, however.[5]

Also indicative of the new historical age was the diversification of the industrial sector of the economy. Railroads arrived in the state in the 1870s and took Texas in new directions. As it linked one town with another, the iron rail gave new life to cotton-growing concerns and other agricultural pursuits and furthered the development of newer industries such as lumber in the Piney Woods of East Texas. Manufacturing also came into its own during this time, and by 1900 the value of the state's manufactured products had reached unprecedented levels. But this still was not the end of the continued economic diversification, for wildcatters tapped the huge Spindletop pool (near Beaumont) in 1901. Other discoveries followed, and these in turn spurred a great many new oil-related businesses.

Further distinguishing the late nineteenth and early twentieth century from the older days were trends toward urbanization (although Texas remained basically agricultural). Houston began to thrive as a point of debarkation for cotton going to the northeastern United States and even Europe. San Antonio experienced immense population growth and economic prosperity with the arrival of the railroad—new buildings featuring modern architectural styles now spread outward from the city's downtown district.[6] El Paso grew into a major site for mining, livestock, tourism, and international trade.[7] Brownsville began modernizing when the St. Louis, Brownsville, and Mexico Railway reached the border city in 1904. In North Texas, the twin cities of Dallas and Fort Worth acted as a commercial center for regional goods heading to markets out of state.[8]

The new Progressive age also had a new style of politics. The reform wing of the Democratic party, for one, took on new crusades to remedy society's ills, among them efforts to battle corruption in big business, improve conditions in which prisoners lived, and bolster the system of public schools. During the early years of the twentieth century, progressives took up further reforms, working to modernize charitable institutions such as state-run homes for the mentally ill, moralize society by prohibiting the sale and consumption of alcohol, grant women the right to vote, and eliminate abuses by politicians. By the early 1910s, good government leagues waged drives to alter the old ways of running city and county business in the lower border, where machine politics had reigned for decades.[9]

THE TEXAS-MEXICAN GENERATION

At least two major features distinguished the Texas-Mexican generation living in the period circa 1880–1910 from the preceding one: the size and origin of the population and a more participatory role for Tejanos. In the first case, the Mexican-American community increased perceptively. In 1880, according to Roberto M. Villarreal, the total Texas-Mexican population (including those of foreign birth) numbered 70,653. This increased to 105,193 in 1890, to 163,617 in 1900, and then to 277,331 in 1910. In 1880, the percentage of native-born Texas Mexicans was 39 percent of the total population, but ten years later this standing had risen to 51 percent and the pattern continued thereafter. In 1900, 57 percent of the Texas-Mexican population claimed the United States as their country of birth, and in 1910, 55 percent did so.[10]

As had been the case before 1880, Mexican Americans predominantly peopled three regions of the state in 1900: about 46 percent of Tejanos resided in South Texas below the Nueces River; 36 percent lived in Central Texas; and the remaining 18 percent were situated in a section of the state west of the Hill Country, including El Paso.[11] But by the last decades of the nineteenth century, Mexicans were advancing in increased numbers towards new areas. They began to settle on Central Texas farms, renting alongside Anglo- and African-American tenant farmers. Migrant farm workers pushed towards Wharton (southwest of Houston in Wharton County) and as far east as the cotton lands adjacent to the Sabine River.[12] In the early years of the twentieth century, these migrant workers traveled in family groups by train and wagons to other parts of the state looking for work in the bountiful cotton fields in their struggle for survival.[13]

Another significant change during this time was an upturn in the Tejano community's involvement in regional, economic, and political activities. Several things may explain this. The rise of communities in South Texas and West Texas made positions available on town councils, police forces, and in public works. The fact that by this time the majority of Texas Mexicans were of native birth meant that the Tejano community had an increased familiarity with American institutions: schools, churches, and other mainstream agencies that helped Tejanos take advantage of new opportunities opening up in a modernizing society. Lastly, Anglo Americans may have encouraged such a participation, ironically as part of the apparatus of control: Tejanos were free to help uplift the growing population of Texas Mexicans, as long as they remained in physically separated areas and did not disturb the Anglo society.

CONTINUED FRAGMENTATION

The transition occurring in late-nineteenth and early-twentieth-century Texas gave rise to a fledgling middle class. This element within the Mexican-American community had remained more or less stagnant since midcentury; census figures for the period 1850 to 1900 show the group to have barely expanded. Indeed, during the last two decades of the nineteenth century, the percentage of Tejano farmers and stockraisers in the total Tejano population declined, from 12.1 percent and 4.2 percent to 8.6 percent and 0.7 percent, respectively. On the other hand, slight increases occurred in the number of Tejanos dealing in trade and transportation during the same period (7.0 percent to 7.6 percent) and in the number of Tejanos in the manufacturing and mechanical fields (7.3 percent to 9.6 percent). Even as modernization dislodged many Tejanos from specific livelihoods, the process ushered in new possibilities. Census figures show that a relatively higher percentage of literate Tejanos found employment in trade, transportation, manufacturing, and mechanical occupations, while illiterate workers predominated in the general labor sector.[14]

The late 1800s and early 1900s witnessed an increase in Tejano participation in the state's business fields. The urbanization of San Antonio, El Paso, Laredo, Corpus Christi, and other Texas cities naturally stimulated economic activity in Tejano sections, and natural reproduction in and recent immigration to the neighborhoods increased the number of customers demanding goods and services. Merchants, therefore, found themselves more involved with Anglo middlemen, negotiating with wholesalers for needed merchandise. As the mercantile establishments expanded, small shop keepers such as watchmakers, jewelers, and grocers had to develop ties with the local power structure, arranging for things such as police and fire protection and necessary business licenses. More ambitious entrepreneurs forged links to state and national markets.[15]

Also involved in the economics of the age were landowners in South Texas, most of whom resided in ranch counties such as Zapata, Duval, Starr, and Webb.[16] During this period several of them engaged in interstate transactions of stock: some imported cattle and poultry from Kentucky, others sold beef to places as far away as the Indian Territory, Kansas City, Missouri, and Chicago. In West Texas, Tejanos also ran successful ranch operations, though not the equals of those in South Texas. Alongside the rancheros were Tejano farmers who experimented with new irrigation and cotton-growing techniques.[17]

The good fortunes of the entrepreneurial class, however, did not filter down to the whole of the community. The bulk of the Mexican-American population lived apart from mainstream institutions, with many families mired in poverty. This impoverishment in part reflected the Tejanos' particular disadvantage, but it also mirrored the times. The great majority of Texans in this period—of every national origin—struggled with a hard life, working as small (often tenant) farmers and ranch hands, day workers, or as part of an urban (industrial) proletariat.

The social differences between the entrepreneurial class and the poor of Tejano society was manifested not only by material standing, but by a cultural and ideological mindset. The well-to-do of Tejano society contained an elite element that identified itself with inherited station, education, and cultural refinement. The historian Elliott Young refers to this select group in Laredo as *gente decente* (decent people, or people of high culture). Probably found in other communities in South Texas, the gente decente tended (or pretended) to be racially "whiter," took great pride in its "Latin" heritage (which, according to members, represented a counterbalance to a decadent Anglo society), and commanded due deference and respect from the rest of Tejano society for their cultural refinement, social activism, and leadership abilities.[18]

POLITICS OF DIVERSITY

Increased political activity also marked the years from the late nineteenth century to the early 1900s, most notably in, but not necessarily restricted to, South Texas. As new towns sprouted up or old ones expanded, they needed officials to oversee civic services, and Tejanos joined the competition for those new positions. Racism, political powerlessness, and restricted opportunities for advancement became unifying forces that stirred fed-up Texas Mexicans into action. Urban problems emerged as points for debate, and reform-minded Texas Mexicans joined the discussion. The new era, therefore, found descendants of the old families and upstart newcomers from different social standings playing spirited roles in community affairs. Commonly, they were part of the machines of power brokers such as Jim Wells, a Cameron County political boss, but others belonged to independent groups grappling with the issues of the day.

Hot rhetoric on the stump (usually in Spanish, but sometimes in English) typified political campaigning in Cameron, Starr, Webb, and other counties of South Texas. Electioneering both for Mexican Americans and Anglo Americans was essential to maintaining political office; a politician had to court Mexican voters or else face their displeasure in the next election. In Laredo and Duval County, politicos thus appealed to political factions such as the *guaraches* (sandals) and *botas* (boots) on issues of community importance. These were local groups whose names had little to do with representing constituents of different class standings as their labels (poor vs. rich) might suggest. In reality, the former represented the ranks of the old guard that had dominated politics since the 1850s, while the latter appealed to newer elements in the region wanting electoral reform.

In these counties Mexican Americans had consistent success in electing public officials from the 1880s through the early 1900s. Tejano campaigners were visible at almost all stages of local politics; their attendance at grass-roots-level conventions even influenced processes outside South Texas by determining who would represent Tejanos at the congressional, senatorial, and state conventions.[19]

Intense political action was also evident in El Paso and its surrounding Rio Grande Valley communities, such as San Elizario, Ysleta, and Socorro. In the late nineteenth and early twentieth century, Tejanos worked resolutely for a political voice in El Paso County and indeed won compromises from the Anglo Democratic ring. Tejanos retained posts, for example, in the county commissioners' court. Among the incumbents was Octaviano A. Larrazolo, a district attorney who later moved to New Mexico and served as that state's governor. Tejano politicians in far West Texas kept abreast of politics by attending the county conventions of the two major parties.[20]

The political fate of San Antonio Tejanos differed strikingly from that of those in South Texas and the valley. As of the last decades of the nineteenth century, Bexareños filled only a few city offices. The situation only worsened in the face of a rapidly increasing Anglo population—by 1900, San Antonio had grown into the largest city in the state—and its efforts to disfranchise Tejanos and subdue their political ambitions. By no means did San Antonio political activism abate during this period, however. Historian Ana Luisa Martínez, in her study of journalist Pablo Cruz, found middle-class leaders in San Antonio engrossed in city politics, among them Cruz, editor of the city's newspaper *El Regidor,* and businessman Francisco A. Chapa. These two men (among others) acted as spokespersons for the San Antonio barrio during the 1890s and early 1900s and ultimately gained political success: Chapa won a post on the San Antonio Independent School Board between 1899 and 1907 (in 1913 he became a municipal alderman, representing the ward in the city that included the Tejano enclave) and Cruz similarly served on the Antonio Independent School Board, winning his position in 1907.[21]

Tejano politicians also took stock of the opportunities available to them under the aegis of political bossism. While on the one hand they used the arrangement for self-aggrandizement, to protect their vested interests, and to see to the preservation of business and regional needs, they also utilized boss rule to derive benefits for their communities. Through organized pressure, especially where they outnumbered Anglos, Tejanos effectively persuaded political rings to concede them patronage appointments. Additionally, Tejano politicians worked with bosses to assist community members facing legal problems or personal tragedy such as the death of a loved one or the loss of a home due to natural disaster.[22]

Among the most prominent Mexican-American politicians serving during this era was J. T. Canales. Between 1905 and 1910, Canales served as the representative for Cameron, Hidalgo, Starr, and Zapata counties in the Texas House of Representatives. In that capacity, he voted for numerous progressive measures, among them education, judicial, and tax reform, modernization of irrigation laws, and the creation of a State Department of Agriculture.[23] Another person who exerted wide influence in South Texas politics was Manuel Guerra. Fluent in English and astute in business techniques, he settled in Roma in the 1870s to care for a new business and to administer the Guerra properties in Starr County. During the mid-1880s, he created a political base in Roma, and until 1915, when he passed away, he used his post on the Starr County Commissioners' Court to rule over county matters.[24]

WORKING-CLASS ACTIVITY

Unpleasant or outright dangerous working conditions, low pay, and limited opportunity for advancement prompted Tejano laborers to take action by launching organizing drives for self-improvement. Though Anglo labor leaders did not aggressively recruit among minorities, working-class Tejanos, individually and collectively, affiliated with receptive labor unions in an effort to combat their impoverishment or enhance the general well-being of their communities.

Surprisingly, such alliances developed early outside South Texas. In 1886, Mexicans living in Galveston joined one of the first labor organizations in the state, the Screwmen's Benevolent Association, and in Central Texas the Texas Knights of Labor courted San Antonio Tejanos for incorporation into industrial unions, although these overtures appear to have been short lived.[25]

Some of the first strikes involving Tejanos erupted in regions far beyond the trans-Nueces. One significant strike that included Mexican-

American participation occurred in the Texas Panhandle: the well-known cowboy walkout of 1883. A man named Juan A. Gómez ostensibly helped lead the work stoppage, for he signed a document listing the cowhands' demands upon the ranch managers.[26] El Paso was also the scene of organized labor activism in the early years of the twentieth century. There, some two hundred construction workers at the El Paso Electric Street Car Company struck in 1901 for an increase in pay, as did smelter workers in the city in 1907, both unsuccessfully.[27] In North Texas, Tejano miners from Thurber engaged in a work protest during the 1890s. But in South Texas, Mexican Americans also walked off the job to protest unwarranted reductions of wages, arbitrary dismissals, and replacement of experienced crews with cheaper laborers. Between 1904 and 1909, for instance, railroad hands in the border region on three separate occasions struck for such reasons, although none of these work stoppages succeeded in winning the desired concessions from management.[28]

In Laredo, Tejano workers voted to affiliate themselves with the American Federation of Labor (AFL) when the national organization undertook a program to integrate Mexican Americans living in the Southwest into its ranks. In that city, Tejanos in the railway shops had organized Federal Labor Union (FLU) No. 11,953 in 1905. A year later, with an AFL charter on hand, the FLU launched a strike against the Mexican Railway Company (connecting Laredo with lines extending north to San Antonio and east to Corpus Christi) for better wages. But railroad management brought in strikebreakers, or "scabs," and court injunctions to weaken the walkout. While the workers won concessions early in 1907, the company relocated across the Rio Grande to Nuevo Laredo.[29]

While at its peak of strength, FLU No. 11,953 helped found a companion union to represent Mexican American miners. For years, Mexican mine workers along the border had railed against management for fixing scales that swindled them of part of the coal they mined, paying them in script redeemable only at the company store, and forcing them to work long hours. Despite threats from company owners, the miners entertained the overtures of FLU No. 11,953, and in 1907 formed Mine Union No. 12,340. Now they pressed the mining companies to address their grievances, but, as had happened to FLU No. 11,953, the miners' union (soon allied with the national United Mine Workers Union) found management too determined in its resolve. By the 1920s, Mine Union No. 12,340 had become a casualty of the national backlash against labor radicalism.[30]

Mexico in Texas

A majority of Texas Mexicans held the traditions and customs of Mexico dear, and they continued to draw upon their immigrant heritage in isolated ranch settlements and segregated enclaves. Others clung to the past out of contempt for the behavior of Anglo Texans. Furthermore, Mexican nationals continuously crossed into Texas pursuing seasonal work on farms and in developing cities, and by the late 1890s and early twentieth century, farmers actively recruited seasonal workers at several border stations.[31] As the immigrants shuttled back and forth between the two countries, they reinforced ties to Mexico and its culture in the Texas communities in which they landed and, in many cases, eventually settled.

HISTORICAL FORCES AND IMMIGRANTS

Since a significant portion of Tejanos were new arrivals from Mexico, they helped maintain the whole group's cultural contact with the old country. Major influxes of people from below the Rio Grande began to occur in the 1890s. In 1880 and 1890, 61 percent and 49 percent respectively of the Tejano community reported their status as being of foreign birth. In 1900, 43 percent of the total Texas-Mexican population of 164,974 reported to have been born in Mexico, but combined with first generation Tejanos, immigrants and their offspring constituted 86 percent of the Mexican-American people in Texas. Of the total 277,331 Tejanos counted in the census of 1910, 45 percent were foreign born, but many native-born Tejanos reported that one or both parents were immigrants.[32]

Isolation from mainstream American institutions strengthened the cohesiveness of the immigrant communities. Residential segmentation was the order of the day in Texas, and physical distance prevented Tejanos from interacting with whites to a great degree.[33] Tejanos who lived along the border towns, furthermore, turned to Mexico as an alternative market, regardless of social class. They read Spanish-language newspapers published in Mexico, sent their children to be educated in the motherland, and traveled south for pleasure or to buy fineries and other luxuries.[34]

Rural residence also acted as a historical force that perpetuated insular group characteristics. Close to 75 percent of the Tejano community during this period was rural,[35] making a living by laying track for the expanding railroad and performing other forms of hard labor, but most commonly working as day laborers on emerging farmlands. As already noted, Texas Mexicans during this era increasingly turned to migrant labor, roaming from the farms of the Coastal Bend of South Texas all the way to those in far East Texas.[36]

Similarly isolated were the New Mexican *pastores* who moved into the Panhandle with their sheep in the late 1870s. Originally, these sheepmen had come with a New Mexican of prominence named Casimero Romero and established homes in the Canadian River Valley; they brought with them some household furnishings, ranch gear, and about 4,500 head of sheep, numerous horses, and a plentiful supply of livestock to furnish them with meat and milk. Other pastores followed, seeking to take advantage of the free grazing on the Panhandle's open plains. Initially these immigrants prospered; the ranchmen marketed their wool in Las Vegas, New Mexico, and as far away as Dodge City, Kansas. But then, in the early 1880s, a series of freezing winters devastated the sheep herds. More ominously, Anglo cattlemen who had moved into the region almost simultaneously began acquiring titles to much of the land that the sheepmen had claimed for years. As they "legitimized" their claims, the cattle ranchers drove out the sheepmen, thus snuffing out the short life of the early Mexican-American settlements in the Texas Panhandle (1874–84).[37]

Concentration in menial occupations also worked to detach Tejanos from Anglo society, further nourishing immigrant cultural forms. The economic changes that took Texas in dramatic new directions in the last half of the nineteenth century allowed some Tejanos to find employment in white-collar positions and the professions, but the number in this group remained modest. As of the turn of the century, 54.5 percent of the Tejano population fell into the sector of the economy classified by the Census Bureau as "unspecialized labor."[38]

Government neglect of the Tejano population may be identified as one more factor that helped to preserve immigrant expressions. Until the 1880s, politicians pursued a laissez-faire attitude toward societal problems in general, but even when progressive reformers tried to improve education, prison life, and the condition of charitable institutions in the early twentieth century, they did not consciously direct their efforts toward improving conditions for Texas Mexicans. Indeed, little happened in Texas comparable to the actions of reformers in the northeastern United States, where educators used the public schools as institutions to acculturate the children of immigrants. To the contrary, the education of Tejanitos remained a remote concern to white society; some Anglos believed in purposely keeping Tejanos as an uneducated proletariat, or, at best, providing Tejanos only the fundamentals of learning.

For that matter, elements within the Tejano community itself rejected the acculturation of young Tejanos into the mainstream Texas society. While some Tejanos of means did send their children to private Catholic schools and American colleges, others enrolled their children in private schools with curriculums emphasizing (in a bilingual format) the values and heritage of Mexico. One such institution was established near Ysleta in 1871, while the popular Aoy School (a Mexican Preparatory School) started in El Paso in 1887. In the 1890s, Mexican-American residents of Hebbronville founded the Colegio Altamirano, and those of Laredo established the Colegio Preparatorio in 1906. The Escuela Particular opened circa 1909 in Zapata County, and another private school started in Laredo in 1911.[39]

THE PLACE OF WOMEN

In their views toward women, Tejanos adhered to an ideal rooted in Mexican culture, though life on the Texas frontier mitigated that notion. There prevailed, for instance, a double standard of morality. Moral codes called for women to be chaste at first marriage (mothers cautioned their daughters: *cuida la honra*—guard your honor) and remain faithful to their spouses thereafter, even if their husbands turned into shameless philanderers. In actuality, this behavior was not confined to the Latin temperament, for similar expressions of masculine traits may be found in other Western cultures. (As an example of such *machismo*, there existed in Texas during the nineteenth century the so-called paramour statute, which permitted a man to kill his wife's lover without fear of legal retribution.)[40]

The Mexican male in the ideal dictated that his daughters and wife remain at home, the latter to raise the children and keep the household. And women themselves may have preferred this domestic role—such a desire was not out of the ordinary, however, for in this sense Tejanas resembled other nineteenth-century women who held similar preferences.[41] But in reality, Tejano society overlooked such gender proscriptions. For one thing, women were compelled to seek employment outside the home in order to subsidize the family income. Statistics bear out this fact. In 1850, working women partly supported some 5.2 percent of Tejano households, but that figure had increased almost fourfold by 1900.[42]

In fact, Tejanas themselves skirted the maxim that they ought to remain homebound. Cases in point are of Mexican-born women such as the aforementioned Sara Estela Ramírez and Santa Teresa Urrea, who assumed activist roles, though in different callings. Ramírez, as noted, participated in labor activism along the border in behalf of the PLM, while Urrea made her mark as a *curandera* (folk healer) who came to El Paso in 1896 fleeing political opponents who charged her with participation in the efforts to incite a popular rebellion against President Porfirio Díaz. During her brief stay in that city, Santa Teresa reportedly healed numerous patients.[43]

TIES TO THE HOMELAND

Curanderos in Mexican society were thought capable of effecting cures through special healing powers. During this period, additionally, folk healers stood as crucial symbols linking Texas Mexicans to the traditional past in a world in rapid flux, according to the anthropologist/folklorist José E. Limón. This is evident in the career of Guadalajara-born Don Pedrito Jaramillo, who practiced *curanderismo* in South Texas from 1881 until his death in 1907. As Texas society changed in the late nineteenth and early twentieth century, Don Pedrito came to symbolize a bulwark against the social transformation. His shrine at Los Olmos (near present-day Falfurrias in Brooks County) provided a sanctuary where Tejanos could identify with the values of the old culture at a time when an emphasis on progress and material advancement subverted the foundations of the familiar pastoral society.[44]

The writing and singing of corridos was an important medium by which people expressed individual or community sentiments. Epic events, for example, could be narrated through the corridos, the subjects of the adventure either glorified or disparaged, depending on the popular feeling. This was the case of *"El corrido de José Mosqueda"* which told of the Mosqueda gang's robbery of the Rio Grande Railroad on January 1, 1891, between Port Isabel and Brownsville. In the 1890s, the ballad related the grief of those victimized by the theft, the anxiety of the men implicated in the crime, and both support for and disgust with the perpetrators who fled across the Rio Grande with part of the plunder.[45]

Border ballads further tell of Tejano discontent with social relations and display the bitterness felt toward the Anglo authority structure. One corrido extolled the exploits of Jacinto Treviño who in July 1910 took on the Texas Rangers after killing a white man who had beaten his younger brother to death. When the Rangers set up an ambush for Treviño near San Benito, he outwitted them, waylaying and, according to legend, killing or injuring four of the officers before fleeing to Mexico. Treviño became a wanted man by law enforcement but a hero within the Tejano commu- nity for his bravery in taking on the hated rinches. In 1970, a college in Mercedes (in the lower Rio Grande Valley) was named after him, though the school closed its doors in 1976.[46]

Corridos also gave voice to a cultural expression of disapproval of the rapidly changing times, a theme Professor Limón detects in the ballad *"El corrido de Gregorio Cortéz."* As mentioned earlier in this chapter, Cortéz had shot a peace officer in Karnes County and, fearing for his life, cut across the South Texas countryside towards Laredo. While white society saw Cortéz as a murderer, Texas Mexicans sympathized with the fugitive and assisted him in his flight to the border by providing him with horses, ammunition, and food. Finally captured after ten days on the run, he was tried and convicted for the killing of a member of the pursuing posse (the governor pardoned him in 1913).

Countless corridos immortalized Cortéz and his escapade with the Anglos. According to Limón, the ballad narrative of Cortéz's heroism and epic struggle helped Texas Mexicans identify with an earlier time, before the economic changes of the early twentieth century had deteriorated the quality of their lives. For Tejanos, the ballad of Gregorio Cortéz conjured thoughts of the time during which they had lorded over the range lands as skillful horsemen.[47]

Ties to the homeland are also evident in the level of political inter- action with Mexico. Tejanos stayed abreast of Mexican politics through family ties or through firsthand information provided by seasonal workers in Texas. On the other hand, many immigrants made Texas their home not only because of better economic prospects there but because they had expressly chosen exile in the state to escape the economic and political tyranny of Don Porfirio (Díaz).

The Texas-Mexican community thus supported Catarino Garza's liberal politics (disseminated through Garza's South Texas newspapers *El Libre Pensador* and *El Comercio Mexicano*) denouncing the Mexican president's stranglehold on the executive.[48] In 1891, Garza (whose attempted murder had led to the aforementioned Rio Grande City riot of 1888) and his army of volunteers set out to stir popular upheaval against the dictator, demanding (among other things) greater political freedom for the people of Mexico, easier ways for ordinary folks to acquire unoccupied properties, and an end to the Díaz policy of letting foreign powers invest in Mexico's economy. On September 15, 1891, a group of somewhere between sixteen and forty men, with Garza at their head, crossed the Rio Grande near modern day La Grulla, Texas. On the Mexican side, they linked up with supporters, bringing their ranks to near one hundred fighters. Following a fierce offensive by the Mexican army to disband and track down the insurgents, Garza retreated across the Rio Grande in late September, but not before his men had suffered several deaths at the hands of the Mexican military. From Duval County and the border region, Garza planned further attacks, though three more guerrilla-style incursions by the Garzistas that year produced little of substance. American officials, meanwhile, moved into the chaparral country to remove Garza and his conspirators but found the population of South Texas uncooperative, choosing to shield the revolutionaries from U.S. troops and Texas Rangers. In February 1892, Garza made his way to Houston, New Orleans, and Key West, where he and his brother became involved in the anti-Spanish activities of Cuban exiles. In 1895, he met his death in Panama (then a part of the nation of Columbia) after joining forces with revolutionaries seeking to overthrow the conservative government in their homeland of Columbia.[49]

Tejanos in a Multicultural Society

Though Anglo Americans by the 1880s controlled practically every mainstream institution affecting Tejanos, and though the economic transformation of the era had adversely affected Texas-Mexican workers, Mexican Americans showed resiliency in adapting to modernity. Tejano entrepreneurs sought to pursue new business opportunities, civic activists attempted to carve out greater roles for themselves in politics, and laborers tried to help themselves and their fellow workers through contacts with national labor unions organizing in Texas.

Tejanos made such efforts at acculturation even as they affirmed their own group identity. Some went about their lives as unreconstructed nationalists stern in their fidelity to Mexican tradition. Many others sought to mold their destiny as part of a syncretic culture: two heritages, two world views. This latter element, diverse in the gradation of acculturation, occupied an uncommon place in Texas society, able to move to varying degrees between the cultural polarity of the recent arrivals from Mexico and that of the Americanized, chauvinistic Texan.

CHAPTER FIVE

Corridors North, 1900–1930

Like other immigrants from Mexico during the last decades of the nineteenth century, Luis G. Gómez went north to Texas with the intention of finding work and building up a nice nest egg. In Central Texas during the mid-1880s, he made the acquaintance of a man named Eleodoro Tamez (a fellow immigrant who had already integrated himself into the local work force, the foreman for an Anglo-American fence-building company) and soon the two entered into a partnership, naming their business Tamez-Gómez and Company. They specialized in a variety of trades, most of them of a back-breaking quality, including land clearing, fence posting, rock busting, road building, and railroad laying. Work for Gómez and his crew (including at times as many as twenty to thirty men) was tough. It necessitated camping out at the place of employment, moving constantly in pursuit of new labor, driving the freight rig from one locale to the next, carrying the tools required for each job, and somehow obtaining provisions for long stays. Crewmembers with families in tow had the additional responsibility of ensuring the safety of their wives and children.

But despite the difficulties, Gómez did well for himself in Texas. He did not mind arduous toil so long as it improved his material standing. On one particular occasion, the Tamez-Gómez Company made a $450.00 profit for two weeks of difficult labor. His work ethic won him the trust of Anglo Americans, and his honesty and decency helped his company land job contracts regularly (especially as his command of English improved). Some of his Anglo employers even took him into their homes and provided him with good references when he requested them. Contrary to what might have been expected, Gómez spoke favorably of Anglos in Texas.

After continuing to manage work crews in and around Central Texas and other parts of the state, Gómez sometime in 1910 settled down with his family to live near Kingsville in South Texas. He never acquired the fortune he sought when he left Mexico for Texas, but he had found living conditions an improvement over what he knew in the old country. Only for visits did Luis Gómez ever return to Mexico.[1]

From the late nineteenth century and continuing until the beginning of the Great Depression, an estimated 1.5 million people like Luis G. Gómez found their way from Mexico to the United States.[2] For a brief time, the immigrants who arrived in Texas tugged at the sentiments of residents of urban *colonias* (Mexican-American settlements) and rural hamlets—using the old country as a point of moral and spiritual reference. Natives and non-natives alike, however, looked no further than their country of residence—the United States—for their identity. This dichotomy—wherein an immigrant and a Mexican-American ethnicity coexisted, even competed with one another—stands as a unique phenomenon in Tejano (and therefore Mexican-American) history.[3] Consequently, the immigrant experience and the Americanization process that unfolded during this era receive equal space in this and the following chapter.

A New Migratory Wave

PUSH AND PULL FACTORS

What caused this unprecedented transborder migration? Generally, students of immigration have broken down the explanation into "push" and "pull" factors. Compelling people to leave Mexico for the United States in the last years of the nineteenth century and extending into 1910 were the distressful conditions many faced under the dictatorship of President Porfirio Díaz. The rural poor were forcibly removed from their common lands by ambitious land barons and faced a dismal life of peonage on the haciendas. Population increases in the late nineteenth century, moreover, weighed on Mexico's semifeudal subsistence economy, pushing the peasantry to search elsewhere for opportunity, often in the United States.[4]

The Mexican Revolution, which broke out in 1910 and lasted until 1920, also became a catalyst for migration. Mexicans fled to the United

States to escape the horrors of war or reprisals from the feuding factions. Even after the fighting had ended, life during Mexico's reconstruction in the 1920s was still precarious, for armed rebels roamed the land, food shortages plagued the population, and unemployment ran amok.

By the 1920s, on the other hand, an economic revolution unfolding along the United States border pulled thousands from their struggling country to try their luck in a more peaceful land. From the 1880s to the early 1900s, thousands of miles of railroad tracks were laid to integrate the vast American Southwest into the United States economy. Mining companies in the region began the excavation of copper and coal. Farmers in the lower Rio Grande Valley transformed old ranchos, which they had recently acquired, into profitable citrus and cotton concerns. Increasingly, railroad contractors, mining companies, and agriculturists in Texas and other parts of the United States looked south to Mexico as a source of needed labor.

The United States' entry into World War I created further labor shortages. The Immigration Act of 1917 had closed the door on European laborers wishing to immigrate; then millions of American workers flocked to new factories or went overseas to serve their nation.[5]

Recently, scholars Gilbert G. Gonzalez and Raul A. Fernandez have called the push-pull theory into question. For them, this explanation does not consider the transnational impact of American capitalism on migration. According to their interpretation, Mexico became an economic dependent of the United States during the late nineteenth and early twentieth century when Díaz opened Mexico's doors to U.S. investors. As Americans poured money into Mexico's railroad lines, ranches, mines, oil fields, and textile factories, the working masses reeled. Peasants now faced expulsion from lands taken up by the foreigners, while laborers in general coped with the ups and downs of an economy in the throes of rapid modernization. In response to the transformation underway, unemployed Mexicans migrated to other parts of Mexico, and by the early 1900s to the United States, where the same transnational economy craved for armies of tractable workers.[6]

Notwithstanding the multiple factors behind migration, Texas farmers welcomed the immigrants, claiming them to have a specific suitability for stoop work. Congressman John Nance Garner of Uvalde rationalized it thusly in 1920 while testifying before the House Immigration and Naturalization Committee, arguing in favor of a more open U.S.-Mexico border:

I believe I am within the bounds of truth when I say that the Mexican man is a superior laborer when it comes to grubbing land. . . . And I may add that the prices that they charge are much less than the same labor would be from either the negro or the white man and for the same time they do . . . a third more—they produce a third more results from their labor than either the negro or white man would do.[7]

So much did growers wish to rely on Mexican hands that a profitable business of smuggling immigrants into Texas fields developed despite statutes forbidding recruiters from contracting labor in foreign nations. Labor agents crossed the border into Mexico and, with promises of higher wages, smuggled workers across the Rio Grande and shipped them to different destinations.[8]

HOW MANY IMMIGRANTS?

Demographers find it difficult to ascertain how many people crossed from Mexico into Texas and the rest of the United States. In the period before the 1920s, there existed a more or less unpoliced U.S.-Mexican border. The U.S. Department of Labor established the Border Patrol in 1924, but its agents were largely preoccupied by the enforcement of customs laws and Prohibition. The government imposed certain stipulations for entering into the United States in 1924, some of which involved entry fees that the Mexican immigrants could not afford to pay. While some immigrants entered legally, many avoided bureaucratic entanglements. Thus, precision in calculating the number of Mexican immigrants that came to Texas is imprecise,[9] but according to the best estimates the figures for the "Mexico-born population," 1900–1930 were:

1900	1910	1920	1930
71,062	125,016	251,827	266,364[10]

RESTRICTIONIST DEBATE

Americans divided on the merits of permitting a dramatic increase in immigration from Mexico. Alarmist warnings regarding the dangers of too many Mexicans in the United States had actually been sounded early in the twentieth century, but nativism grew pronounced by the 1920s. The debate over immigration took two paths. Advocates of an open border insisted that the matter was a harmless one. Restrictionists, on the other hand, saw many perils in a Mexican human floodtide.[11]

The debate turned on both economic and racial convictions. The advocates of an open border advanced the economic argument that U.S. agriculture could not survive if the government interrupted immigration. Growers maintained that immigrants worked hard and did not demand the high wages wanted by Anglo field workers. Antirestrictionists also tried to assure those fearing social ruination that the "Mexican Problem" was manageable. They conceded that Mexicans were a degenerate people and posed some moral and political dangers to the country, but maintained that Mexicans were, all in all, docile and law-abiding and made good citizens (actually, good "second-class" citizens, as Texans did not realistically contemplate extending Mexicans full political rights). Finally, they assured their fellow Anglos, the immigrants could be controlled by restricting their employment opportunities to the fields, where they would not jeopardize the fabric of white society.[12]

Small-scale farmers and Anglo field hands, conversely, challenged the notion of free admittance into the country. For these opponents of an open border, Mexicans threatened U.S. national identity. The influx of Mexican workers, they argued, might create a peonage system that would bring into question the American guarantee of economic freedom; their willingness to work at low wages would rob U.S. citizens of their "inherent" right to work. Labor unions also sought to arrest easy entry into the country, fearing that Mexican immigrants might, once across the border, reject farm work and seek employment in mines and factories. A cast of politicians, educators, concerned citizens, and racists argued further that racially backward Mexicans would increase the rates of disease, crime, and various other social problems.[13]

By the end of the 1920s, the restrictionists triumphed over the antirestrictionists as the United States government directed consuls to exercise greater controls in granting passports to Mexicans. Though the number of entrance visas granted to Mexicans fell after 1929, by then the Great Depression had begun to hamper immigration northward from Mexico.[14]

DISPERSAL

Many of the Mexican immigrants who came to the United States between 1900 and 1930 arrived in border towns such as El Paso and Laredo by train, for railways by the latter part of the nineteenth century connected numerous points in Mexico to Texas. From these settlements on the Rio Grande, and San Antonio in the interior, the immigrants dispersed into all parts of the state,[15] even venturing into those sections only lightly pioneered by the Texas Mexicans during the nineteenth century.

The areas most heavily affected by immigration, expectedly, were the older Tejano strongholds of the trans-Nueces and the El Paso and San Antonio areas. South Texas attracted Mexican nationals because it was not far from Mexico and because farming in the Rio Grande Valley offered many seasonal jobs picking cotton, vegetables, and some fruits. In Nueces County, where the economic transformation from ranch to cotton farm unfolded between 1900 and 1910, the immigrants worked crops on lands that they had recently grubbed of brush.[16]

The El Paso Valley and the newly settled West Texas region similarly saw tremendous expansion in their foreign-born Tejano populations. "El Paso symbolized to Mexicans what New York had represented to European immigrants: the entranceway to what they believed would be a better life," explains the historian Mario T. García. From the 1880s until the early decades of the twentieth century, this border town and its environs offered employment for down-and-out Mexican workers as it became a booming metropolis—El Paso's population increased from 39,571 in 1920 to 58,291 in 1930—and the valley around it developed into a thriving cotton-farming section.[17] At the same time, small, emerging settlements in West Texas needed a great influx of range hands to handle sheep and cattle as well as field workers for new cotton-farming operations.[18]

San Antonio lured its share of immigrants because of its proximity to the border but also because burgeoning businesses needed unskilled workers. Immigrants, furthermore, saw it as a good home base for seasonal migration. Between 1900 and 1930, therefore, the Alamo City's Mexican population increased from 13,722 to 82,373, a substantial percentage of this number claiming foreign birth.[19] From Béxar, Mexicans sojourned north or to nearby farms (where some became sharecroppers alongside African-American and Anglo renters). San Antonio, noted one observer, "poured out Mexicans into the cotton fields with such speed that by 1920, the greatest density of rural Mexican population in Texas was not along the Rio Grande but in Caldwell County in sight of the dome of the State Capitol." By 1930, several counties around the cities of Austin and Waco contained fledgling Mexican enclaves.[20]

Mexicans were not only entering new geographic locales during this period but also settings that lacked the old Hispanic ambience still evident in South Texas and the Béxar region. These new places, furthermore, contained overwhelming white and black majorities. Certainly, such descriptions applied to East and North Texas, which also received Mexican immigrants. Work on *el traque* (railroad tracks) lured many Mexicans to Houston by the 1910s, for instance, but the Bayou City's incredible rise as a major oil and gas production center opened many other sorts of employment for immigrants, as did the completion of the Houston Ship Channel, which spurred even greater activity in the cotton compresses, the textile mills, and construction companies. By 1910, some 2,000 Mexicans had settled in Houston just since the 1880s and 1890s. Twenty years later, the city's Mexican-origin population stood at 15,000, many of them immigrants. Mexicans could also be found in Beaumont and Galveston by the 1910s.[21]

In North Texas, the Dallas–Fort Worth area saw the beginnings of Mexican settlements similar to those in Houston. By the 1910s, immigrants fleeing the Mexican Revolution mixed with Tejano day laborers working with local railroad companies and founded a barrio (which came to be called "Little Mexico") just north of Dallas's central business district, there joined by others doing pick-and-shovel work on gas and sewer systems, streets, and street-car lines. In the 1930s the U.S. Census counted nearly 6,000 persons of Mexican descent in Dallas, many of whom had made their way north from Mexico and lived in "Little Mexico" and in newer barrios with such names as "Indiana Alley" and *"Los Altos de Juárez"* (Juarez Heights).[22] In Fort Worth, the Mexican population stood at 4,426 in 1920, but declined to 3,955 ten years later. Mexicans had first arrived in the city during the 1870s, and by the early decades of the twentieth century, some eight different barrios existed, among the most prominent being *El Papalote* (the Windmill), the North Side, and *La Fundición* (the South Side). From the several barrios, residents walked to their places of work, generally the nearby stockyards, the slaughterhouse, the railroad grounds, the foundries, or downtown restaurants, hotels, or laundries where they performed unskilled labor.[23] Like San Antonio in Central Texas, Dallas and Fort Worth turned out Mexicans into neighboring cotton counties, among them Ellis and Kaufman.

But immigrants found other places in North Texas offering employment, such as Milam County, where they worked on farms and in lignite mines, in McLennan County and Robertson County, where some became cotton pickers and wood choppers respectively, and in Denton County, where they turned to farm, ranch, or railroad jobs. As of 1930, however, the number of Tejanos in North Texas in no way compared to figures in the southern and far western regions of the state.[24]

The Immigrant Generation

For the most part, those who came to Texas from Mexico descended from the class of poor folks. These economic refugees were the ones to cause the aforementioned immigration policy debates of the 1920s: they worked cheaply and performed labor shunned by whites yet were seen as a social danger to the United States because of their alleged illiteracy, propensity to commit crime and spread disease, and reluctance to acculturate.

An upper class of *ricos* (wealthy people) and a middle class of professionals also fled northward, hoping to stay in Texas temporarily until politics stabilized in Mexico. These included exiles whose ties to the Porfirian order made their stay precarious in Mexico; others were landowners trekking to Texas to escape the wrath of vindictive peasant armies. In the 1920s, the political emigrés were followed by refugees escaping the turmoil in Mexico created by the anti-Catholic administration of President Plutarco Elías Calles. Though not as significant in number compared to the bulk of immigrants who descended from the lower class, the ricos could be influential due to their backgrounds as people of education and means. These families were typically found in the lower Rio Grande Valley, San Antonio, Laredo, El Paso, and Houston.[25]

In Texas this corps of elites played significant roles in ethnic enclaves. They promoted a Mexican past through the distribution of Mexican books, magazines, musical records, and Spanish-language newspapers from Mexico City. They sponsored speaking engagements and theatrical performances and editorialized or extolled the virtues of *la patria* (Mexico, their native country). Meantime, they formed their own clubs and held exclusive cultural activities. They maintained a commitment to preserving Mexican nationalist sentiments within the community of immigrants.[26]

IMPLANTATION

Many of the immigrants had planned to stay in Texas only so long as to make enough money to permit them to live a more comfortable life back in the homeland. Consequently, they did not pursue American citizenship. In their view, Americans in Mexico were not any more inclined to naturalize, even as they benefited immensely from the natural resources (such as oil) of that nation. Moreover, many felt Mexico a better country, especially in cultural terms, than the United States. Since they had every intention of returning to the old country, the visitors asked why they should be expected to become U.S. citizens.[27]

Thus, in the period from the early twentieth century until the Great Depression, numerous Tejano communities throughout Texas took on a "foreign" quality. Recent arrivals integrated themselves into the local Spanish-surnamed population, renting or building shacks in the Mexican section of town or finding work with Texas-Mexican crews, spending part of their wages in *cantinas* (bars) in the barrio, frequenting Mexican-American gatherings, and even courting the daughters of Texas-born Mexicans.[28] Together, this mass of laboring poor and the rico exiles came to constitute what historians refer to as the "Immigrant Generation."[29]

A NONNATIVE WAY

The look to Mexico is discernible in the persistent attachment of the foreign-born to traditional cultural conventions. In Texas there thrived concepts from south of the Rio Grande concerning family cohesion, gender roles, the customary age for marriage (by late adolescence), adherence to Catholicism, and the preference for use of the Spanish language. Reinforcing the above precepts were corridos and other songs, poems, folklore and other oral traditions, and Mexican-style ceremonies and social gatherings occasioned by weddings, funerals, and religious holy days.[30]

Within such a context, immigrant women did not fare too well. Immigrant males, like Texas-born Mexican-American men, still held the attitude that women's chief duties consisted of raising children and keeping house, but financial need at times still compelled women to find employment. The jobs they took, however, were hardly profitable: most did "women's work" as laundresses or domestic servants in the border cities. For the most part, they joined the ranks of fellow immigrant women who rounded out the labor pool in the urban centers as garment workers, pecan shellers, and cigar rollers, or in the rural areas as cotton pickers toiling for $3.00 to $5.00 a day.[31]

To be sure, middle-class women fared better. They enjoyed an improved standard of living and joined exclusive clubs, especially charitable organizations designed to assist the less-fortunate members of the colonias. Some became activists, like the sisters Teresa and Andrea Villarreal of Coahuila, who after arriving in San Antonio to escape Díaz's thugs, lobbied for the release of incarcerated Mexican revolutionaries in the city (pre-1910) and through *Regeneración*, a woman's group, lent support to the Mexican Revolution, which they viewed as part of a struggle to end the oppression of women in Mexico.[32]

In the countryside life may have been more restrictive. There, male heads of families discouraged women from attending school or learning English, as some felt education for women disrupted traditional male-female relationships. Wives and daughters typically stayed back on the farm when fathers and sons went into town. Once married, preferably early, women bore babies successively; most lacked knowledge of birth-control measures, but men also preferred to have large families, considering a succession of offspring as a mark of their virility (and recognizing the economic benefits to having many children). An older family member, such as a grandmother, or a *partera* (midwife), helped deliver babies at home.[33]

Habitually, the immigrants also used Mexico as a moral compass for proper behavior. Journalists advised parents, for example, to teach children the ways of propriety, and to instill in them racial pride. Cultural and rec-reative clubs emphasized the need for the preservation of Mexico's good name, as well as its customs and traditions. *Fiestas patrias* celebrations, which dated back to the 1820s in Texas, became yearly rituals for the display of allegiance.[34] Various kinds of entertainment nurtured *"méxico de afuera"* (Mexico in the United States). Theatrical companies, relocated to Texas because of the Mexican Revolution, gave dramatic performances and the accordion-led ensemble, called the *conjunto,* diffused the music popular in northern Mexico throughout the state.[35] The Immigrant Generation proclaimed their Mexican heritage proudly, and they patriotically upheld the honor of the homeland.

Conversely, many of the recent immigrants held denigrating views toward the United States and even Mexican Americans, who, despite their earnest efforts to Americanize, were still treated as second-class citizens by white society. Recent immigrants singled out the women, criticizing them for mimicking American customs and fashions. The newcomers referred derisively to Tejanos who adopted American habits as *pochos* (cultural hybrids).[36]

LOYALTY TO THE LAND OF BIRTH

The foreign born did not forgo their concern for the old country either, and in many cities Tejanos maintained connections to specific areas in Mexico, usually their hometowns. Some colonias formed associations to raise funds for the relief of victims of natural disasters in Mexico or for other worthwhile projects in the old country, as when in 1921 the San Antonio community undertook a fundraiser to subsidize the construction of two public schools in Guanajuato. Other fund-raising drives might involve unique projects. In 1919, the people of San Antonio heeded a local call to raise money so that the old country could purchase a merchant vessel.[37]

But immigrants also engaged in causes of greater magnitude. The immigrant community included a contingent of political exiles who used Texas as a plotting ground. In addition, poor laborers regularly crossed the Rio Grande as part of their migratory pattern of labor and saw their country's despair firsthand. Furthermore, family ties to people directly affected by the tyranny of Don Porfirio and the Mexican Revolution after 1910 motivated the refugees to support one cause or another. Others felt moved to act in face of Díaz's brazen mistreatment of ordinary citizens. Among these was Leonor Villegas de Magnón, who during her stay in Mexico City in the early 1900s, became so incensed with the dictatorial regime that she joined anti-Díaz elements attempting to remove the president. Returning in 1910 to her home in Laredo, Villegas de Magnón opened her home to refugees fleeing Díaz. In 1914, she founded *La Cruz Blanca*, a volunteer medical unit that bravely went into the war zone to assist combatants injured in the Revolution. In Houston, the refugee community established *La Sociedad Mexicana "Vigilancia"* in 1914 to aid the forces of Venustiano Carranza, who led a movement to remove the Díaz surrogate Victoriano Huerta.[38]

The most prominent case of revolutionary activity in Texas against Díaz involved the aforementioned Ricardo Flores Magón and his PLM, which intrigued to remove the Mexican dictator in the hope of implementing significant changes that would, among other things, bring relief to the lower classes through land reform and prolabor policies.[39] PLM newspapers in the years before the Mexican Revolution were located in San Antonio, Del Rio, and El Paso,[40] and through *Regeneración*, the PLM's primary journalistic organ, Magón appealed to Tejano workers who identified with their comrades in the homeland or were dissatisfied with job conditions in the state. Though it is difficult to measure the ideological impact of the PLM, the party had followers as far north as Central Texas. The PLM local *"Tierra y Libertad"* of Austin, for instance, organized an impressive rally at Uhland, Texas, on Labor Day of 1912, which roughly one thousand people from other PLM chapters in Central Texas attended.

After inspirational speeches that urged societal changes in Mexico and the United States, delegates dispersed to campaign in their own communities for the goals of the PLM.[41] In actuality, most immigrants in the early twentieth century stayed out of movements that appeared to be radical for fear of jeopardizing their work or risking extradition, though some obviously participated in the labor struggles of the era.[42]

The PLM also exhorted women to join its ranks and fight on behalf of workers and women's emancipation. Indeed, women members of the PLM participated as speakers and fundraisers in forums and rallies held in El Paso, Brownsville, and Zapata and Frio counties on the eve of the Mexican Revolution. Among the PLM's several women activists was Sara Estela Ramírez, mentioned in the previous chapter.[43]

By no means was the PLM alone in work related to political developments in Mexico. There was, for example, *La Grán Liga Mexicana*, formed in 1909, which, in contrast to the PLM favored Díaz. This organization collaborated with local workers' groups in San Antonio to try to help the dictator continue his prolandholder and probusiness government.[44]

SELF-HELP SOCIETIES

Mutual aid societies first appeared among Texas Mexicans in the 1870s, but they proliferated with the coming of the Immigrant Generation and by the 1920s could be found in most regions of the state including the Big Bend and North Texas. Such organizations emerged, in part, in reaction to the abuses many Tejanos experienced at the hands of white society: public humiliation, violence, and poverty, to list only the most salient. Despite their root cause, mutualist societies tended to be nonconfrontational, concentrating on improving conditions for their members and other working-class people, assisting members in financial distress, especially after the death of a loved one, and job placement. They also attempted to uplift their compatriots through intellectual and spiritual stimulation, social camaraderie, and the creation and maintenance of a congenial and familiar environment in an adopted home.[45]

Several characteristics marked these societies as a product of the immigrants' temperament, though their memberships usually included U.S.-born Mexicans. First, they promoted a Mexicanist identity and cultivated what historian Emilio Zamora, a student of Texas-Mexican labor, calls an "ethic of mutuality," committed as they were to such ideals as fellowship, humanitarianism, and reciprocity.[46] Generally, the societies carried the name of a national hero from Mexico such as Benito Juárez. Members preferred to use Spanish when conducting business. Organizers emphasized Mexican ideals and values and held reservations about assimilation and integration into a racist society, though they were not opposed to joining the American mainstream on an equal basis.[47]

Because of common concerns, *obreros* (laborers) founded labor *mutualistas*. Shunned by the American Federation of Labor—which had, as mentioned, made some gestures towards incorporating Mexicans though soon began to look upon them as strikebreakers—and Mexican consuls who feared alienating the U.S. government, immigrant laborers looked to the customs of Mexico, where craftsmen traditionally organized into mutualistas. In San Antonio, for instance, bakers founded the *Sociedad Morelos Mutua de Panaderos,* which struck for decent wages and working conditions in 1917.[48]

Women participated in mutualistas as officers and committee heads and even founders. For example, María L. Hernández and her husband Pedro of San Antonio, Texas, organized the *Orden Caballeros de América* (Order of Knights of America) in 1929 to help solve educational problems for Tejanos and to promote civic and political activism beneficial to Mexicans, whether native or foreign born.[49] Still, scholars today disagree on the roles women played in these mutualistas. Like men, some women joined them for self-protection and probably did not advocate a feminist agenda. Some of the middle-class female members did, however, assail the double standard and urged women in general to take stands against the consumption of alcohol, war, and the subordination of women.[50]

THE IMMIGRANT PRESS

Spanish-language newspapers, often owned by political refugees and read by thousands of new arrivals (not to mention native-born Texas Mexicans) served as vehicles that maintained Tejanos' connection to Mexico. These presses praised Mexico and its people and denounced white Americans for abusing immigrants and Mexican Americans. They devoted extensive and continuous coverage to national causes in the old country.[51] Additionally, these newspapers stressed the need to preserve the old way of life, published creative pieces of literature, praised musical artists and theatrical companies performing in nearby towns, and gave much coverage to religious and secular celebrations in the community.[52] Simultaneously, they condemned practices and policies that appeared incompatible with the sense of social justice proclaimed by Americans.

Among the most widely read such paper was *La Prensa* of San Antonio, established by Ignacio E. Lozano in 1913. A daily distributed throughout many parts of the United States and the northern states of Mexico, *La Prensa* had a readership comprised of refugees, especially the rico class, and consequently denounced the string of revolutionary governments that took power in Mexico during the 1910s and 1920s. Though Lozano's elitist politics hardly harmonized with the sentiments of the many poor refugees, his efforts did influence the manner of political sentiments in Texas, for *La Prensa* disseminated the thoughts of Mexico's most prominent intellectuals during the 1910s and 1920s, among them José Vasconcelos.[53]

Summary

In the early decades of the twentieth century, waves of immigrants from Mexico re-invigorated native-born Texas-Mexican enclaves (both urban and rural) and even helped morph some of them into largely immigrant communities.[54] In these colonias, barrios, and neighborhoods resided an array of groups differing in class, status, and political visions, with numerous clubs, newspapers, labor associations, churches, and other institutions vying to meet the diverse expectations of the community.

The presence of such large numbers of foreigners modified, albeit temporarily, the nineteenth-century adaptation of Mexicans to Texas. Briefly, a Mexican "presence" vied for ascendancy with an American "presence" in the Tejano community. But this struggle would last no more than a generation, for the sentiments of many born in the United States, or others who took a liking to its institutions, would increasingly turn away from the old country to the country of their birth or adoption.[55]

CHAPTER SIX

The World War I Years and the 1920s

On August 14, 1912, Francisco Gutiérrez (age 70) and his son Manuel (age 42), approached a dwelling in Webb County in which one Alonzo W. Allee had taken up residence. Some time ago, Allee had moved into the property (the rancho *La Volanta*) which belonged to don Francisco. Allee had settled there without the notification and permission of the don. Father and son, therefore, rode up to Allee's quarters to inquire about the matter.

The two men wished to know how Allee thought he had a legitimate right to stay at La Volanta, and they brought along a lease they hoped he might sign. But when the rancheros presented Allee with the agreement, things turned violent. Only one other person had been on the premises, and from an adjoining room had picked up on the argument. According to his testimony, he next heard Allee walk across the room and, upon going to investigate, saw Allee fetch his gun and blurt out something along the lines of "I am as good a man as any Mexican!" At this point don Francisco asserted that the question at hand did merit the use of firearms. Allee responded by mortally shooting the younger Gutiérrez before turning on don Francisco and killing him as well. An immediate investigation revealed that don Manuel had apparently been able to get one shot off before dying but that don Francisco's gun still lay in its holster.

Allee stood trial in Laredo in May 1913 for the murder of Manuel Gutiérrez, wherein the jury shortly acquitted him. Allee's lawyers (from prominent law firms in South Texas) argued that the defendant, who had a broken leg at the time, had been physically assaulted by the two landowners and had killed them both in self-defense. The district attorney subsequently decided that Allee need not be tried for the murder of don Francisco, as the evidence that had resulted in the earlier acquittal would be the same used in any new trial.[1]

During the nineteen-year span between 1910 and 1930, Texas entered an age of modernity. While it was the case that men along the South Texas border still carried guns when traveling through the countryside, that disputes might well be settled by gunfire, and that justice favored Anglos able to afford good legal counsel, Texas in the new century was now part of a powerful nation pursuing an overseas empire, and with a booming national economy tied to international markets. Still, the new order did not exactly improve the quality of life for the majority of Texans of Mexican descent (Roberto M. Villarreal estimates their numbers at some 695,000 as of 1930.[2]) In many cases, in fact, the arrival of the new age only exacerbated a bad condition.

Tejano Life in the Modern Age

ON THE FARMS

By the early decades of the twentieth century, cotton had already established its reign as "king" in Texas. Along the border in South Texas, farmers arrived from states in the Midwest and North, and by the 1910s they had ushered in a veritable farm revolution (this influx of Anglos diluted the Mexican population advantage throughout South Texas).[3] Central Texas farms continued to harvest the old staple; there, tenant farming and sharecropping had become a fact of life for numerous poor whites, African Americans, and even recently arrived Tejano workers. The region of West Texas beyond the 100th meridian had also embraced the switch to cotton, and even the El Paso Valley, situated in one of the most arid regions of the United States, had yielded to cotton growing by the 1910s, primarily along a stretch of fertile land parallel to the Rio Grande east of El Paso.[4]

This transformation in the rural sector affected Tejanos in several ways. Economically, it shocked the landed aristocracy of South Texas, as the newly arrived Anglo farmers displaced more of the old rancheros through forced sales, strong-arm tactics, and legal acquisitions when Tejanos faced uncertainty due to taxes, unpaid loans, and an unpredictable market for their livestock. More fortunate were Tejano counterparts in predominantly ranch counties such as Webb, Zapata, Kenedy, Brooks, and Jim Hogg, where the topography was better suited to livestock raising. Also able to weather the encroachment of the Anglo farmers were some of the Tejano stockmen in Duval and Starr counties who had switched effectively to careers in agricultural husbandry.[5]

For common folks, the cotton-based agricultural order produced newer labor arrangements. By the 1920s, the majority of Tejano farm workers made their living in one of two ways: as various types of sharecroppers or, most commonly, as migrant seasonal workers on commercial farms.[6] Tejanos picked cotton in South and Central Texas (in 1910, for wages of 50 cents per hundred pounds; this increased to $1.00 after World War I) but began heading *"pal wes"* (*para el west*, or to West Texas) where the new farms lured them in unprecedented numbers.[7] By the 1920s, Tejanos traveling in family units were staying after the cotton-picking season and taking up residence in towns such as Sweetwater, Lamesa, Rotan, Tahoka, Littlefield, Muleshoe, Lubbock, and Plainview. In this early period, however, most such folks remained migrant workers and returned annually to South or Central Texas.

The agricultural transformation of the age also affected Tejanos politically, certainly in the rural communities of South Texas where the new Anglo farmers, through reform groups and alliances, sought to dislodge the old Democratic bosses. The recent arrivals worked specifically to deprive Mexicans of the vote, through the establishment of poll taxes (which many Tejanos could not afford) or the new practice adopted by the White Man's Primary Association that required those wishing to vote in primary elections to go before a committee and declare, "I am a white person and a Democrat." By the late 1910s, much of the Mexican-American population in the farm counties of South Texas had been disfranchised through white primaries (party primary elections in which only whites could vote), threats of firings from their jobs or of bodily harm, state legislation excluding translators from the voting booth, common intimidation by Texas Rangers, and various methods that might include not informing Tejanos about scheduled elections. Exception again must be made of the ranch counties of the region, where Mexican officeholders remained active in politics.[8]

PANHANDLE

SOUTH Plains

Amarillo

Hereford

Muleshoe
Plainview
Littlefield

Lubbock

Tahoka

W E S T

Lamesa
Rotan

Sweetwater

NEW MEXICO

El Paso
Ysleta
Socorro
San Elizario

FAR

WEST

TEXAS

Garden
City

T E X A S

Pecos

San
Angelo

Fort
Stockton

Alpine

Rio

Rocksprings

Del Rio

Grande

Eagle
Pass

MEXICO

Rio

0 miles   100   200   300

0 kilometers 100   200   300

Twentieth Century
Texas

OKLAHOMA

Red River

ARKANSAS

Dallas

Piney

Thurber

Fort Worth

Cross Timbers

Sabine

Woods

Nacogdoches

Brazos

Trinity

Waco

Colorado

River

Thorndale

River

Austin

Beaumont

LOUISIANA

Hill Country

Kyle

Bastrop

San Marcos

Houston

Lockhart

New Braunfels

San Antonio

CENTRAL

Wharton

Castroville

Ganado

Galveston

Crystal City

Pearsall

TEXAS

Victoria

Edna

Three Rivers

Kenedy

Winter Garden

Cotulla

Goliad

Carrizo Springs

R.

Beeville

Nueces

Corpus Christi

Robstown

Coastal Bend

Laredo

San Diego

Alice

Driscoll

Nuevo Laredo

Kingsville

Hebbronville

Falfurrias

Gulf of Mexico

Rio Grande

Roma

Rio Grande City

Edinburg

Edcouch-Elsa

Rio Grande Valley

Mission

San Benito

San Juan

Port Isabel

Mercedes

Brownsville

IN THE TOWNS

For many Tejanos living in cities, survival meant taking on occupations that were not much better than seasonal wage labor on the expanding farms (as noted, Mexican migrant workers used urban sites by the 1920s as home bases for their migration). Poverty for urban Tejanos was still as much a reality at the time of modernity as it had been in the nineteenth century. Old, dilapidated housing, rough and dusty roads, and the lack of sanitary facilities typified El Paso's south side, San Antonio's west side, and Houston's budding east side. Malnutrition and disease plagued the barrios of the state's municipalities. Barrio residents faced extremely high rates of infant mortality, tuberculosis, and other maladies.[9]

The Mexican sections remained separate enclaves within the state's cities. While no legal restrictions outwardly prohibited Mexicans from living in the better homes in more desirable neighborhoods, racial segregation persisted due to a combination of poverty, a preference many Tejanos had for living in an in-group environment, and the strengthening of Jim Crow laws and attitudes, for values of white city dwellers often chimed with those in the state's rural areas. In the Anglo communities, new and popular notions charging that Mexicans were unhygienic barred Tejanos from admittance to eating establishments, drugstores, barbershops, banks, movie theaters, and miscellaneous other public places.[10]

Segregated schools were the rule in most towns, and neither the Texas government nor the general society was particularly committed to educating Texas-Mexican students. Texas farmers wanted to have a readily available supply of field workers, something they might hope to sustain by discouraging Mexicans from acquiring an education. Thus, schools for Mexicans in Texas typically lacked proper facilities or provisions. Furthermore, some towns prohibited Mexicans from advancing further than the sixth grade. According to a survey taken in 1928, some 40 percent of the school-aged Tejano children received no instruction between 1927 and 1928.[11]

While the above experiences applied to the majority of Texas Mexicans in the new age, a middle class still remained. In communities such as El Paso, Brownsville, and Laredo, Texas Mexicans were employed in city or county government, taught in the public schools, and worked as compositors, printers, and salespersons. These cities even had some Tejano doctors and lawyers.[12] Furthermore, new immigrants as well as Mexican Americans continued to operate small-scale enterprises that serviced the

Mexican population. Women, naturally, made up part of this entrepreneurial sector. Many established restaurants, among the most successful of whom was Faustina Porras Martínez, whose small eating establishment in Dallas eventually grew into a chain of restaurants named El Fenix. In Houston, the downtown Mexican commercial district that catered to Tejanos included retail stores, barbershops, restaurants, bookstores, doctors' offices, pharmacies, and a theater. Tejano customers even rode the trolley cars into the district from their homes.[13]

SHIFTING LOYALTIES

Diverse ideological and philosophical expressions characterized the Tejano community during this time. Naturally, many residents still had strong ties, both familial and cultural, to old Mexico. Also, many Texas-born Mexicans proudly upheld the traditional values of their upbringing in colonias and remote rural villages. In their views toward the role of women, for example, some Tejanos insisted on adhering to old ways: girls were to be strictly chaperoned when in the company of boys and were to accept without question their role as exemplary wives, mothers, and homemakers. Some parents looked askance at American customs; to many of them, United States traditions represented disobedience, a loose morality, elopement, and a high rate of divorce.[14]

But residence in Texas had over the years induced many Tejanos to embrace the very system that sought to shut them out. Even as Tejanos may have faced nativism, political disfranchisement, and the old and severe problems like land loss, violence (such as lynching), and scarce economic opportunities, forces of socialization during the new era seemed to hold out a middle course between the worldview of the less-acculturated masses and those who hoped to succeed in the mainstream. Tejanos residing in the cities (some 25 percent lived in metropolitan areas in the 1920s, according to some estimates)[15] came in contact with Americanizing agents, among them emerging ideological currents, modern innovations, and the new consumer culture. By the 1920s Mexican Americans, like all Americans, had been swayed by seductive advertising that talked them into coveting the latest labor-saving devices, the "fashions" of the day, and the most-recent line of cosmetics. Entrepreneurs lured customers into spending with easy credit terms and progressive sales techniques, which along the border included the hiring of Spanish-speaking clerks. Tejanos also had contact with mainstream institutions that penetrated even the segregated barrios. By World War I, for example, Mexican theaters showed (in addition to films produced in Mexico) American movies starring Charlie Chaplin and Mary Pickford. Charity and reforms groups in cities such as San Antonio, El Paso, and Houston acted as liasons that Americanized barrio residents by sponsoring classes on health, holding sporting activities, and teaching teenage girls numerous American crafts. Parochial schools, furthermore, taught children allegiance to the United States and instilled in the students' minds the notion of the American dream. Church social centers and even Catholic Youth Organizations assisted in acculturating impressionable youngsters.[16]

Public schools also helped to shape Tejanitos' sensibilities, even as segregated school facilities left much to be desired. Educators considered Mexican Americans and Mexican immigrant students as intellectually inferior, and Anglo-controlled school districts commonly discouraged their attendance. But, Progressive educational reformers of the era actually advocated the Americanization of non-English-speaking children so as to nudge them toward the mainstream. Using an English-only pedagogy, classroom teachers emphasized to their charges the value of learning the English language. Fluency in English would help foster positive feelings toward the United States and American principles, as well as prepare Tejanos for self-improvement.[17] By this time, moreover, the number of school-age Texas-Mexicans had increased, so that educators prompted state officials to implement curriculum reforms that attended to issues such as Tejano poverty, illiteracy, juvenile delinquency, and disease.[18] Thus by the 1920s, a generation of American-raised-and-educated young Tejanos seemed poised to undertake campaigns for the improvement of Mexican-American society. As Jovita González, a writer and folklorist, put it at the end of the decade:

> Young Texas-Mexicans are being trained in American [schools]. Behind them lies a store of traditions of another race, customs of past ages, an innate inherited love and reverence for another country. Ahead of them lies a struggle in which they are to be the champions. It is a struggle for equality and justice before the law, for their full rights as American citizens. They bring with them a broader view, a clearer understanding of the good and bad qualities of both races. They are the converging element of two antagonistic civilizations; they have the blood of one and have acquired the ideals of the other.[19]

WORLD WAR I

During World War I (following passage of the Selective Service Act on May 19, 1917), the U.S. government and society at large made conscious efforts to co-opt the Mexican-American population into the course of national life. As war-related manpower shortages deepened, federal, state, and local authorities called upon all elements of the Texas-Mexican community to join in the defeat of the Central Powers. Spanish-language newspapers, for one, hastened U.S.-born Mexicans to display their patriotism and called on those of foreign birth to provide a sympathetic hand to the country that sheltered them. In urging young men to become part of the war mobilization, a contributor to San Antonio's *La Prensa* on June 6, 1917, declared: "The future will know that we fulfilled our obligation, that we sacrificed everything we could on behalf of our country and our fellow man."[20] Members belonging to the small Tejano middle class played a more important part in rallying localities to arms. Prominent citizens such as J. T. Canales of Brownsville and Clemente Idar of Laredo acted as intermediaries between Anglo officials and the Mexican community. Additionally, middle-class Mexican Americans sponsored fundraisers and challenged audiences to make contributions at Liberty and War Savings Stamp gatherings: on more than one occasion, the middle-class businessmen and ranchers of South Texas donated generously to such undertakings. Tejanas complemented the war effort by joining local chapters of the Red Cross, hosting fundraising events, and engaging in propaganda campaigns to persuade fellow Tejanos to support America's involvement in the European conflict.[21]

While not all Tejanos responded eagerly when called to service—a small percentage of them resisted the draft on moral grounds and some recent immigrants pled loyalty to Mexico and returned there—overall, according to José A. Ramírez, an authority on Tejanos and World War I, most Tejanos answered draft calls and appeals to join the armed forces ungrudgingly. They did so for a variety of reasons: out of ethnocentric pride in being "Mexicano," or conversely, to prove their fitness as upstanding Americans, a sense of patriotism, a desire to experience less stifling social conditions than they found in Texas, and in the hope that they would earn better pay and embark on new adventures. In the end, some 5,000 Texans of Spanish surname participated in World War I, many of whom fought in the trenches on the western front and earned a laudable record for valor.[22] One of them, Marcelino Serna, a Mexico-born resident of El

Paso, earned Italy's Cross of Merit, France's Croix de Guerre and Military Medal, Britain's Medal of Bravery, the Distinguished Service Cross, and two Purple Hearts. His feat of single-handedly taking twenty-four prisoners probably qualified him for the Congressional Medal of Honor, but, in the estimation of historian Carole E. Christian, "He probably did not receive [the Medal] due to his inability to read and write English."[23] The highest honor bestowed on a Tejano for gallantry on the field of battle went to David Cantú Barkley, a native of San Antonio born in Laredo to a Mexican American mother and Anglo father. Barkley died in France on November 9, 1918, while swimming back across the frigid Meuse River (which traverses France and Belgium) following a mission to gather intelligence on German positions and troop strength. The information he collected (alongside a fellow soldier who survived to deliver the particulars) helped the Allies defeat German forces in one of the last campaigns of the war. For his actions, the Allies posthumously recognized Barkley with the U.S. Congressional Medal of Honor as well as the French Croix de Guerre and the Italian *Croce al Merito di Guerra*. About 100 Tejanos died in WWI action.[24]

World War I, then, may be identified as a point of departure in mainstream U.S. society's concern for Tejanos. In an effort to make maximum use of the nation's manpower, federal, state, and community officials launched serious drives to incorporate a wider spectrum of the population, including immigrants and Mexican Americans. Following the war, government no longer looked upon them as stepchildren, and society even came to display greater awareness of the Mexican presence. Texas Mexicans themselves became optimistic about the prospects for real integration and acceptance, but they would be disappointed in their hopes.[25]

IN THE WORKPLACE

According to Emilio Zamora, a common sense of *Mexicanidad* (Mexicanist identity) in part motivated Mexican Americans and Mexican immigrants to launch organizational efforts to challenge adverse working conditions. Between 1910 and 1930 shared experiences in Texas—with social, economic, and political institutions—and robust nationalist feelings engendered a spirit of solidarity that united diverse elements of Tejano communities behind labor-organizing initiatives.[26] These included the nativist response to recent immigration from Mexico (for it touched Mexican-descent people regardless of nativity), increased politicization among the Americanized sectors of the population, persistent job discrimination, and even social interaction with fellow *obreros* (workers) at the barroom, in the mutualist hall, or on the street corner. Collectively, such factors explain some of the early activism on behalf of the exploited laborers.

Tejanos pursued various means to improve conditions on the job, explains Zamora. Most practically, they walked off the fields or breached agreements with growers in order to take jobs on neighboring farms offering better wages. These actions were bold for the time given the traditional reluctance of pickers to negotiate with farmers, who held the advantage in labor relations. More commonly, however, Tejanos established their own labor organizations. Among the most prominent of these independent bargaining bodies was *La Agrupación Protectora Mexicana* (Mexican Protective Association) established in San Antonio in 1911. Composed primarily of farm renters and laborers (all Mexicans, whether native- or foreign-born, qualified to join), La Agrupación sought legal protection for its members whenever they faced Anglo-perpetrated violence or illegal dispossession of their property.[27]

Tejanos also formed coalitions with different unions, even as Anglo labor leaders ordinarily rebuffed Mexican initiatives to participate in the broader national labor movement. Tenants, field hands, and an array of city workers in Central Texas, for example, joined affiliates of the Texas Socialist party, such as the Land League of America (1914–17). Worsening economic conditions, exacerbated by the presence of the new immigrant farm hands who depressed wages, explain Tejano motives for joining socialist organizations, but so does the influence of the revolution in Mexico and of newspapers that offered radical alternatives for dealing with the plight of workers. The number of Tejano laboring people involved with socialist organizations is difficult to determine, though one contemporary member placed it at nearly one thousand. It was about 1915 when the Texas Socialist party began to disintegrate due to government suppression and a World War I–inspired frenzy against radicalism. Mexican socialist organizing faced a similar fate.[28]

Texas-Mexican craftsmen also joined the Texas State Federation of Labor, the state arm of the American Federation of Labor (AFL). They did so as the AFL, for the first time since World War I, extended a helping hand (to ensure influence over all sectors of the labor force), recruiting Laredoan Clemente Idar to travel the state and organize among Texas Mexicans. Though Idar succeeded in his work to some extent, Tejano obreros generally founded local unions on their own initiative, then sought association with the AFL.[29]

Expectedly, most Texas-Mexican unions (regardless of affiliation) were segregated. In El Paso, two such examples in the 1910s were the International Clerks' Protective Association and the Laundry Workers Union. But labor unions with a mixed ethnic membership did exist. In that same border city, one could find a few Mexican laborers with membership in the Carpenters' Union, the Painters' Union, the Musicians' Union, the Pressmen's Union, and the Freight Handlers' Union.[30]

At present, it is difficult to determine the extent of strikes and violent confrontation between Tejano laborers and management. The historian Mario T. García notes that El Paso was a setting for labor agitation and that numerous small unions, such as those involving clerks, laundry persons, and city public-works employees, struck for workers' rights during the decade of the 1910s.[31] Other scholars have also documented worker discontent and strike activity in San Antonio during the World War I years, one incident involving Tejano protest against the contract system used in a local federal building project, another being the bakers' strike mentioned in the previous chapter.[32] In the North Texas town of Thurber, Mexican members of the United Mine Workers' Union took part in a strike in 1926.[33] Ordinarily, strikes taken up by Tejano workers proved unsuccessful, though some did produce slight gains. Management could always hire scabs, use police power, or deport foreign-born laborers to squelch organizing movements.

COLLECTIVE PROTEST

Besides the Tejanos who took an active part in unions to improve their working situations, there were others who participated in protest movements. Such persons challenged miserable living conditions, as have been discussed in previous chapters, continued societal injustices, the murdering and lynching of innocent Mexicans, and the common custom followed by courts of forgoing penitentiary time for Anglos accused of killing Mexicans.[34]

One expression of Tejanos' political resolve occurred in the West Texas town of San Angelo in September 1910 when Texas-Mexican parents protested school segregation and the inferior education afforded Tejanitos by demanding either the admission of the Mexican children to the white schools or the location of white and Mexican school buildings on the same grounds. When the school board refused to compromise (on the grounds that integration would demoralize the entire school system), Tejano parents initiated a school boycott. For the next several years (1910–15), parents sent their children to the local Catholic school and a Mexican Presbyterian Mission school that opened late in 1912. By 1915, however, the boycott of the public schools had lost its momentum and faltered.[35]

A more expressive act of political assertiveness involved the gathering in Laredo of some four hundred delegates—including representatives of mutualistas, various newspaper publishers and reporters, spokespersons for women's causes, and other Tejano leaders—at the invitation of Nicasio Idar and his son and daughter Clemente and Jovita (editors and writers for *La Crónica*) to discuss inequality and discrimination in a public forum. At the *Primer Congreso Mexicanista* (the first Mexican Congress of Texas), held during the week of September 14–22, 1911, speakers addressed the need for unity and denounced inferior schooling, lynchings, labor exploitation, and land loss among Texas Mexicans. Women participants in the assemblage forcefully presented a plank of issues pertaining to women and also established *La Liga Femenil Mexicanista* (the Mexican Feminine League of Texas) whose purpose was to struggle for recognition of individual rights for all Texas Mexicans and more specifically to advance education for Tejanos. The delegates also created a statewide league, *La Grán Liga Mexicanista* (the Grand Mexican League of Texas), entrusted to carry out the goals of the Congreso and specifically to monitor the manner in which Texas Mexicans were treated in society. In the end, however, the promise of unity advocated by the conference lost its fervency. Several of the mutualist societies preferred autonomy and did not wish to relinquish authority to an umbrella organization.[36]

The most conspicuous example of Texas-Mexican collective protest outside of mainstream politics occurred during the time of the Mexican Revolution (1910–20) when turmoil in northern Mexico spilled over into South Texas. Tejanos then joined militia-type units in support of the *Plan de San Diego* (PSD). Supposedly written in San Diego, Texas, in Duval County, the PSD advocated the elimination of "Yankee tyranny" by the waging of a rebellion in February 1915 and the subsequent founding of a new republic constituted of the states lost by Mexico in the War with Mexico.[37]

The origins of the PSD remain obscure. They have been attributed to German intrigue and to Mexico's President Venustiano Carranza's use of the border raids as an instrument to acquire U.S. diplomatic recognition in 1915, and the next year to pressure the United States into withdrawing General "Black Jack" Pershing's troops from Mexican soil. Connections have also been made to the PLM, as PSD leaders were familiar with *Regeneración* and had been influenced by Flores Magón's anarchist ideas of rebellion as a means of dealing with problems such as those people in South Texas faced. But according to revisionist historians, the PSD was a response to the prejudice and disdain with which whites treated Texas Mexicans in the border region.

Leaders of the movement included Luis de la Rosa and Aniceto Pizaña, both from the lower Rio Grande Valley, who recruited freely in northern Mexico and South Texas, where the PSD gained support. From both sides of the border these men launched guerrilla attacks, at times leading parties numbering as high as one hundred men. Border Mexicans and Tejanos joined the insurrectionists to strike back for past and present injustices: landgrabbing; displacement from the old pastoral society; racially motivated violence; and the contemptuous attitudes of the newly arrived Anglo farmers. They attacked and often destroyed farm and ranch operations, irrigation pumps, and transportation lines.

To stem the disturbances, the Texas government dispatched more Texas Rangers to the border and federal troops intensified their patrol of the area. Meantime, volunteer Anglo groups invoked the tradition of nineteenth-century justice, applying lynch law and perpetrating other outrages against defenseless Texas Mexicans and others thought to be in support of the Plan de San Diego.

The border conflict inflicted untold damage on South Texas. The attacks and counterattacks, waged intensely from 1915 to 1917, interrupted the economic development of the region, destroyed property, and resulted in the deaths of an untold number of people and the homelessness of thousands. Still, the PSD failed to meet its objectives because of poor coordination on the part of its leaders, violence directed at rank-and-file supporters, the militarization of the border, and, very significantly, President Carranza's decision to stop supporting the raiders. As of late 1916, he was still fighting a civil war in Mexico and needed diplomatic recognition from the United States in order to ward off his enemies. Once President Woodrow Wilson recognized Carranza's government, Carranza barred the raiders' use of northern Mexico as a base from which to launch their expeditions.[38]

POLITICS

Simultaneously, Tejano political participation through mainstream channels reached a low ebb. As noted, political representation at the regional
and community levels in the El Paso Valley and in the trans-Nueces
may have increased in the late nineteenth and early twentieth centuries,
but a decline in the number of Tejano officeholders and involvement in
grass-roots decision making followed in the 1910s and 1920s, save for
ranch counties such as Zapata, Duval, Webb, and Starr.[39] Several factors
in addition to those listed earlier help explain this downturn, among
them bitter Anglo reprisals for the suspected Tejano complicity in support of the PDS, demographic shifts such as those that had occurred in
South Texas, San Antonio, and El Paso (which had diluted the former
predominance of Tejanos), as well as the Progressive reaction to nonwhite
peoples who supposedly had corrupted democratic rule. To ensure honesty
in government, for instance, the Progressives instituted citywide elections,
and while this reform was designed to fight bossism, it eliminated the
old ward system under which minorities had commanded at least some
sort of representation.[40]

By the 1920s, then, the political structure that had previously
allowed Tejano politicians opportunities to hold office had changed.
Political machines such as those that had emerged in San Antonio in
the late nineteenth century no longer encouraged but rejected Mexican-American political activity. Tejano voters living in the Alamo City
in the 1920s voted according to the dictates of Anglo bosses if they
wished to keep working for the city or county.[41] In the greater South
Texas border region, a reversal of bossism took effect. The Progressive
offensive weakened the powerbase of the old politicos, and Mexican-
American fortunes tumbled commensurately. From the 1880s to 1920,
for example, the political boss Jim Wells dispensed patronage to members
of propertied Mexican families who occupied several significant elective
positions in the city and county. With Wells's downfall in 1920, farmers
comprising the new Anglo order sought to minimize Tejano occupation
of new political seats. In far off El Paso, Mexican-American politics
entered a transitional period during the late 1910s and into the 1920s.
Now Texas-Mexican leaders were reduced to acting as intermediaries
between the Mexican-American immigrant community and local Anglo
government in the city.[42]

About the only Tejano politicians able to weather the changes in the 1910s and 1920s were some of those in the aforementioned ranch counties of South Texas. The agricultural development that spread throughout the section did not penetrate the westernmost valley counties, and Manuel Guerra, for one, was particularly successful at surviving numerous challenges to his machine. (Guerra's sons continued to hold power in Starr County until after World War II.) In Duval County, Archie Parr dispensed offices to faithful Tejano supporters (the Parr machine inherited by Archie's son remained entrenched until 1975).[43] Anglo-dominated bossism in lesser degrees extended to other South Texas communities.

Aside from Guerra, the most prominent Tejano politician of South Texas was J. T. Canales. As already noted, this Brownsville attorney had served in the Texas legislature from 1905 to 1910. Reelected to the state legislature in 1916, Canales took stands in support of prohibition and woman suffrage and against the Progressive effort to place restrictions on Texas-Mexican voters. In his boldest crusade, Canales called upon the legislature to probe Ranger atrocities committed against Tejanos during the PDS incident and to reorganize the legendary law enforcement body. Canales failed to persuade the legislature to heed his suggested reforms, but his investigation did result in the dismissal of several Rangers accused of having committed extralegal acts upon Mexicans. In 1920, Canales retired from the legislature. Not until the late 1930s would another Tejano win election to the state house.[44]

A New Generation

Meanwhile, a new generation of Mexican-American leaders rose up to undertake fresh approaches for reform. Their U.S. citizenship, their involvement in World War I (either as combat soldiers or as civilians on the homefront), and the aftermath of the PDS motivated them to succeed, both personally and in the name of their race.[45] World War I had seemed to offer a serendipitous opportunity for the social improvement of Texas Mexicans. After all, Mexicans had cooperated fully and responded patriotically to the general mobilization. America's concerted effort to integrate all segments of society in support of the war suggested more openness in the future. In the perception of those with an eye towards politics, the future augured long-deferred prospects for social advancement.

In the early years of the twentieth century, finds historian Benjamin Heber Johnson, people of business and social rank (among them J. T. Canales and the Idar family of Laredo) began advocating a progressive platform they hoped would better the lot of Texas Mexicans. Tejano Progressives saw the uplifting of Mexican Americans in their participation in the farm revolution then taking place in South Texas, in their acceptance of the mainstream culture (while retaining their ethnicity), and in their accommodation to the American way of life.

Then the PDS ideology and the violence that accompanied the proclamation placed Tejano Progressives and their ideas in jeopardy. Many Texas Mexicans found the PDS—with its promise of establishing racial equality, retaking of their lost land, and regaining the rights of citizens—appealing, so they joined the insurrectionists in raiding Anglo ranches and otherwise sabotaging the infrastructure of the region. Anglos responded to the PDS and its proponents with vigilantism, lynching, and a general portrayal of Mexicans, including the Tejano Progressives, as un-American. Notwithstanding such actions, the Progressives found comfort in the more neutral stance taken by the federal military and by outside officials who arrived in South Texas to preserve order and safeguard everyone's civil rights. This stand by the U.S. government in protecting constitutional principles without prejudice confirmed for Progressive leaders the wisdom of tying themselves to the nascent farm order and joining a political structure that extended Mexican Americans fundamental civil guarantees. Ironically, the PDS solidified the Progressive vision advocated before 1915.[46]

Thus, Tejano Progressives, veterans, professionals, and socially conscious women picked up the struggle when race relations reverted to the pre–World War I standards. Though most still lived in barrios and entertained a deep appreciation for their Mexican upbringing, such individuals were slightly better off than the majority of other Tejanos and by the 1920s were gaining greater esteem for their status as U.S. citizens.[47]

Tejanas came to be visible agents in the resurgence of the age. As historian Julie Leininger Pycior points out, women during the 1920s were active on many fronts, among them *mutualista* endeavors to uplift their condition, efforts to establish small libraries, and working with adults to combat illiteracy. Women also participated as members of auxiliaries to the Woodmen of the World (WOW) so that the *leñadores* (as the woodmen were called in Spanish) might help their fellow Mexicanos. Other Tejanas joined the *Cruz Azul* (Blue Cross), a charity group intended to help the poor and distressed by providing health care and legal assistance. Still other Mexican-American women joined the Spanish Speaking Parent Teacher Association (SSPTA), chartered in 1927, in order to voice Mexican-American concerns regarding the condition of education for Tejanitos.[48]

But the new activism was most pronounced on the civic front, on which a new generation of leaders founded organizations designed to help Tejanos better integrate into national life. Such was the intent of the *Orden Hijos de America* (Order of Sons of America, or the OSA), founded in San Antonio in October 1921. Compared to precursor groups, the OSA consisted of members born in the United States, extolled loyalty to America, and sought citizens' rights through institutional channels. Soon, Sons of America chapters appeared in South Texas, from Corpus Christi to Brownsville to Pearsall, fighting for educational equality, the desegregation of public places, the right to serve on juries, and the right to bring suit against a white person (in the 1920s courts refused to hear cases involving Mexican Americans attempting to sue whites).[49]

The OSA splintered soon after its birth, and defectors founded the Order of Sons of Texas in San Antonio in 1922, and others the *Orden Caballeros de América* (the Order of Knights of America) in 1927. These new groups still abided by the philosophy of the OSA and appealed to Tejano citizens to pay their poll tax and vote and encouraged them to become involved in civic and political affairs, stressing the necessity of being bilingual. This too was the philosophy of another civic organization, the League of Latin American Citizens, founded in the Rio Grande Valley by war veterans J. Luz Saenz and Alonso S. Perales.[50]

At this point concerned Tejano leaders, some of whom had been brought into the war mobilization campaign, initiated a unification drive to create a stronger league in the struggle for equality. In 1929, at Corpus Christi, the agents of compromise brought together the various splintered societies—the OSA, Knights of America, and the League of Latin American Citizens—to form the League of United Latin American Citizens (LULAC). Several of these World War I veterans and civic activists went on to become LULAC officers during the league's early years or served in leadership capacities that enhanced LULAC'S growth into a statewide organization.[51]

ETHNIC TRANSITION

In the era between 1910 and 1930 (actually, until the start of World War II), loyalties to Mexico and the United States vied for dominion within the Tejano community. Diverse strains of thought manifested those loyalties, and some of these sentiments may be found in the content of community newspapers of the epoch. Representing the Mexican view was *La Prensa*.

More disposed to express the syncretization found in many communities were San Antonio's *El Imparcial de Texas* and Edinburg's *El Defensor*. Edited by Francisco A. Chapa, a Mexico-born Tejano who had achieved both business and political success in Texas, *El Imparcial* voiced the acculturation of many Tejanos and revealed a nascent biculturalism. *El Defensor*, founded in 1930 by Texas-born and college-educated Santiago G. Guzmán, embodied the loyalties of the up-and-coming Tejano middle class that was outspoken in its allegiance to the United States. Thus, *El Defensor* emphasized the dual heritage of some Tejanos and reflected a state of mind shaped by those having grown up in two cultural spheres.[52]

As second and third generations of immigrants do universally, this cohort assimilated the values of the nourishing culture(s): they worked hard, displayed courtesy, respect, and hospitality, cared for their loved ones, sympathized with the downtrodden, and worshiped a Christian being. They also spoke Spanish, esteemed their parents' homeland, identified with or joined mutualistas, ate Mexican dishes, sang corridos, and dressed in a Mexican style, but these same people also spoke English, admired their nation of residence, became members of the upstart OSA or LULAC, partook of American foods, listened to mainstream radio hits of the 1920s, and kept abreast of U.S. fashions. Over time, increased numbers of Tejanos would be absorbed into the process of cultural change from a Mexican to an American identity.

CHAPTER SEVEN

To the U.S. Born, 1930–1945

During the Great Depression, one of the most readily obtainable, yet most undesirable, occupations available in San Antonio throughout the winter months was pecan shelling. A work force of almost 12,000 people needing any kind of employment that would sustain them through the hard times took it up as a kind of last alternative. The job required tedious manual dexterity, enduring dreary and uncomfortable work conditions, and acceptance of abusively low wages. Maximum weekly earnings for entire families ordinarily amounted to no more than $1 to $4. Women constituted nearly 90 percent of the work crews, with most of them being Mexican American.

On January 31, 1938, twenty-two-year-old Emma Tenayuca led a strike of some 6,000 to 8,000 pecan shellers. To pressure plant owners into conceding higher pay and a better work environment, Tenayuca—a natural leader whose organizational skills had been honed through activity since 1935 with the Trade Union Unity League, a Communist organization with a council in San Antonio—coordinated mass demonstrations and rallies, some of them attended by as many as 5,000 supporters. In the end, the revolt proved to be a short-lived one. Industry opted for mechanization, a decision that left the strikers jobless and in the same state of unemployment in which so many others across the state languished.

Tenayuca's daring came at a personal price. Married to a Communist (from whom she later separated) and herself a member of the Communist Party (which later she also renounced), Tenayuca spent time in jail during the walkout, having been accused by the police of being a Communist subversive. For questioning the social and racial status quo, she incurred the scorn of political leaders in the Alamo City, who rationalized the use of violence by law enforcement officials against strike participants. Tenayuca faced such strong pressures from so many quarters (among them the Tejano middle class in the city, which included the membership of LULAC) that she departed Texas for San Francisco in the aftermath of the pecan-shellers strike. In the City by the Bay she acquired an education, not returning to San Antonio until the 1950s. During the decades that followed, she earned her living as a schoolteacher in the city. She retired from teaching in 1982 and passed away in July 1999.[1]

The Great Depression

Unemployment and the kind of social ostracism that befell Emma Tenayuca paled by comparison to deportation drives and repatriation initiatives launched against the Tejano community at large during the 1930s. Deportation involved efforts on the part of the U.S. Bureau of Immigration (under the Department of Labor) and local public and private welfare agencies to expel foreigners on relief roles, who—according to unemployed Anglo-Americans—took jobs away from American citizens, or who resided in the United States illegally. Ordinarily, the deportees would be gathered at some center, then transported to the border by train, truck, or car caravan. Repatriates, on the other hand, departed the state voluntarily for two primary reasons: some found it difficult to eke out a living in a white society that gave Anglos priority in employment and in the allotment of relief funds; and, in some cases, the Mexican government offered people jobs in public works projects (building roads or irrigation facilities) and opened up opportunities for the repatriates to buy real estate in the motherland. Some 250,000 Mexican immigrants and their children, many of whom had been born in the United States, are estimated to have returned to Mexico from Texas between 1929 and 1939.[2] The 1940 U.S. census placed the figure for Mexican-descent people in Texas at 484,306, but this total represents a serious undercount, one lower than Roberto M. Villarreal's adjusted figure of 695,00 for 1930.[3]

Aside from problems related directly to the Great Depression, Tejanos still had to endure old forms of bigotry. As in the 1920s, the Anglo notion that Mexicans were somehow dirty and inferior persisted, fostering continued segregation. Thus, many businesses barred Mexicans, fearing that Anglo customers might resent their presence. Catholic churches scheduled separate masses to avoid contact between the two groups. Real estate agencies followed rules that encouraged ethnic-based separation, and sprouting subdivisions enforced similarly restrictive policies.[4] School boards designated specific accommodations for Mexican children. Additionally, society still deterred Texas Mexicans from serving on juries and generally discouraged them from voting.

ECONOMIC AND SOCIAL STANDING

Obviously, the depression impeded economic mobility for the Tejano population. In the rural communities, Tejanos faced lean times as they subsisted by taking onerous and low-paying jobs, often working as maids, cotton pickers, kitchen helpers, slaughterhouse workers, cannerypersons, and warehousemen. According to surveys conducted in the 1930s and during World War II, poor folks living in South Texas and the Winter Garden area inhabited small wood-frame dwellings, ordinarily two-room hovels with earthen floors, no windows, and open-pit privies. People cooked in the open since many of the shanties lacked kitchens. Poverty-related diseases such as diphtheria and tuberculosis thrived in such unsanitary living conditions. Midwives ordinarily delivered babies, many of whom died by the age of one as a result of premature birth, pneumonia, influenza, and diarrhea enteritis.[5]

To find steadier or better-paying work, rural Mexicans followed the cotton crop. Even sharecroppers and tenant farmers during the 1930s resorted to migrant work, for federal programs enacted by the administration of President Franklin D. Roosevelt dislodged them from rented lands. In order to boost prices for agricultural products, New Dealers instructed landowners to reduce the amount of acreage under cultivation and even compensated them for keeping lands unplanted. Under such arrangements, landlords no longer needed full-time, year-round help, and they certainly had no desire to share government subsidies with others. Ousted from rented lands, Tejano sharecroppers and tenants wandered from place to place in search of work during the harvest season, the only time when landowners now wanted to hire them.[6]

It was, therefore, in the years of the Great Depression that the so-called "Big Swing" intensified, as workers followed the cotton season from South Texas, through the central portion of the state, up to the West

Texas–Panhandle region, then back to their points of origin. Many pickers traveled by car, but scores of others relied on contractors who negotiated with growers and then trucked the workers to the preagreed destination. In the fields, the *troquero* (as the trucker was called), weighed the cotton sacks, kept track of the number of pounds picked by each field hand, then compensated the migrants from wages paid him by the farmer.[7] In actuality, the migrants' earnings barely offset their travel costs: the Texas State Employment Service in 1938 calculated (on the basis of the prevailing wage of 50 cents per hundred pounds picked) that migrants made only about $37.50 per person during a six-month harvest period.[8]

By routinely making the Big Swing to the northwestern cotton lands, migrant workers either replenished old or founded new West Texas and Panhandle Tejano communities. Though treated as a necessary evil in the cotton fields, given little in the way of shelter or toilet facilities and barred from public places in the neighboring communities, many migrant field workers became attached to the places they visited each year. Some of them found employment opportunities in the oil fields of West Texas, performing hard, menial tasks such as digging ditches and cleaning storage tanks. Others, however, remained in the new communities after the termination of the picking season with their entire family, which often included grandparents and grandchildren, simply because they were unable to afford the journey back to their home.[9]

During the depression Tejanos living in large urban centers endured living conditions as wretched as those in the rural sections. Shacks in the Mexican district of San Antonio lacked proper floors, plumbing, indoor toilet facilities, and electricity. Tuberculosis and intestinal diseases lurked throughout the Mexican quarter, menacing every inhabitant. By the time of World War II, the Alamo City had the highest rate of death from tuberculosis in the entire nation, almost half of the victims being Mexican Americans. In Houston and Dallas, inquiries made during the war years by the Works Progress Administration (WPA) and sociologists, respectively, found Tejanos living in deplorable conditions, some of them managing to support entire families on yearly incomes of about $600 and residing in cheap, congested, tumbledown houses.[10]

Even as these conditions plagued so many Tejanos, a middle class still held on in cities such as Corpus Christi, Houston, San Antonio, El Paso, and others in the greater South Texas region. According to some estimates, this small middle class of managers, proprietors, salespersons, clerical workers, professionals, and craftsmen comprised about 15 percent of laborers listed in the 1930 census. Exiles and refugees from Mexico, enterprising Mexican-American merchants, and old-line families in the ranch counties of South Texas who still managed to hold on to their lands were among those who composed this "petit bourgeoisie."[11]

LA PATRIA

Several forces between 1930 and 1945 continued to reinforce the ties that Mexican Americans wished to retain with Mexico. Segregation in Texas and the rest of the nation prolonged a separate Mexican ethnicity. *"La patria"* (the motherland, Mexico), moreover, seemed to care about the welfare of barrio residents in a foreign land. Efforts by the Mexican government to relocate them in Mexico during the depression pulled on the sentiments of the lower class, much as it did on the small cohorts of ricos and professionals who had taken refuge in Texas during the Mexican Revolution but still remained deeply interested in the politics of Mexico. Many members of this latter group ended up returning to their mother country when Mexico granted a general amnesty during the latter years of the Great Depression. The continued activities of Mexican consuls in Texas also perpetuated ties between Mexico and unnaturalized citizens. Indeed, the consular officials who represented Mexico's commercial interests in the state acted vigorously as spokespersons for Mexican nationals, especially in cases in which they had been the victims of violent crimes.[12]

Then there were several influences that fanned the feelings of Mexican nationalism. Throughout the state one could find Spanish-language newspapers from Mexico as well as from Texas, among the latter being the aforementioned *La Prensa,* that reported on news of local and international importance in an attempt to perpetuate the bonds between Tejanos and the motherland.[13] Religious occasions, among them weddings, funerals, and church carnivals, acted as collective cultural activities for those of different classes, as did the Mexican national holidays of the Cinco de Mayo and Diez y Seis de Septiembre, during which representatives from Mexico, if not the consuls, used the opportunity to remind assembled celebrants of their common Mexican heritage. Professional and amateur artists organized small-scale theater companies that presented secular dramas and vaudeville acts in the various settlements. Also, movie theaters in the barrios splashed the silver screen with images of the latest film and stage idols of Mexico, while Spanish-language radio programs broadcast the news, commentary, and popular songs of Mexico.[14]

Social and recreational clubs as well as self-help organizations further catered to those who venerated la patria. The 1930s, however, witnessed the decline of many of the mutual aid societies. Repatriation and the increased financial assistance given by the societies to those suffering from the economic hard times reduced their membership. At the same time, new federal assistance programs such as Social Security offered similar financial benefits, radio and movies slowly replaced the entertainment functions of the mutualistas' regular meetings, and political clubs after the 1930s siphoned off the more politically minded mutualista members.[15]

To the U.S. Born

The 1930 census in Texas reported about 60 percent of the Mexican-stock people as U.S. born (during the 1930s, meantime, the immigrant population declined due to repatriation and deportation efforts). New and powerful forces now confronted young Tejanos who knew only the United States as their country of origin. In the years preceding World War II, for instance, Mexican junior and senior high schools—although segregated—appeared in increasing numbers in order to accommodate more Tejanitos. Students embraced the English language as well as American traditions, fashions, and attitudes about family, faith, and loyalty. During this decade, many New Deal relief programs shunned Mexican-American applicants, but some federal organizations, especially the National Youth Administration (NYA) did recruit young Tejanos. In South Texas, youths (ages sixteen to twenty-five, both male and female) enrolled in the NYA often provided the only source of income for their struggling families. Such overtures from the federal government confirmed for many Tejanos the magnanimity of the United States and buttressed their sense of U.S. belonging.[16]

Churches of different sects, meanwhile, brought mainstream outlooks and practices directly into the barrios. While both Catholic and Protestant clergymen generally conducted services in Spanish (and tried to deliver their messages to their congregations in ways relevant to the Spanish-speaking), in most cases their ministerial work was grounded on time-tested Euro-American beliefs and approaches. On the premise that Americanization produced "better citizens," for instance, Catholic parochial schools emphasized the learning of English, and the faculty (many of them nuns) instructed their charges to aspire to lofty American principles and proper American behavior. Lay personnel helped impart

American ideals on youths by sponsoring parish dance clubs and encouraging participation in sports. Some of the means Protestants employed for instructing Mexican American youngsters during the 1930s, moreover, derived from Anglo models, among them the tradition by the Methodists, Baptists, and Presbyterians of sponsoring youth camps for the purpose of reinforcing the faith among young people, undertaking youth caravans that allowed teens to gain on-the-job training during an eight-week missionary excursion, and holding Sunday Schools for instructing the youngest church members.[17]

Association with school teachers, government representatives, and church agents, therefore, bolstered the Tejanos' identity. Newspaper contents revealed a bicultural consciousness. The aforementioned bilingual *El Defensor,* for instance, emphasized that readers take pride both in their Mexican heritage and U.S. citizenship. The newspaper published advertisements for American products and historical bits from both the Mexican and American past and encouraged adolescents to consider a university education. Mexican-oriented papers such as *El Continental* of El Paso reported the public spirit displayed by Tejanos on occasions such as the Fourth of July.[18]

Creative writers during the 1930s and the World War II era expressed similar sentiments. Mexico-born but Texas-educated novelist and short story writer Josefina María Niggli, for one, sought to familiarize U.S. readers with the experiences of Mexican Americans through books and articles that she began publishing during the late 1920s. (Her career as an author of novels and essays continued until the 1960s.) In the early 1930s, Jovita González became one of the first Mexican Americans to publish English-language translations of traditional Tejano stories (related over generations orally), submitting articles to various scholarly outlets, including the yearly publications of the prestigious Texas Folklore Society. González continued to write sketches, short stories, and poems during the 1950s. Elena Zamora O'Shea believed her native South Texas and her Mexican-American forebears had not received fair treatment in mainstream Texas history books, so in 1935 she produced *El Mesquite,* a fictionalized account of Tejano community life in the trans-Nueces from the colonial era to the early twentieth century.[19]

U.S.-born-and-raised leaders, a cohort that included Tejano Progressives from the World War I era, military veterans, and a small middle class of entrepreneurs and professionals, spearheaded notions about adopting American customs and habits into a bicultural heritage, accepting loyalty to the United States, and gaining access to mainstream institutions on the basis of equality. Articulating such an outlook were what historians now refer to as the "Mexican American Generation," some of whom had founded LULAC in 1929. These leaders included Ben Garza, who served as the League's inaugural president (1929–30), Alonso Perales, LULAC's next national director (1930–31), and M. C. Gonzales, the organization's third president (1931–32).[20] From their base in San Antonio, the latter two emerged as the League's organizer-intellectuals of the 1930s. Perales and Gonzales, both attorneys, commanded large followings within Hispanic communities and imparted the LULAC doctrine most persuasively. According to the historian Richard A. García, "Everyone knew them, respected them, and listened to them."[21]

LULAC maintained a commitment to improving the human condition for all within the Mexican community regardless of class, even nativity. Though the organization restricted membership to the native born, it did accept those who were naturalized (the organization argued that the foreign born had their defenders in the Mexican consul, but LULAC leaders worked closely with the consuls in cases involving Mexican nationals). Ideologically, LULAC sought to redress old problems. LULACers still combated the entrenched racist sentiments holding that Mexicans were "unclean" and the Anglo contention that Mexican Americans were not "white folks."[22] In response, the organization launched efforts to secure civil liberties and access to opportunity by trying to overturn segregation; in their view the practice stood out as the most personal and visible reminder that Anglo Americans considered Mexican Americans as second-class citizens.[23] Further, they fought to assert their contention that they were Caucasian, as LULACers did in 1936 when the U.S. Bureau of the Census ruled that Mexicans be identified as "non-whites." Protest from LULAC councils across the state forced the Census Bureau to retract the categorization. Similar pressure exerted upon the Social Security Administration that same year forced the Social Security Board to accept the application of Mexican Americans as whites.[24]

Similarly, the League worked doggedly to overturn obstacles that impeded the educational achievement of Mexican Americans. LULACers ran up against the theory, then prevalent among educators, that Mexican culture embodied deficits that foiled Mexican Americans' success in the classroom (and elsewhere for that matter). League activists also tangled with the issue of school segregation (and its by-product, a second-rate education).[25] In addressing the matter of separate schooling (justified by educators, in part, on the concept of cultural deficiency), LULAC in 1930 pushed forth the case of *Independent School District, et al* v. *Salvatierra* (1931) arguing for an end to the deliberate segregation of Mexican children in Del Rio. A Texas Court of Civil Appeals ruled that arbitrary segregation was unjust but sided with school officials who contended that the students' retention of the Spanish language made school segregation necessary.[26] Without funds to follow up on *Salvatierra,* LULAC pursued other tactics, such as going before school districts and conferring with administrators to argue for better teaching for Mexican-American children. To disseminate their faith in education, LULACers organized evening schools in barrios and conducted meetings that focused on the topic of U.S. citizenship. They also undertook fundraisers to subsidize the education of especially good students who might, with the proper education, go on to become skilled workers, lawyers, doctors, and teachers.[27]

POLITICS IN THE 1930s

Little political remonstrance in the vein of the Primer Congreso Mexicanista or the Plan de San Diego occurred between 1930 and 1945, although Tejanos did launch reform drives to call for change. Such was the case in San Antonio, where in 1934 a diverse assemblage of community-oriented societies, behind the leadership of Eleuterio Escobar, united under the name of *La Liga Pro-Defensa Escolar* (School Improvement League) to reject segregation and persuade school officials to provide better facilities and a modern curriculum to the Mexican settlement in the city's West Side. Although *La Liga* won concessions from the San Antonio School Board in 1935 to build three new elementary schools and improve existing structures, the impact of the depression and the dawning of World War II stifled further action, and the League entered a temporary hiatus.[28]

Also appearing during this time was the *Confederación de Organizaciones Mexicanas y Latino Americanas* (Confederation of Mexican and Latin American Organizations, COMLA), founded in the late 1930s in the Gulf Coast area. (There apparently was a parallel organization with a similar name in El Paso.) The Houston/Galveston COMLA intended to act as an umbrella organization for the various lodges, societies, and civic groups throughout Texas, and though the prime movers were the Mexican consuls in these two East Texas cities, the confederation purported to work toward the well being of all Mexicans as well as "Latin Americans" (as it called Mexican Americans). In its early years, the COMLA initiated serious efforts to overturn racist policies, such as Jim Crow discrimination and segregation. It never succeeded, however, in accomplishing its goal of uniting the Gulf Coast's several societies and civic groups in a common struggle.[29]

In the realm of electoral politics, things remained near the nadir reached during the preceding two decades. This statement applied particularly to the regional and state levels, though some Tejanos did campaign for certain offices. In the 1930s, the first Tejano since J. T. Canales won election to the state legislature: Augustín Celaya from Brownsville. John C. Hoyo from Béxar County joined him in the state house in 1941.[30]

Political movements by Tejanos in this era were not, however, completely absent. They turned up, in fact, wherever reformers founded LULAC chapters, notes Richard A. García: in San Antonio, a city that contained an activist Tejano middle class and a large Mexican population; in South Texas towns like Brownsville, Corpus Christi, Kingsville, Alice, and Laredo; and in West Texas sites such as San Angelo, though this last region of the state lacked the level of leadership found in South Texas, perhaps because of its relative isolation from the rest of Texas or the numerical disadvantage of Tejanos there. The famous *Escuadrón Volante,* or "Flying Squadron," composed of the League's San Antonio leaders, made frequent trips throughout the state in order to help establish new councils and spread the LULAC word. By the beginning of World War II, LULAC had reached its pinnacle of strength. But then, as many LULACers enlisted in the service of the U.S. military in the aftermath of the attack on Pearl Harbor in December1941, the organization found its ranks reduced.[31]

In the 1930s, also, LULAC members took it upon themselves to perform a variety of civic and political responsibilities. They participated in Red Cross and Community Chest fundraisers, volunteered as leaders for local units of Boy Scouts and Girl Scouts and the Salvation Army, sponsored programs such as Latin American Health Week, and organized PTAs in barrio public schools. Committed to increasing the rate of U.S. citizenship and voting registration among Tejanos and to securing adequate representation in public office, LULACers went before city commissioners to press for the resolution of specific problems, organized assemblies, acted as intermediaries between the Mexican enclaves and bureaucrats, and conducted poll-tax raising drives.[32] Though claiming LULAC a nonpolitical entity, individual members nonetheless joined political groups that went by names such as the League of Loyal Americans (in San Antonio) or the Latin Sons of Texas (Houston). Through these political organizations, Tejanos protested their impoverished condition in the Mexican quarters, confronted local businesses that did not serve or hire Mexicans, introduced political candidates (both Anglo and Mexican) to Texas-Mexican voters, endorsed slates of office seekers, and joined in presidential campaigns such as that of Franklin D. Roosevelt. LULACers abided by a prescribed code of conduct and avoided extreme methods of protest, militant confrontation, strikes, and marches.[33]

Women, too, joined in the various LULAC programs, for in 1933 LULAC incorporated women's auxiliaries. Whether single or married, Mexican-American women members in that era resisted the notion of male LULACers that wives belonged at home, and though female members did not enjoy equality with their male counterparts, women did make important contributions to their communities (albeit in deeds closely related to "women's work"). They did volunteer work in orphanages and health clinics, sponsored youth activities, participated in voter registration drives, raised scholarship funds, taught English, and helped Mexican nationals study for U.S. citizenship exams.

Among the most prominent women to serve LULAC in the era were Mrs. J. C. Machuca of El Paso and Alice Dickerson Montemayor of Laredo. Firm in her thinking that women should share authority with their male counterparts, Machuca organized the League's first Ladies Council, assumed the office of Ladies Organizer General, and indefatigably worked to establish more Ladies Councils,[34] among them one in Laredo that brought into LULAC its first feminist, Mrs. Montemayor. Between 1937 and 1940, Alice Dickerson Montemayor served on several national posts, advocating (through articles published in *LULAC News*) independent insights that questioned notions of male dominance. She also favored a policy that women should work together to improve the general status of all women. In the 1930s, however, male-dominated LULAC councils were not disposed to hear such points of view. For reasons unknown, Montemayor left LULAC in 1940.[35]

LABOR PROTEST

The wellsprings for the subdued but undaunted struggle to improve the lot of laborers in the 1930s lay in the hardships of the masses, on renewed efforts by leftists to recruit Mexicans into labor unions, and, in the agricultural sector, in New Deal labor legislation that neglected the plight of farm workers.[36] Though most mainstream labor unions still excluded

Mexicans from membership, Tejanos in various parts of the state addressed the need to remedy conditions faced by commonfolk Mexican-American and immigrant laborers. In West Texas, cotton pickers in the El Paso area rallied behind the Fabens Laboring Men's Protective Association in 1933 to demand better wages for their toil; facing formidable opposition from local growers, police, federal and state officials, and the Immigration and Naturalization Service, their strike of that year eventually collapsed. Around the San Angelo area, where many Tejanos sheared sheep for a living, 750 members of the Sheep Shearers' Union of North America struck against low wages and exploitive employment practices in 1934, though threats, the use of strikebreakers, arrests, and vigilante harassment defeated the movement.[37]

The more vigorous labor-protest activity, expectedly, occurred in South Texas. In Crystal City, for example, spinach workers joined the Catholic Workers Union in 1930 and reached a settlement with local growers and processors concerning working arrangements, low wages, and child labor. In Laredo, *La Asociación de Jornaleros* (Association of Journeymen Workers), an independent union founded in 1933, led an abortive strike of some 3,000 onion pickers in the irrigated farms near the city in 1935. The next year, upon being chartered as the Agricultural Workers' Union No. 20212 by the AFL, the body continued to push to organize similar locals in other farming sectors of the state.[38]

Then, in 1938, the United Cannery, Agricultural, Packing, and Allied Workers of America (UCAPAWA) located operations in the lower Rio Grande Valley, though efforts to organize agricultural hands did not yield significant victories. Following a period of decline, UCAPAWA resurfaced in the greater South Texas region to represent Tejano truck drivers, shed packers, and field hands belonging to Spinach Workers' Union Local No. 87. In 1942, the union won a slight pay increase from producers in the Mathis area but then faltered. The following year, the Texas Fruit and Vegetable Workers' Union Local 35 (also UCAPAWA chartered) attempted to organize the citrus fruit and vegetable industry labor force in the lower valley. The local won some concessions but little is known of its existence after 1945.[39]

Similar efforts at union organization were undertaken in urban areas. In El Paso, workers at the major smelters and refineries joined the International Union of Mine, Mill, and Smelter Workers in 1939 and by 1946 had earned union recognition, maximum-hour limits, and wage benefits among other privileges.[40] In 1938, at the height of the pecan-shelling season, Emma Tenayuca led Tejano pecan shellers belonging to the UCAPAWA-chartered Texas Pecan Shelling Workers' Union in a walkout at some 170 San Antonio plants. In the Gulf Coast city of Houston, Mexicans joined initiatives by UCAPAWA to organize cotton compresses in 1941. In a contract negotiated with management, workers won overtime pay, time off on ethnic holidays (such as Diez y Seis de Septiembre) and a salary increase.[41]

Women played significant roles in the unionist fervor of the era, and, according to one historian, women participants in San Antonio outnumbered men in activities that challenged subsistence wages and abject conditions in the workplace.[42] In 1933 and 1934, Tejana cigar rollers and tobacco strippers in San Antonio walked off the job at the Finck Cigar Company, complaining of ill-furnished bathrooms, poor plumbing, and an unhealthy environment. Scabs broke the strike, so management never addressed the workers' grievances. Also in San Antonio, Tejanas joined the International Ladies Garment Workers Union (ILGWU)—in 1939, 80 percent of the 1,400 San Antonio women who belonged to this union were Mexicans—and while their strikes against local plants often ended unsuccessfully, one such strike in 1937 against the Shirlee Frock Company (manufacturer of infants' attire) did produce union recognition and the concession of a 20-cents-an-hour wage. ILGWU organizing of Tejanas in San Antonio continued until the war years, and many of the garment workers came under the protection of union contracts, at least until the 1940s when union activity across the state fizzled out. In Laredo, Tejana home workers organized *La Unión de Costureras* (the Seamstresses Union) in 1934, then sought affiliation with the ILGWU in 1936 to win decent wages and improved working conditions.[43]

In the end, the pre–World War II union movement among Texas Mexicans made little headway. Too many factors acted to prevent victories, among them labor surpluses, the precarious nature of the economy, the antiunion climate pervasive throughout Texas and the nation, and the basic contention among Anglos that Mexicans did not deserve better working conditions. Such factors would continue to inhibit union organizing after World War II.[44]

WORLD WAR II

World War II hardly opened up new employment opportunities for Texas Mexicans. The call for cooperation touched numerous barrios and ranchos and mobilization brought Texas Mexicans close to Anglos in a common cause of security and survival, but economic advancement for Tejanos still proved elusive. Relatively few Mexican Americans found work in war-related industries, and those who were hired performed common or unskilled labor. In addition, the paltry job openings that did open up to the Mexican-American community had more to do with the military emergency than with the relaxation of Jim Crow attitudes. The exigencies of the war produced the Fair Employment Practices Committee (FEPC) to monitor job discrimination among federal agencies and private businesses contracting with the government, though not until 1943 did the FEPC undertake operations. Companies then began to promote Mexican Americans into the semiskilled and skilled openings, but even that was done begrudgingly.[45]

When it came to contributing to the nation's war effort, however, Tejanos were ready, able, and more than willing to help, and Texas Mexicans joined up with patriotic zeal. Tejanos born and raised in the larger cities as well as in rural hamlets and small towns of the state answered the call to arms for a variety of reasons: military duty expedited naturalization for the foreign-born; scant numbers met the criteria for draft deferments; some looked at the armed forces as a way out of poverty; and most of them genuinely believed in the democratic ideals of their nation.[46] As in all wars, some saw duty only in support capacities, as in the case of mess cooks, administrative personnel, and Tejanas who joined the WAVES (Women Accepted for Voluntary Emergency Service). At the battle front, Tejanos saw duty in integrated companies, though others belonged to all–Mexican-American units like the Company E. 141st Regiment of the 36th (Texas) Division, which fought with distinction in the European theater. Five Texas Mexicans—José M. López, Macario García, Cleto L. Rodríguez, Luciano Adams, and Silvestre Herrera—won the Congressional Medal of Honor for heroism in Europe and the Pacific theater. While in the service, Tejanos came to know a treatment by whites that was more tolerant than that prevalent in their hometowns.[47]

KEEPING THE FAITH

If the 1920s turned out to be years that dampened the World War I generation's hope for integration, the Great Depression era all but drowned them. Unemployment during the 1930s inflicted greater misfortune upon Texas Mexicans than it did upon the general society, not only because preferences for possible job openings went to white folks, but because society questioned Tejanos' U.S. citizenship—and thus their eligibility for jobs. Indeed, to be Mexican made one a candidate for possible deportation. Jim Crow, moreover, feasted on intolerant times. Disfranchisement, enduring patterns of segregation, and substandard schooling further aggravated the misery of the age. The "Big Swing" across the state may have been an adventure to the young, but for parents migrant work seemed to lead only toward an unceasing cycle of drudgery and uncertainty.

Nonetheless, the pre–World War II years produced imaginative responses from Tejano communities. The new depth of desperation moved Tejano leaders of every political stripe to act on behalf of the forlorn. Those concerned with working-class compatriots sought to help them through means as diverse as the imposition of impromptu work stoppages, affiliation with the AFL or the Communist party, even violence. In the bigger cities, alarmed Mexican-American spokespersons organized different types of groups in an effort to counter their people's nagging woes. San Antonio established the Liga Pro-Defensa Escolar. Houston and El Paso addressed the needs of their people through COMLA. These cities and several smaller communities throughout the state founded LULAC councils to overturn barriers that circumscribed equality.

LULAC activism, in fact, continued during World War II, even as responses to calls for volunteers and the draft reduced its membership. As early as 1941, LULAC leaders (among them M. C. Gonzales and Alonso Perales) pressed the state legislature to enact a law permitting Mexican Americans equal access to public places. The times seemed ripe for such action as the nation, in its war against the Axis alliance, needed the unqualified support of Mexican-American communities and other western hemispheric countries—Mexico in particular, for the neighbor to the south held a reservoir of workers needed to fill the unprecedented labor demands of U.S. agriculture during the conflict. Using its connections to government officials in Mexico (and supported by an array of community activists, civic organizations, and the Spanish-language press, among other interested groups), LULAC led at least three separate attempts during the war years to see legislation passed guaranteeing the civil rights of Mexican Americans (though not of African Americans). While these efforts failed, they did bear fruit. In 1943, the state legislature passed the "Caucasian Race–Equal Protection" resolution, which though more of a statement (and not a law), discouraged discrimination in business establishments, municipal swimming pools, theaters, and other public facilities. Dissatisfied with the strength of the resolution (which did not, for example, impose penalties on those who discriminated against individuals of Mexican origin) the Mexican government refused to extend the *bracero* program (discussed in the next chapter) to Texas. Governor Coke Stevenson, in a gesture of concession, created the Good Neighbor Commission (1943) to deal with discrimination involving those of Mexican descent; still, Mexico did not permit braceros into Texas until 1947. During World War II, then, LULAC's push for equal rights became a transnational venture, though ultimately it achieved only minor gains. The political strategy of the 1930s and World War II years, consequently, would be carried on by "Latin Americans" in the postwar era.[48]

Los Tejanos: A Photoessay

Top: "Coronado on the High Plains" by Frederic Remington. Copied from a reproduction in *Collier's Magazine*, Dec. 9, 1905. *The UT Institute of Texan Cultures at San Antonio, No. 68-2015.*

The *pobladores* (settlers) turned to the environment for materials with which to build homes on the Texas frontier. *Photograph by E. K. Sturdevant. Daughters of the Republic of Texas Library.*

Top: The *Corrida de la Sandía* (Watermelon Race), part of the celebration of the Día de San Juan. *Painting by Theodore Gentilz. Yanaguana Society Collection, Daughters of the Republic of Texas Library.*

Bottom: Martín De León. *The UT Institute of Texan Cultures at San Antonio, No. 7201799.*

Right: José Antonio Navarro, 1795–1871. *Prints and Photographs Collection, CN 03861. The Center for American History, The University of Texas at Austin.*

Skinning a beef on the Johanna C. Wilhelm Ranch. Stefan de los Santos (with hat on, right) was sheep boss for the ranch. *The UT Institute of Texan Cultures at San Antonio,* No. 72-1770.

Petra Vela de Kenedy (1825–1885) was already a wealthy woman when she married the prominent rancher Mifflin Kenedy in 1852 and was well known for her philanthropic work. *Reprinted from* Petra's Legacy *by Jane Clements Monday and Frances Brannen Vick by permission of the Texas A&M University Press.*

Above: Juan Nepomuceno Cortina. Photo taken by Deplanque, Brownsville, and Matamoros, 1866. *The UT Institute of Texan Cultures at San Antonio, No. 73-8426.*

Bottom: Tejano wood haulers (*leñeros*). *Texas State Library and Archives Commission.*

Tejano and Anglo (French) students and their teacher outside their school in El Carmen, Texas, ca. 1896. *The UT Institute of Texan Cultures at San Antonio, No. 78-561.*

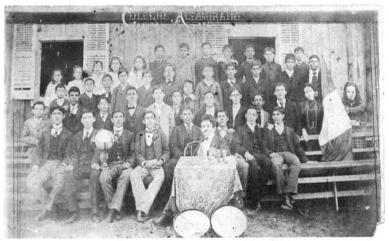

Colegio Altamirano, 1898. *E. E. Mireles & Jovita González de Mireles Papers, Special Collections & Archives, Texas A&M University–Corpus Christi Bell Library.*

Right: Members of the Teodoro Zambrano family and others gathered at a baby's funeral in early 1900s. Cemetery located in either Karnes or Bee county, Texas. *The UT Institute of Texan Cultures at San Antonio, No. 81-154.*

Left: Unidentified woman holding a parasol with a U.S. flag used as a backdrop. Attributed to a studio photographer in Beeville, Texas, ca. 1910s. *The UT Institute of Texan Cultures at San Antonio, No. 81-149.*

Sociedad Concordia, Corpus Christi, Texas, ca. 1910s. *Rafael, Sr. & Virginia Galván Family Papers, Special Collections & Archives, Texas A&M University–Corpus Christi Bell Library.*

Mexican American Women's Auxiliary to the Woodmen of the World, Corpus Christi, Texas, ca. 1917. *Rafael, Sr. & Virginia Galván Family Papers, Special Collection & Archives, Texas A&M University-Corpus Christi Bell Library.*

Corpus Christi business-
man Rafael Galván, Sr.
and Virginia Reyes Galván
Wedding Portrait, 1919.
*Rafael, Sr. & Virginia
Galván Family Papers,
Special Collection &
Archives, Texas A&M
University–Corpus Christi
Bell Library.*

Las Aguilas baseball team, Corpus Christi, Texas, ca. 1920. *Rafael, Sr. & Virginia Galván
Family Papers, Special Collection & Archives, Texas A&M University-Corpus Christi Bell
Library.*

Corpus Christi Mexican American Organizations, ca. 1920, in front of Obreros Hall. *Rafael, Sr. & Virginia Galván Family Papers, Special Collections & Archives, Texas A&M University–Corpus Christi Bell Library.*

J. T. Canales (1877–1976) was a South Texas lawyer who served in the Texas legislature from 1905–1910 and 1917–1920, and was among LULAC founders. *House Composite of the 36th Legislature (detail of J. T. Canales);Courtesy State Preservation Board, Austin, TX; Accession ID: CHA 1989.534; Photographer: Jesse Herrera; 2/1/1995, post conservation.*

Interior of *La Prensa* newspaper, ca. 1923–1928. *The UT Institute of Texan Cultures at San Antonio, No. 83-408.*

Salomé Rodríguez, 110 years old, as he joins a caravan of Mexican repatriates on their way back to Mexico from Texas. Published October 19, 1931. *The* San Antonio Light *Collection. The UT Institute of Texan Cultures at San Antonio, No. 1310-A.*

Emma Tenayuca at age nineteen, in the
courthouse waiting to see Mayor Quin
about better facilities to distribute relief
supplies, San Antonio, Texas, July 16,
1936. *The* San Antonio Light *Collection.*
The UT Institute of Texan Cultures at San
Antonio, No. 1006-B.

"Baile de los Gallos" (the Cock Fight Dance), performed by Alex Moore and his
group, at Fiesta La Villita. San Antonio, Texas, 1940s. *The UT institute of Texan*
Cultures at San Antonio, No. 83-164.

Teenagers during the 1940s were part of bicultural communities such as those in Houston. *Courtesy Houston Metropolitan Research Center, Houston Public Library Houston, Texas.*

Dr. Hector P. García, founder of the American G. I. Forum, ca. 1948. *Dr. Hector P. García Papers, Special Collections & Archives, Texas A&M University–Corpus Christi Bell Library.*

Two members of Conjunto Alamo: Leandro Guerrero (left) and Frank Corrales. Taken at KCOR radio station (in Calcasieu Building) where they played each morning, 6:00 to 6:30, San Antonio, Texas, 1949. *The UT Institute of Texan Cultures at San Antonio, No. 91-147.*

Family members view the body of Félix Longoria, killed in the Philippines and refused service at the local funeral home chapel in Three Rivers, Texas. About to be interred at Arlington National Cemetry, February 16, 1949. *Dr. Hector P. Garcia Papers, Special Collections & Archives, Texas A&M University-Corpus Christi Bell Library.*

Trucks such as these transported Tejanos from the cotton fields of South Texas to those of the Panhandle during the era of the "Big Swing." *Photo courtesy of UT Institute of Texas Cultures at San Antonio, No. 96-1184; courtesy of Rev. Mak and Alice Mae Williams.*

Left: Two boys sitting on a concrete slab outside toilet facilities in a housing complex on San Antonio's West Side, 1960s. *The UT Institute of Texan Cultures at San Antonio, No. 82-546.*

Below: Dr. Américo Paredes. *Courtesy of The University of Texas at Austin and Dr. Américo Paredes (neg. #388, 1970).*

Top: Young Mexican laborers picking cotton and loading it by hand, near San Benito, Texas, August 1972. *The UT Institute of Texan Cultures at San Antonio, No. 72-3583.*

Bottom: Cinco de Mayo celebration at the birthplace of General Ignacio Zaragoza near the La Bahía Presido, Goliad, Texas, 1972. *The UT Institute of Texan Cultures at San Antonio, No. 72-3609.*

La Raza Unida Party, whose influence in Texas politics reached its high point during the 1970s, marches in solidarity with Mexico's Partido Socialista de Trabajadores at the International Bridge in Laredo, Texas, and Nuevo Laredo, Tamaulipas, January 1980. *Photo from the Maria Elena Martinez Papers, Nettie Lee Benson Latin American Collection, University of Texas Libraries, The University of Texas at Austin.*

Singer Lydia Mendoza (1916–2007) in 1999 receiving the National Medal of Arts from President Bill Clinton. *National Endowment for the Arts.*

Representative Henry B. González, 20th District, Texas (1961–1999). *Courtesy of Representative González.*

José (and wife Lidia) Lopez, of Tyler, Texas, who with other plaintiffs, filed suit in 1977 for the right of immigrant children to acquire a free education in Texas. *The Dallas Morning News/Richard Michael Pruitt, June, 2007.*

U.S. Army General Ricardo S. Sánchez, born and raised in Rio Grande City, commanded coalition ground forces (2003–2004) during the Iraq war. *Official U.S. Army V Corps photo.*

Eva Longoria, born and educated in Corpus Christi, Texas, rose to stardom in the ABC television series *Desperate Housewives* (2004 to present). *Photographer: Paul Chouy*

CHAPTER EIGHT

"Latin Americans" *in the Postwar Era,* *1945–1960*

Like other Tejanos during World War II, Felix Longoria joined the U.S. Army because "everyone else was going off to fight." Leaving a wife and a four-year-old daughter behind in November 1944, he recognized the risks that war posed to himself and his family. He never could have imagined, however, the impact that his wake and burial would have on the history of Texas.

Longoria came from Three Rivers, a small South Texas town some seventy miles west of Corpus Christi. Since a young man, Felix had worked as a manual laborer, mainly for his father, who managed a small fence-building company, but also as a roughneck in the nearby oil fields. When he arrived in the Philippines with his army unit, Longoria adjusted quickly to the strange surroundings and shortly won several medals for acts of bravery under fire. But death came just as promptly to Longoria when a Japanese sniper felled him on June 16, 1945. His comrades buried him in Luzon, where his remains stayed until his rendezvous with history.

In January 1949, the army telegraphed his wife Beatriz that Longoria's body would soon be arriving in the United States and asked her where the services for her husband would be held. Naturally, she replied, it would be in Three Rivers, but the local mortician refused to hold a wake for a "Mexican" in his funeral home. Distraught over the slight of a war hero, Beatriz sought the counsel of Dr. Héctor P. García of Corpus Christi, himself a World War II veteran who had recently organized a veterans group by the name of the American G.I. Forum. García, already known for his activism in behalf of Tejano causes, called on his contacts in the press and in government circles, and the case of injustice and racism soon widened into a national, even international, incident. Longoria's body was ultimately interred at Arlington National Cemetery in Washington, D.C., on February 16, 1949.

In death, however, Longoria had contributed more to Tejano history than he had as a common citizen from Three Rivers or a World War II hero. The dispute over his wake had cast a bad light upon the State of Texas, drawing attention to the institutionalized discrimination, segregation, and racism that daily haunted Tejanos. His death also galvanized the American G.I. Forum, which morphed into an active spokesgroup for Tejanos and for many decades thereafter went on to challenge the many wrongs brought to public awareness by the wake of Felix Longoria.[1]

Some features of the Texas landscape obviously did not change much after World War II, and would not do so until the late 1950s. Politics, for example, retained its conservative bent. On the one hand, many Texas Democrats preferred disassociation with the national party in protest of its support for labor unionism and the civil rights of African Americans, while, on the other, Texas Republicans refused to relax their opposition to constitutional liberties and welfare assistance, which they equated with socialism. In race relations, the strength of Jim Crow sentiments led to the passage of several segregationist laws in 1956–57, and while their purpose was to prop up long-standing discrimination against African Americans, by implication they extended to those of Mexican descent.[2] Meantime, right-wing extremism prevailed as the campaign of Wisconsin senator Joseph McCarthy against Communists at the national level found supporters throughout Texas. Reactionaries demanded the removal of controversial books from libraries, the dismissal of teachers considered too liberal for local standards, and the suppression of left-wing ideas.[3]

Nonetheless, Texas began to take new directions in the postwar era (especially towards the late 1950s) that opened up fresh possibilities for Texas Mexicans. In that period, the old agrarian order long committed to the subordination of Tejanos lost the political advantage to urban commercial interests, farm ownerships made a transformation from individually owned concerns into mechanized corporate entities, and many who had been field hands moved to the cities to take better-paying industrial jobs. By the mid-1950s, furthermore, McCarthyism was on the wane, and no longer a political issue handicapping "foreigners" from pursuing the American dream.[4]

Texas-Mexican Society at Midcentury

The interruption in population growth that occurred during the 1930s ended during World War II and the 1950s; the number of Tejanos now increased from about 1 million in 1950 to 1.4 million in 1960. According to the census of 1960, 86 percent of white persons of Spanish surname in Texas were native born.[5]

Like the rest of the state's population, Texas Mexicans in the post–World War II years became more urbanized. During the war, many people abandoned rural areas for the cities to explore new occupational prospects in growing industrial sectors, and improved wages in the 1950s persuaded still more to relocate from the farm to the city. At the same time, farm hands were supplanted by mechanization and new techniques that permitted farmers to produce more with less human labor.[6] Whereas 57 percent of Texas Mexicans resided in urban areas in 1940, 78 percent of Texas Mexicans did so by the 1950s, and the pattern accelerated thereafter.[7] By 1960, some 30,000 Mexican Americans lived in Dallas, 75,000 in Houston, and 243,000 in San Antonio (by then, only Los Angeles, California, had more Mexicans than did the Alamo City). In the 1950s, Texas Mexicans made up 50 percent of El Paso's population.[8]

In their socioeconomic standing, close to 75 percent of Texas-Mexican males remained members of the proletariat. According to the 1950 U.S. census, Tejanos lived on a yearly median income of about $1,000. Anglo Americans at that time made twice that much.[9]

Many Tejano city dwellers faced the same conditions that had plagued their parents and grandparents. These included neglect from city government concerning squalid living conditions, high rates of infant mortality, and epidemic diseases such as tuberculosis, diarrhea, and typhus. The 1950 U.S. census identified 33 percent of urban homes owned or rented by Tejanos in the state as substandard.[10]

In rural areas, living conditions for Tejanos were even more bleak. Seasonal work in the cotton fields, for which farmers paid around $1.25 per hundredweight (that is, per hundred pounds picked), remained a dismal option for survival, as families participating in the migrant cycle made less than $400 per year during the 1950s.[11] In face of the lean wage rates and competition from Mexican illegals (called "wetbacks" during the era, *mojados* in Spanish) whose numbers mounted during World War II because of alleged labor shortages in state agriculture, Tejanos took off for the midwestern United States in large numbers. There, lodging in the sugar beet and tomato fields was as primitive as it was in Texas, though wage rates exceeded those in the Lone Star.[12]

Other workers joined the intrastate migration, either in family units or with troqueros. They responded to the beckonings of farmers for whom they had previously worked, then followed the well-traveled "Big Swing" from South Texas, through the Coastal Bend area, into Central Texas, and then to West Texas. Along the way they encountered all too familiar problems: having to improvise to find shelter (usually in the fields but more commonly beneath the protection of bridges or deserted sheds or chicken coops); entering towns that lacked parking areas for trucks as well as accessible bathing facilities and toilets; and inadequate means to battle disease, especially dysentery, due to the poor sanitary measures afforded them. Those who returned to their hometowns (many did not, depleting Tejano communities along the migrant trail) awaited the new planting and picking seasons by working in whatever jobs they could find. The migrant workers' children meantime, tried to obtain schooling for a few months in the spring.[13]

At the same time, the resilient Tejano middle class continued to grow, primarily in the urban sites. The 1940s and 1950s constituted auspicious years for Mexicans in terms of opportunities for socioeconomic advancement. In 1950, the percentage of Tejano men employed in middle-class occupations (as professionals, managers, proprietors, clerical, sales, and craftsmen) rose to 25 percent, up from the 15 percent reported for 1930.[14] Felix Tijerina, the Houstonian restaurateur, symbolized the example of many other successful entrepreneurs who during the era thrived financially by gaining a niche in the wider Anglo-American consumer market.[15]

A Dual Identity

The expansion of the middle class at mid-century could not help but to foster a sense of class difference and even of separate identities within Tejano communities. Those with a better education and socially on the climb, those who held blue-collar jobs that paid above the average, and those in professional capacities interacted more frequently with whites and Anglo institutions and tended to regard themselves as somewhat apart from common Tejanos. They had certain cultural preferences (perhaps dancing to middle-class music, such as that of the *orquesta*, whose arrangements borrowed from the American big-band sounds of the era). And their aloofness was clearly perceptible to those in the lower stratum, who mocked and ridiculed them for their pretentiousness, referring to them as *gente jaitona* ("high-toned folks") or *"agringado"* (American-ized).[16] Social mobility derived from changing historical circumstances and from individual or group effort, but it carried consequences for those who strayed too far from remaining "Mexican."

In point of fact, only a small percentage of folks within Mexican-American communities approached full Americanization. Many influences still tugged at Tejanos inside the colonias that discouraged their greater acculturation. There was, for one, the Catholic Church (to which most belonged). Traditional customs and traditions practiced by the Church reinforced "lo mexicano": most families observed holy days such as *el día de la virgen de Guadalupe,* mothers set up *altarcitos* (home altars), and parents insisted that their children be duly baptized or that their grown children have a Church wedding.[17] Then there was Spanish, the predominant language used in the home, the barrio, and even the school grounds. Its usage also blunted Anglicization and daily reminded everyone of their Mexicanness. By mid-century, many Tejanos (especially middle-class youths) held a fairly good command of English—indeed, a major reason given for the decline of readership for *La Prensa* of San Antonio in 1957 was "the younger generation of Latin Americans being able to read English and the dwindling [numbers] of the non-English reading generation"—but seldom used it at the expense of dropping their mother tongue. A pattern unfolding by this time, the historian/anthropologist Manuel Peña reminds us, was bilingual code-switching, in which Mexican Americans artfully integrated words from both languages when engaged in in-group dialogue. One could only code-switch by having fluency in Spanish; language thus acted as still another force arresting total accul-turation.[18] Bombarded by Anglo influences but still attached to the world of their immediate environment, many who were part of the generation of the postwar era lived in dual cultures.

Labor Movements in a Conservative Age

Texas-Mexican labor organization declined somewhat in the postwar era. As noted, labor historians consider the 1930s to have been a time of heightened union activity. That intensity lessened between 1945 and 1960 because of the probusiness sentiments that seemed endemic to the state, apprehension among activists of being branded Communist agitators or labor racketeers and therefore incarcerated for un-American activities, the many options available to employers to suppress walkouts, and because many unions discouraged Tejano workers from membership. In the case of the ILGWU, for instance, the national office showed reluctance to invest money in Texas to organize and train union leaders. The result was more workers in the state's garment factories during the 1950s but a decline in union membership.[19]

Overall, it appears that the postwar era consitituted one of setbacks in the face of self-organization. In 1948, workers at the Rio Grande Valley Gas Company in Harlingen sought to organize a union, but management hired undocumented aliens to replace the organizers and their supporters.[20] Then, in 1951, Mexican-American women garment workers belonging to the ILGWU staged a walkout of a Houston plant, but the factory went out of business shortly thereafter.[21] In El Paso, the Amalgamated Clothing Workers of America (ACWA) struck Hortex in 1952 over alleged "unfair labor practices" on the part of the garment company, but the union proved ineffective in representing its members.[22] In early 1959, Mexican-American women struck against the Tex-Son Company of San Antonio, which specialized in the making of young men's wear. Beating of strikers by the police ensued, but workers and sympathizers continued to picket outside the stores of merchants carrying Tex-Son products and appealed to the public, religious groups, and fellow unions in San Antonio for assistance. Ultimately replacements and antilabor legislation weakened the job action, and by 1962 the strike had foundered.[23]

Postwar Politics

Though World War II was very much a watershed in opening of new opportunities for Texas Mexicans, civil rights between 1945 and the late 1950s hardly came to Tejanos automatically. With the end of the war, white society once again regressed toward old attitudes. One West Texan veteran, for instance, groaned that he and fellow G.I.'s had not fought Hitler to have "ill-smelling Mexicans" now clamor for integration.[24] Public establishments still refused to serve Tejanos, even recently discharged soldiers, among them Medal of Honor winners. White neighborhoods, eating places, movie theaters, tonsorial shops, public swimming pools, and even hospitals were considered off-limits to Mexican Americans. Throughout the state, police officers and other law enforcement agencies such as the Border Patrol—an agency of the Immigration and Naturalization Service responsible for keeping immigrants from entering the United States illegally—regularly reminded Tejanos of their second-class citizenship through disparagement or physical intimidation.[25] On the job, a similar backslide from the racial tolerance exhibited by whites during the war years occurred. Employment opportunities for Tejanos diminished quickly. Those who had occupied skilled positions during the war now faced demotion, even dismissal, while new employees found little available beside unskilled tasks.[26] In South Texas, the press, influential businessmen, and farmers no longer preoccupied themselves with workplace or living conditions for Texas Mexicans. Governor Coke Stevenson's Good Neighbor Commission, created during the war to better relations between Texas and both Mexico and Mexican Americans came to be staffed by personnel with little commitment to alleviating discrimination.[27]

Politically, Texas Mexicans in the immediate postwar years still had to pay the poll tax and cope with other voting and office-holding restrictions. They were handicapped by the lack of necessary funds to field candidates from their own neighborhoods and had to campaign against Anglos who still regarded politics as their exclusive domain. Moreover, bossism still survived at midcentury. In South Texas, businessmen and farmers possessed enough economic power to control the vote.[28] The political condition of Texas Mexicans thus remained at a level only slightly improved since the 1920s, when the Anglo-American domination of the border towns from South Texas to far West Texas dealt a crushing blow to the Mexican-American presence in public offices.

But a resurgence of Tejanos in politics occurred by the 1950s, as "progressive" Anglo business leaders in the cities stood up to the power of the old guard that had long dominated the machines. The challengers tried to incorporate middle-class Mexican Americans into local government so as to establish a climate conducive to business expansion. In San Antonio, especially, power brokers by the early 1950s sought to enlist black and Mexican-American candidates for progressive slates, though Tejanos who did win by tacit agreement of these movers and shakers often found it difficult once in office to work effectively for Tejano causes because of their ties to Anglo sponsors.[29] In 1956, however, an independent, grass-roots campaign resulted in the election of Henry B. González to the Texas legislature, making him the first Tejano to serve in the state senate in the twentieth century. Voter registration and a get-out-the-vote campaign in El Paso led to the election in 1957 of Raymond Telles, the city's first Mexican-American mayor. He won reelection two years later without opposition.[30]

Compared to the other sections of the state, South Texas and far West Texas had produced more prominent civic leaders, been the primary centers of activism in the Tejano community, and generally held an edge on the number of Tejanos in office. Indeed, of the six Tejanos in the state house in 1960, two were from San Antonio, one from El Paso, and the other three from the South Texas border area.

At midcentury, therefore, it was still difficult to organize Mexican Americans in the rural counties of West and Northwest Texas due to their physical isolation.[31]

Renewed Struggles for a Better Life

World War II and the Korean War (1950–53) produced politically minded Mexican-American veterans and other similarly conscious Tejanos who set out on a concerted course to erase the inequalities that their people faced. The military experience had defined for veterans the meaning of citizenship and exposed them to the inconsistencies of a nation that espoused equality but did not practice it. In San Antonio, therefore, civic leaders took activist stances through organizations such as the Loyal American Democrats, the West Side Voters League, and the Alamo Democrats. Eleuterio Escobar revitalized *La Liga Pro-Defensa Escolar* in 1947 to press once more for equal and adequate educational facilities and more educational opportunities for Mexican-American children.[32]

Also organized in San Antonio that year by business and professional men was the Pan American Progressive Association (PAPA). As a nonpartisan entity, it sought ways to improve the lives of the Mexican-descent population of the city, including the integration of residential areas in San Antonio. But PAPA's life appears not to have extended beyond the early 1950s.[33]

In Corpus Christi, World War II veteran Dr. Héctor P. García in 1948 founded what evolved into the most vigorous advocacy organization of the postwar period, the American G.I. Forum. Originally established in an effort to expedite federal benefits for Mexican-American ex-servicemen, the G.I. Forum attained a new standing in 1949 with the aforementioned Félix Longoria affair at Three Rivers, Texas. The courageous stand that the G.I. Forum took on the incident vaulted the group into the role of spokesperson for disadvantaged Mexican Americans.[34] G.I. Forum chapters from across the state now united with LULAC councils to press for sociopolitical advances. Involved in these struggles were leaders from the 1930s and World War II years, among them Alonso Perales, M. C. Gonzales, J. T. Canales, James Tafolla, George I. Sánchez, and Carlos E. Castañeda. Joining them in the era between 1945 and 1960 (and after for that matter) were Gus García, Ed Idar, Cristobal Alderete, John J. Herrera, and, of course, Dr. García.

Also part of this activist cadre were women from the two organizations. Representatives of Ladies G.I. Forum Auxiliaries and Ladies LULAC Councils engaged in programs established to buy milk tickets for children whose parents suffered from tuberculosis, purchase eyeglasses for needy students, distribute toys to the poor at Christmas time, raise funds to provide clothing for children in hospitals, and donate money to the March of Dimes and the Polio Drive. Alongside men, women helped back Little League baseball clubs to help adolescents build a positive self-esteem, worked in poll-tax raising drives and rallies, and were often the prime figures in the establishment of new councils throughout the country by spearheading efforts to integrate public accommodations and voice the concerns of Mexican-American women. Many women gained recognition within their respective organizations as exemplary models of commitment to the cause of Mexican-American rights.[35]

SCHOOL DESEGREGATION EFFORTS

For years activists had decried the lack of education for Tejanos as the major stumbling block to Mexican-American progress. The presence of inferior "Mexican Ward" schools, especially, stigmatized children as being less than full-fledged citizens, hindered their ability to learn the English language, and impeded their participation in matters relevant to the community.[36] Because middle-class leaders recognized schooling as a gateway to social betterment, they sponsored efforts to educate Tejano children by means that included back-to-school drives, public-service announcements over radio, community rallies, teenage hops, and king and queen balls.[37]

The middle-class leaders also undertook legal measures, this according to historian Guadalupe San Miguel's study of the Texas-Mexican campaign for educational equality. Following World War II (but before the founding of the G.I. Forum), LULAC took the lead in seeking legal reversals to educational wrongs. In California, the League contested the pattern of segregation in *Méndez* v. *Westminster School District* (1945), and the subsequent ruling by the Ninth Federal District Court in Los Angeles—that segregation of Mexican-American children indeed infringed on guarantees made by the Fourteenth Amendment—had inspired the drive to desegregate schools in the Lone Star State.[38] Therefore, in January 1948, Minerva Delgado and several parents in Central Texas counseled by LULAC alleged that school segregation in the region was in breach of the U.S. Constitution. Soon thereafter, the G.I. Forum closed ranks behind LULAC with moral support and financial contributions garnered from across the state. In *Delgado* v. *Bastrop ISD* (1948), a district court agreed with the aggrieved plaintiffs, declaring that separating students in different buildings violated the law.[39]

Despite this legal pronouncement and supportive regulations issued by the state superintendent of public instruction to integrate, most school districts generally overlooked the mandates of the *Delgado* decision. Undaunted, Mexican-American leaders took other segregation cases to court, including the significant *Hernández* v. *Driscoll Consolidated Independent School District* (1957). In this complaint, LULAC and the G.I. Forum argued that the segregation of Mexican-American children in the first two grades and their subsequent detention at that level for a total of four years was an unreasonable practice predicated on notions about race or ancestry. In January 1957, a federal district court agreed with the charge. Despite such significant victories, school districts devised ways of evading court orders. These included gerrymandering districts (dividing districts unfairly to ensure segregation), building schools for specific neighborhoods, and offering freedom-of-choice plans that allowed Anglos to select the school they preferred to have their children attend.[40]

The commitment to educational matters produced, in 1957, what came to be known as the "Little School of the 400." The brainchild of the Houston restaurateur and then National LULAC President Félix Tijerina, the program, first implemented in Ganado, Texas, by seventeen-year-old Isabel Verver, sought to teach preschool Tejanos four hundred English key words and phrases that would allow them to succeed in their first year in school. Implemented initially in Jackson County, the project proved so popular by 1958 that the Houston entrepreneur enacted similar programs in other parts of the state and gained the endorsement of Price Daniel, the governor of Texas. The next year, the state legislature funded Tijerina-type schools to the tune of $1.3 million. The concept of the "Little School of the 400" survived into the 1960s, though budget cutting undermined it by the middle of that decade. The federal government, however, later modeled its Head Start program on Tijerina's creation.[41]

HERNÁNDEZ V. TEXAS

LULAC and the G.I. Forum also joined forces to have Mexican Americans recognized as a class whose rights Texans transgressed. To this end, Gus García took the case (with the assistance of attorneys John J. Hererra and James de Anda) of Pete Hernández, who had been accused of murdering Joe Espinosa in Edna, Texas, on August 4, 1951. In his motion against the state, García contended that the omission of Mexican Americans from jury service in Jackson County violated their right as a class to equal protection under the law. Hernández was tried nonetheless, and the jury rendered a guilty verdict and condemned him to life imprisonment. García next turned to the Texas Court of Criminal Appeals, but without success.

Then the United States Supreme Court in October 1953 agreed to hear *Hernández v. State of Texas* and LULAC and the G.I. Forum members supplied the needed funds for the attorneys' Washington stay. In May 1954, the High Court, basing its opinion on the premise that local norms and attitudes could identify Caucasians (such as Mexican-descent individuals) as non-whites, agreed unanimously that Texas practices discriminating against "other whites" (such as Mexicans) did in fact defy the rights and assurance granted by the Constitution. Hernández was retried and again found guilty (though given a lesser sentence), but the Supreme Court's decision was far-reaching as it acknowledged that Tejanos (to whom Jim Crow laws did not ostensibly apply) had long been the victim of discriminatory treatment. The verdict did not change race relations in Texas immediately, but future generations of Tejanos would profit from its implications.[42]

THE ACSSP

In the background of such efforts to protect the legal rights of Mexican Americans in the United States existed an organization rediscovered by the historian Ricardo Romo called the American Council of Spanish-

Speaking People (ACSSP). Founded in 1951 by the educator George I. Sánchez, ACSSP pursued litigation in the area of civil rights and assisted sister civic-action groups in other parts of the United States. With monies received from the American Civil Liberties Union, it helped LULAC and the G.I. Forum with several civil rights cases during its brief period of existence, among them *Hernández* v. *State of Texas* (1954) and *Hernández* v. *Driscoll Consolidated Independent School District* (1957). By the late 1950s, however, the ACSSP faced decline as Sánchez and other members of the Council found less time to dedicate to the organization and fundraising became more difficult. In 1959, the ACSSP passed into history, having set an example as a courageous attempt to utilize the legal system as a recourse for redress on behalf of Spanish-speaking Americans.[43]

LOS DEL OTRO LADO

In seeking to improve the lives of Mexican Americans after World War II, both LULAC and the G.I. Forum resisted what Tejanos of the era referred to as the "Wetback Problem." In the eyes of these organizations, the presence of *braceros* (day laborers from Mexico brought to the United States on contract) and "wetbacks" cheapened wages for Texas-Mexican residents, supplanted them in agricultural jobs, intensified health problems in the colonias, and generally gave "Latin Americans" (the preferred self-referent used by Mexican-American leaders circa the 1930s to the 1950s to combat the image held by Anglos that Tejanos were not "Americans") a bad name. The braceros were part of an official labor agreement negotiated between the United States and Mexico during the World War II years to provide field hands for United States farm estates facing extreme labor shortages. Although Mexico had banned the movement of braceros into Texas because of the state's well-known racism, it relented in 1947 and removed Texas from its "blacklist." Illegal entrants ("wetbacks"), on the other hand, had arrived in Texas after 1942 in response to the state's great demand for farm workers and continued to be preferred by growers as they could be hired without bureaucratic interference and could be easily exploited by greedy farm managers.[44]

To deal with the "Wetback Problem," the G.I. Forum and LULAC lobbied to extradite illegals, to terminate the bracero program, and to have the border better patrolled in order to halt unauthorized crossings into Texas. In 1953, the G.I. Forum published an investigative report entitled *What Price Wetbacks?* as part of its ongoing efforts to combat the presence of undocumented workers in the United States. The pamphlet illuminated the exploitation of wetback labor and explained the effects these laborers had on health standards in border communities. The survey further faulted law authorities for a lax enforcement of the immigration statutes.[45]

Politicians seemed indifferent to the Forum's concerns (preferring to ignore the wetback issue because it helped the nation's growers maintain a supply of cheap labor), but the public ultimately became alarmed over the "wetback menace." With popular support, therefore, the Immigration and Naturalization Service in July 1954 ventured upon a wide-sweeping campaign called "Operation Wetback." In collaboration with local and federal authorities, the Border Patrol mounted raids into rural areas of Texas to arrest illegals and deport them to Mexico. The drives affected many American citizens of Mexican descent who witnessed close relatives forcibly repatriated. The American G.I. Forum and LULAC both countenanced the project, though they did make attempts to ensure that the rights of the Texas-Mexican citizens facing deportation were respected. Nonetheless, their accommodationist stand caused friction within the ranks of the Tejano community, leading many to question the sensitivity of the Forumeers, LULACers, and other supporters of the xenophobic campaigns.[46]

Academicians and Writers

In the postwar era, academicians, intellectuals, and others with a talent for composition contributed to the scholarly record on Texas Mexicans. Noteworthy writers include the renowned historian Dr. Carlos E. Castañeda. A professor of history at the University of Texas from the 1930s until his death in 1958, Castañeda wrote numerous works during the period between the Great Depression and the 1950s that sought to explain the Spanish/Mexican contribution to Texas history, among them the now-classic, seven-volume study, *Our Catholic Heritage* (7 vols; Austin: Von Boeckmann-Jones, Co., 1936–58). His lifetime bibliography of eighteen books and close to fifty articles contributed to Texas and borderlands scholarship by identifying the debt American history owed to Spain and Mexico.[47]

Dr. Américo Paredes, a University of Texas folklore teacher, writer, and poet educated in the Brownsville schools, in 1958 published *"With His Pistol in His Hand": A Border Ballad and Its Hero* (Austin: University of Texas Press, 1958), a book studying the relationship between the corrido and the real historical events surrounding the episode of Gregorio

Cortéz. The lay historian Mercurio Martínez coauthored *The Kingdom of Zapata* (San Antonio: The Naylor Co., 1953), and Cleofas Calleros in numerous pieces preserved the history of Spaniards and Mexicans in the El Paso Valley.[48] The public school official and educator Edmundo E. Mireles during the 1940s and 1950s wrote several textbooks for use as instructional materials in primary and secondary Spanish-language classes and published numerous articles on a variety of topics in popular periodicals and academic journals. Some of his publications were coauthored by his wife Jovita González, the folklorist, and Mireles's fellow teacher in Corpus Christi.[49]

New Mexico–born-and-educated George I. Sánchez, who taught in the Department of History and Philosophy of Education at the University of Texas from 1940 to 1972 (when he passed away), authored or edited some fifty books, monographs, and special reports as well as some eighty articles, many of which dealt with his deep concern with the quality of education for Mexican-American students. As a graduate school professor at the University of Texas, Sánchez directed in excess of sixty-five master's theses and twenty-eight doctoral dissertations, and he taught as a visiting professor in universities both in the United States and overseas.[50]

Activists also contributed to the literature issued during the period. J. T. Canales, the former legislator from Brownsville, authored several essays between 1930 and 1945 on behalf of civil rights causes; in 1945 he paused to reminisce in "Personal Recollections of J. T. Canales." After that he produced other historical pieces, among them *Bits of Texas History in the Melting Pot of America* (2 vols; Brownsville: privately printed, 1950, 1957) as well as works on his kin Juan Cortina, among them *Juan N. Cortina Presents His Motion for a New Trial* (San Antonio: Artes Gráficas, 1951).[51] Alonso Perales, the LULAC activist, published *El méxico americano y la política de sur de Tejas* (San Antonio: Artes Gráficas, 1931) and *En defensa de mi raza* (San Antonio: Artes Gráficas, 1936 and 1937) to highlight the political disadvantages of Tejanos in South Texas.[52] In 1948 he compiled a volume of statements on discrimination and published them in *Are We Good Neighbors?* (San Antonio: Artes Gráficas, 1948).

The End of an Era

From 1945 to 1960, Texas Mexicans continued to experience oppression and exploitation, most severely in the rural regions in which racial attitudes relegated Tejanos to a second-class status.[53] But circumstances in the late 1950s for Texas Mexicans no longer resembled those of the 1940s. Within the community, for one, improved familiarity with American mainstream society offered more promise. While Tejano society had command of the Spanish language, observed Mexico's national holidays, and enjoyed Mexican music and other traditions of the motherland, a number of factors strengthened Mexican American attachment to United States institutions: World War II had acquainted Tejano veterans with an Anglo-American world they had previously known only vicariously; the G.I. Bill of Rights had proved instrumental in the education of many ex-servicemen; compulsory–school attendance laws were more strictly enforced; and the consumer culture of the era seduced the multitudes, many of whom were U.S. born and knew no other than American life. Continued cultural syncretization improved Tejanos' chances to capitalize on the age's new opportunities.[54]

Meanwhile, de facto Jim Crow traditions for Texas Mexicans in the urban areas faced new threats due to the increasing influence of Mexican-American leaders and their sympathizers in the NAACP and labor unions as well as to initiatives undertaken on the national level by government and the courts to integrate public education and juries. By the late 1950s, political circumstances conspired to weaken racism against Tejanos. The liberal wing of the Democratic party experienced a resurgence, and Texans in Congress such as Lyndon Baines Johnson and Ralph Yarborough did not look upon Jim Crow as an appropriate system for the modern age. In Austin, legislators such as Henry B. González and Abraham Kazen initiated campaigns to overturn segregation.[55] As the decade closed, however, much remained to be accomplished in the struggle for equality. The 1960s and 1970s would see newer approaches in the campaign to achieve that end.

CHAPTER NINE

The Sixties and El Movimiento, *1960–1976*

The early 1970s were heady days for Chicanos in Texas. Many belonged to a third party named La Raza Unida, which had been gaining statewide attention by replacing or diluting Anglo American political control in various small ranch and farm towns in South Texas. In Robstown, a farm community of about 11,000, *Familias Unidas* emerged as the barrio counterpart to similar politicized groups elsewhere, many of which identified with Raza Unida ideology. Familias Unidas grew out of student complaints of unfair treatment at the hands of the high school's Anglo-American faculty and the school district's administration. When student efforts to gain concessions from the school board (which included a mix of Mexican Americans and Anglos) failed, activists in town organized Familias Unidas. They worked on the premise that a change in the schools—and city politics for that matter—would not occur until the old political establishment was replaced. In their attacks on the "system," therefore, Familias Unidas members blamed not only Anglo leaders in the city but their Mexican-American political allies whom the militants accused of colluding with Anglos to perpetuate the status quo.

Playing the race card and highlighting the role that Mexican American *vendidos* (sellouts) played in abetting local conditions, Familias Unidas won seats in both the Robstown city council and school board in 1973. By 1976, however, it became evident that Familias Unidas could not compete successfully with the powerfully entrenched bloc of Anglo Americans and their Mexican American partisans, and their candidates lost the elections that year. But Familias Unidas and the militancy of the 1970s left a legacy. After the 1980s (as a result of white flight from the community), Robstown became more than 90 percent Tejano, with almost all positions in city government and school administrations occupied by Latinos.[1]

The 1970 federal census estimated the Mexican-American population in Texas at approximately 2 million, a figure that represented about 20 percent of the state's total population.[2] By that time, Tejanos could be found in just about all parts of the state, but principally in the agricultural counties of South Texas, the cattle- and sheep-raising sections of West Texas, the towns of the South Plains such as Lubbock, Amarillo, and Hereford, the El Paso region, and the inner cities of large metroplexes such as San Antonio, Houston, and Dallas.

Socioeconomic differentiation characterized the Tejano population more than ever. Some 60 to 70 percent of Mexican-American male workers in the state were solidly in unskilled and semiskilled blue-collar occupations (machinists, craftsmen, laborers, service, farm workers and farm managers, and other unspecified positions). The Tejano middle class, meantime, continued to expand to as much as 40 percent of the Tejano community. The census listed increased numbers of Mexican-American craftsmen, clerks, salespersons, managers, proprietors, and professionals.[3]

Politics in the 1960s

In the early 1960s, many veteran activists began subscribing to political notions that diverged from the moderate approaches to change that had characterized the postwar era. Several factors explain the turn. By the 1960s, new heights seemed attainable for Texas Mexicans. The matter of race was no longer a major issue, and many of the barriers and obstacles against which the LULACers and G.I. Forumeers had fought since their organizations' inception had tumbled, among them school segregation, discouragement from jury service, and even the poll tax, which was barred by the 24th Amendment to the U.S. Constitution in 1964. Legislative and judicial intervention in the 1960s and 1970s, moreover, removed numerous handicaps that had restricted political participation. In 1962, the United States Supreme Court declared the principle of one man, one vote, thereby strengthening Texas-Mexican political representation. The federal Voting Rights Act of 1965 ensured fair elections at the local level. In 1969, the Texas legislature repealed the segregationist laws passed by that body in 1956–57.[4] With many old issues settled, Tejano activists took on newer causes.

Numerous problems persisted, however, as part of an entrenched past. Although change was in the air, Anglo Texans generally remained conservative and cautious, especially those living in the many rural regions, in their concessions toward a people they still considered as inferior. Discrimination seemed different only in its newfound subtlety; standard practices of segregation in residential areas, schools, and hiring practices died hard. Tejanos still stood in fear of the Texas Rangers, the Border Patrol, and even the local Sheriff's Department, remembering the long history of mistreatment at the hands of these police bodies. Poverty stalked the great majority of rural Tejanos, especially the *campesinos* (farm workers) who toiled in the fields with practically no help from an insensitive government, both state and federal. In rural and urban areas, many Tejano parents had no choice but to keep their children from attending public schools and send them to work instead in order to help make ends meet in the tight family budget. Education for Tejanos, in fact, still lay mired in a shameful condition: Mexican schools remained segregated and underfinanced and many times under the control of racist administrators. The resentment and frustration that this generated, as well as the realization that traditional political approaches toward solving these problems had never yielded significant results, helped give rise to a new brand of Mexican-American politics in the 1960s and 1970s.

An early manifestation of the 1960s politics was Henry B. González's effort in 1958 to gain the Texas governor's seat. A San Antonio native, González had, during his term in the Texas senate in the 1950s, taken on struggles against Jim Crow, and González's quest for the governor's mansion had attracted political organizers of the era, primarily those working with the G.I. Forum and LULAC. González's gubernatorial run proved unsuccessful, but the campaign nonetheless inspired supporters to take on new battles.[5] In 1961 González went on to win election to the U.S. House of Representatives—a seat he would hold for thirty-eight years (1961–99)—in a newly formed congressional district that comprised most of Bexar County's Mexican barrios. In 1964, Eligio "Kika" de la Garza of South Texas joined González in the House.[6]

Then, in 1961, Mexican-American organizers who had helped John F. Kennedy win the presidency through "Viva Kennedy" Clubs—only to face a let down when the new president did not deliver on his promise of federal appointments for Hispanics—established the Political Association of Spanish-speaking Organizations (PASO). Indignant over what seemed to be a lack of progress for Mexican Americans, PASO challenged the credibility of Anglos and even of the old Mexican-American leadership and encouraged greater community involvement. By the mid-1960s, this political organization had extended its denunciations to all levels of government, blaming local and federal authorities for the impoverishment of Tejanos. Though PASO declined as the 1970s approached, it (as well as the Viva Kennedy clubs that had spawned it) had made earlier reform causes a political issue and had elevated Mexican-American politics to a national dialogue.[7]

By the tumultuous 1960s, then, Tejano middle-class leaders stood prepared to join the ranks of liberal politicians to call for increased action on the part of government and to pursue political office more diligently. Protest movements at the national level for the civil rights of gays, women's equality, and against the United States' involvement in the war in Vietnam (1964–75) incited bolder action. Mexican Americans themselves drew inspiration during the mid-1960s from unionizing efforts in California led by a labor activist named César Chávez. In June 1967, a former Evangelist preacher named Reies López Tijerina launched a highly publicized campaign to regain land grants previously owned by Mexican Americans in New Mexico. In Texas proper, in 1963, PASO and the Teamsters Union masterminded a political upset in Crystal City, helping to elect an all–Mexican-American ticket to the city council. Finally, strike activity among the campesinos in South Texas farms and a subsequent "Minimum Wage March" during the summer of 1966 fomented a broad movement calling the entire American political system into question.[8]

THE MINIMUM WAGE MARCH

In June 1966, Tejano farm workers walked off their jobs in the fields and continued to walk, all the way from the Rio Grande Valley to Austin. Governor John Connally, who opposed receiving the protestors at the statehouse, drove out to meet them at New Braunfels, where he rejected their plea for a special session of the legislature on the spot. Nonetheless, throngs of supporters—among them members of LULAC, the G.I. Forum, and PASO—waited for the marchers at the outskirts of Austin and accompanied them on to the capitol grounds. The several-hundred-mile trek and the passion it created, together with the governor's crass conduct, brought together diverse sectors of the Texas-Mexican community.[9]

The result was what came to be known as the "Chicano Movement" (the Movement or *"el movimiento"*), an expression of dissatisfaction that brought to light in dramatic fashion the many adverse conditions that still afflicted Mexican Americans and their communities. The emergence of the movement was not an isolated incident in which a group tried to find its identity or restless young people ran amok due to frustration with the status quo. Instead Mexican Americans—many with working-class roots—now opted to include militant tactics as part of a reformist struggle for self and group improvement. Chicano activists and their supporters during the era came mainly from the ranks of those who had experienced barrio or migrant life, and thus spoke from firsthand knowledge: in the process, they even reproached Mexican-American politicians who represented the old guard and who, presumably because of their middle-class upbringing, did not understand the needs of poor folks. The 1960s/1970s Chicano Generation believed that the ideas and strategies espoused by those who had predated it—among them views toward political approaches, assimilation, and American institutions—were ineffective and no longer viable.

The Movement produced what the historian Ignacio M. García calls a militant ethos, specifically "that body of ideas, strategies, tactics, and rationalizations" that the activists used to address problems still plaguing Tejano communities. Their thinking and political tactics stemmed from common negative experiences that shaped the solutions they offered for treating the nagging problems of racism, oppression, and poverty. It was this "militant ethos," in García's view, that rallied others to *chicanismo,* a nationalistic sense of self and community that, unlike earlier philosophical outlooks, was neither pro-Mexico (the Immigrant Generation) nor pro–United States (the Mexican-American Generation), but instead a mixed appreciation for Mexico's history and cultural richness, the consciousness of growing up in the United States, and the realities of life as distilled in the barrios and the fields. Intellectuals, political spokespersons, members of the politically moderate middle class, farmworkers, and many others fell in behind the activists as part of the new militant ethos.[10]

The Middle Class and the Movement

The Movement, therefore, consisted of a mix of moderate and militant thinking. Within the ranks of LULAC and the G.I. Forum, exasperation had prevailed over the neglect of the Mexican-American population in President Johnson's Great Society programs. In response to his critics, Johnson scheduled cabinet committee hearings on Mexican-American affairs to be held in El Paso, Texas, in October 1967. Because the list of participants omitted the emerging leaders of the Movement such as Chávez, Tijerina, and Rodolfo "Corky" González of Colorado, some of the delegates chose instead to attend a rump convention organized in El Paso's barrios. The delegates to what became known as the Raza Unida Conference tended to be combative in their criticism of white society and their discourse tended to exalt the superiority of Mexican-American culture over that of Anglo Americans.[11]

As part of the Chicano Movement, the members of older groups such as LULAC and the G. I. Forum tapped their connections to Washington; among programs that these organizations enacted in the mid-1960s, with the assistance of millions of federal dollars in aid, was a job-training and placement project for the unemployed poor called Operation SER (Service, Employment, and Redevelopment).[12] Simultaneously, middle-class activists took an interest in Mexican-American political campaigns as well as in school walkouts and different forms of public demonstration being led by the more aggressive elements within the Movement. PASO, for its part, took notice of these forms of protest but focused its energies on getting the candidates it endorsed, regardless of race, into office, where they could effect positive change for Mexican Americans. By the late 1960s, however, PASO yielded to the more militant strain of the Movement, as its middle-class philosophy served to put distance between itself and a community becoming more receptive to militant politics. Thus, it lost the chance to lead an important movement which in some ways it had set forth.[13]

But newer middle-class organizations also surfaced out of el movimiento, among them the Mexican American Legal Defense and Education Fund (MALDEF), founded in 1968. Funded by government grants and private corporations, MALDEF—adopting a posture between the old guard from the Mexican American Generation and the newer militancy—worked through the courts to protect Mexican-American rights. It assailed, for instance, practices that marred equal educational opportunities, such as discriminatory school funding or continued segregation. In so doing, it took several cases into the courts, among the most famous being *Cisneros* v. *Corpus Christi Independent School District* (1970).[14]

As school officials utilized the accepted Mexican-American classification of "white" as a subterfuge in school desegregation and continued
the pattern of excluding Mexican Americans from Anglo schools, lawyers
for Mexican Americans moved away from the old claim that Mexican
Americans were white people. Attorneys adopted the position that Mexican Americans must be recognized as an "identifiable ethnic group." This
new categorization would circumvent the ploy used by Anglo-controlled
school boards of using Tejanos (classified as white) to "integrate" certain
schools. The Mexican-American community was gratified when in June
1970 a federal district judge ruled that Mexican Americans could be
considered an identifiable ethnic minority and that the equal protection
of the law guaranteed under the Fourteenth Amendment applied to
them. Though the case was appealed, in 1973 the United States Supreme
Court acknowledged the separate legal status of Mexican Americans. For
MALDEF, the decision provided an important legal mechanism for its
desegregation cases.[15]

Middle-class organizations such as LULAC, the G.I. Forum, and
MALDEF had always made education one of their priorities, and they
heeded complaints by students who grieved that school systems treated
them unfairly in many ways. Principals and teachers, they protested,
criticized their heritage, editorialized about politics and the negative
role of Mexican Americans in history, enforced a "no Spanish" rule, discouraged them from involvement in certain school functions, neglected
their needs when it came to charting out career plans, and overlooked
Mexican-American applicants when hiring teachers and administrators
who might have acted as positive role models. By the mid-1970s, however,
school districts had conceded many of these demands.

Of all the called-for reforms, however, Mexican Americans were most
adamant about bilingual education, a program enacted by Congress in 1967
to alleviate the educational problems Mexican-American students faced.
Bilingual education seemed to give students a sense of self-esteem and
facilitated teaching, at least according to national studies that argued that
instruction in a native language enhanced the learning process. Further, it
circumvented the "no Spanish" rule and permitted a positive interpretation
of Mexican Americans' role in history. Moreover, necessary modifica-
tions made in the curriculum would try to meet the particular needs of
Mexican Americans. But despite the merits of these reforms, Mexican
Americans failed to pass state legislation that would have implemented

a strong program of bilingual education during the late 1960s and early 1970s. State Representative Carlos Truán (Democrat–Corpus Christi) did succeed in having a bilingual education act passed in 1969, but the law only asked local school districts to consider voluntarily beginning the program. Without state and judicial mandates, such efforts did not effect much progress.[16]

El Movimiento "Chicano"

MEXICAN AMERICAN YOUTH ORGANIZATION

The events of 1966 and 1967 set in motion another struggle, more militant in style and headed by the Mexican American Youth Organization (MAYO). Formally organized in 1967 by José Ángel Gutiérrez and four other activists, MAYO sought to act upon long-standing problems confronting Mexican Americans, among them segregation, harassment from law-enforcement authorities, and inferior schooling. MAYO activists adopted the militant style of African-American radicals and emulated the striking campesinos in California who had turned to the heritage of the pre-Columbian peoples of Mexico for cultural symbols and heroes. Many MAYO activists were students recruited from colleges, but their ties were to the grassroots, the segment of the Tejano community that MAYO purported to represent.[17]

This MAYO-influenced strain of the Movement adopted the self-referent term "Chicano" as suggestive of the resurgent cultural awareness. Chicanos rediscovered their Aztec and Mayan heritage and proclaimed it chauvinistically. Like some Anglo counterparts, they grew long hair and beards and donned the defiant Hippie garb of the period. In their politics, the militants damned mainstream society for its long history of oppression and criticized middle-class leaders as sellouts to *la raza* (the Mexican American people).[18] Beatings of Mexican Americans at the hands of policemen, alleged injustices inflicted by school administrators upon Chicano students, and electoral machinations were cases that activists cited when publicizing their cause, thus winning new adherents to their columns. School boycotts also became a strategy for making the educational system responsive to the needs of Mexican Americans, and student walkouts were initiated in institutions in numerous towns from the Texas Panhandle to the greater border region between the late 1960s and early 1970s.[19]

CRYSTAL CITY

Meanwhile, another activist group, *La Raza Unida* party (RUP), guided the militancy of the era, according to Ignacio M. García, one of the most knowledgeable students of the party. RUP's earliest victories came in 1970 in Crystal City, the small rural town in Zavala County that had been the setting for the aforementioned victory in 1963. It also happened to be the hometown of José Ángel Gutiérrez, one of MAYO's founders. When Gutiérrez returned to *Cristal* (as it is known in Spanish) in the spring of 1969, he organized Mexican-American high school students who were at that time in a state of complete discontent over the preferential treatment that the school faculty accorded the Anglo student minority.[20]

Things came to a head in October 1969 when the Crystal City High School Ex-Students Association proposed that it be permitted to select a queen and her entourage for the approaching homecoming game. It was a school requirement, however, that all candidates for homecoming queen have a father or mother who had received a degree from their town's high school, a criterion that severely limited the pool of Mexican-American prospects. When the angry students and their parents, organized by Gutiérrez and his wife Luz, failed to persuade the school board to reject the Ex-Students Association's petition to use the school campus for their activities, the young people walked out of classes on December 9, 1969.

For almost a month, through the Christmas holidays, the boycott remained in place, reaching a high of 65 percent total student absenteeism. As disbursement of state funds figured on attendance, the school system suffered gravely, so during the first week of January 1970 the board arranged a truce with the students, acquiescing to many of their requests. The protestors then lifted the boycott.[21]

RAZA UNIDA PARTY

Spinning off the confrontation was *Ciudadanos Unidos* (United Citizens), a political alliance founded by the parents of the boycotters and other sympathizers who sought to sustain the political momentum in Cristal following the resolution of the school issue. In the spring 1970 city and school board elections, Gutiérrez turned to Ciudadanos Unidos to help contest Anglo electoral dominance of the town.[22]

In January 1970, Ciudadanos Unidos created the Raza Unida party, whose antecedents harked back to 1967, when MAYO sponsored several

Raza Unida unity conferences at which leaders from different parts of the nation encouraged young people and prospective followers to get involved in the Chicano movement; the organizational meeting of the Raza Unida conference, of course, had been held in El Paso in that same year. Now, as Crystal City students boycotted in December 1969, MAYO met in Mission, Texas, and called for the formation of a third political party. Following RUP's founding, MAYO members directed their priorities to politics, and as a consequence their organization began to fade. By 1971, RUP supplanted MAYO as the main force of Chicano political organizing in Texas.[23]

In the 1970 elections, the slate Gutiérrez assembled took posts on the Crystal City school board and city council and soon gained dominance of both. Numerous reforms followed. In the schools, the new officers implemented bilingual instruction, developed Chicano history courses, established a free-lunch program, and hired Mexican-American personnel to replace teachers who found the new environment uncomfortable. At the city level, the party replaced Anglos with Raza Unida people and aggressively pursued federal monies. The Chicano "takeover" of the town gained widespread notice, inasmuch as it symbolized what Chicanos in other parts of the nation might hope to achieve with commitment and sound organization.[24]

Confident that the Crystal City success story could be duplicated elsewhere, RUP supporters from throughout the state gathered in San Antonio on October 31, 1971, to contemplate RUP's direction. Delegates decided to establish RUP as a statewide party that would run candidates in the 1972 elections.[25]

Most visible of the RUP candidates that year was its nominee for governor, Ramsey Muñiz, a Corpus Christi native who held a law degree from Baylor University and who, at the time of his selection as a gubernatorial candidate, was a MAYO organizer in the Waco area. As the RUP candidate, he spoke for a leftist-liberal platform that the party had hammered out in June 1972. The plank stressed education, calling on schools to implement programs to meet the needs of Mexican Americans and demanding that the state's school funding be dispersed more fairly. It called on government to partition cities into districts so that barrios would receive equal representation in ruling bodies. Among other things, the RUP platform addressed foreign policy, healthcare, and the standard of living. It supported ratification of the Equal Rights Amendment and demanded that the Texas Rangers be disbanded. When the ballots were counted, Muñiz received 6.28 percent of the vote to the Democrat's 47.8 percent and the Republicans 45.08 percent. By drawing votes away from the Democrats, RUP made the old, major parties recognize it as a possible alternative in Texas politics.[26]

Between 1970 and 1973, RUP compiled an impressive list of victories throughout several South Texas towns. RUP-backed candidates in Cotulla (La Salle County) and RUP sympathizers in Carrizo Springs (Dimmit County) triumphed in 1970, the same time that Gutiérrez and his supporters had won in the Crystal City school board and city council. In Robstown (Nueces County), as mentioned earlier, Familias Unidas made headway in gaining positions in city government between 1973 and 1976. In Kingsville (Kleberg County), RUP activities duplicated the Robstown feat. Pearsall, San Juan, and Edcouch-Elsa in the lower Rio Grande Valley, and Eagle Pass, Kyle, San Marcos, Lockhart, Hebbronville, Beeville, and even smaller communities in far West Texas's Brewster and El Paso counties were among the other places in which RUP or its sympathizers won local offices during the early 1970s.[27]

WOMEN IN THE MOVEMENT

Throughout Texas, women played significant roles in el movimiento. Women had been part of the Movement since its beginnings; their ranks came from veteran activists such as Virginia Músquiz, believed to be the first Mexican-American woman to run for the state legislature (1964) and a participant in the Crystal City movimiento in 1969, as well as María L. Hernández, founder of the *Orden Caballeros de América* in 1929, who campaigned for RUP candidates in the early 1970s.[28] The greater number of women activists, however, were college students who had joined MAYO in the late 1960s. Following the founding of RUP, some women, several from the working class, won political office under the RUP banner and others (like Martha P. Cotera and Evey Chapa) played prominent leadership roles as members of *Mujeres Por La Raza,* a woman's caucus in the party.[29]

Women's role in el movimiento, however, was not limited to traditional politics, as many advocated feminism and urged assertiveness for women. Leaders directed themselves toward the amelioration of such problems as poor educational standings, discriminatory wage structures, the right of women to control their own bodies through access to birth control and abortion, and family care. To address these issues, Tejanas convened in Houston in May 1971 in what is considered to be the first national conference ever organized to specifically deal with Mexican-American women's concerns. This *Conferencia de Mujeres por la Raza* (National Chicana Conference), was attended by hundreds of women from diverse sections of the nation. Certainly, this conference was only one of many similar meetings Tejanas held during the first half of the 1970s.

Middle-class Mexican-American women advocated similar goals. LULAC's Women's Affairs Committee held its first state convention in Houston in November 1972, which approximately 250 women from Texas and elsewhere attended. They passed resolutions encouraging LULAC to work for more significant government appointments for women. They resolved to reform the prevailing role of the Mexican-American woman as a homemaker and to inspire women to assume a more visible role in society and political affairs.[30] By their involvement in the Movement, women (whether working class, collegian, or professional) countered the old prescribed gender roles by asserting their leadership: picketing and participating in mass demonstrations; campaigning for political office; or engaging in debate over the division of family responsibilities. Women's strong presence as part of la causa forced the Movement to address points of special concern to women. Since the 1970s, women's issues have remained a part of the Mexican-American political agenda.[31]

LA IGLESIA AND EL MOVIMIENTO

Until about the mid-twentieth century, Mexican Americans had an ambivalent relationship with the Catholic Church. The Church (to whom most owed their fidelity) looked after their spiritual needs and in many cases provided them a comfort zone in which they might find solace from a life of toil, poverty, and despair. In their association with the Church, however, many Tejanos dealt with church personnel who treated the Mexican faithful (often in segregated parishes) as ignorant, inferior, and even quaint. Both clergymen and parishioners accepted the precept that it was not the Church's responsibility to seek proactive solutions to society's ills.

During the Chicano movement, however, many activists (joined by politicized parishioners) began denouncing the institutional Church as racist, elitist, and a silent partner of the Establishment. They insisted that the Church play a larger role in helping to solve the problems plaguing Tejano neighborhoods. Some church officials responded defensively, arguing that the Church's duties lay in the realm of the spiritual, not in that of liberation politics.

But there were those within the Church who disagreed with the old line and wanted to help better the communities they served. These included Mexican American priests who in San Antonio in 1969 formed *Padres Asociados para Derechos Religiosos, Educativos y Sociales* (PADRES) with the intent of persuading the Church hierarchy to respond to community calls for participation in the campaign for equality. Two years later, Mexican American nuns organized *Las Hermanas* (The Sisters) for a purpose akin to that of PADRES: forcing the Church to change its position regarding its social responsibilities to the barrios. Also seriously involved were local clerics and nuns who supported labor struggles, as was the case with Father Patricio Flores (subsequently to become Bishop Flores) who gave vocal support to the farm workers movement of the 1960s. Others endorsed some of the militants' actions, supporting school walkouts, joining rallies and demonstrations, and helping with various community projects. By the time the 1970s ended, however, the commitment of the Catholic Church to social causes seemingly unraveled. As the political climate of the age changed, the Church reverted to its more traditional function of caring for their charges' spiritual condition.[32]

THE DECLINE OF EL MOVIMIENTO

By the mid-1970s, el movimiento faced a downturn, as attested to by RUP's inability to follow up on earlier gains. Political victories were limited to Crystal City and Cotulla in the spring of 1974, and in Cristal, divisiveness now smoldered, as two factions of RUP vied for the same offices. The new group accused the older, Gutiérrez-led wing of seeking self-aggrandizement and of having become despotic. Then, Ramsey Muñiz's second run for the governor's mansion in November 1974 proved less significant than had the first: the meager result prompting many to reassess the prospects of the party at the state level. Back in Cristal, Gutiérrez did win the position of County Judge in 1974, and RUP won other county offices. But Gutiérrez's talk of getting Anglo ranchers to pay more taxes on their lands and the rise of the new faction in Cristal that challenged Gutiérrez on ideological grounds did not bode well for effective rule from Raza Unida.[33]

Numerous factors conspired to exhaust el movimiento. Ideological splits hurt it. The difficulty of fundraising constrained the party's ability to wage effective campaigns. Harassment of RUP organizers by Texas Rangers, legal attacks, and sub rosa efforts designed to cast a shady image on activists dispirited RUP supporters. The defeat of the Gutiérristas in Crystal City in April 1976 by the opposition RUP faction (with the support of some Anglo Democrats) did not help the Movement. Then, the power of Texas governor Dolph Briscoe came down hard on Gutiérrez's plan to establish a collective farm in Zavala County. Calling it an effort to establish a "little Cuba" in Texas, the governor succeeded in lobbying against the use of a $1.5 million federal grant to fund the project and convinced many voters to regard the RUP experiment as an adventure in socialism.[34]

Just as critical to the decline of the Movement was the earnest devotion most Mexican Americans now had to the principles of integration into the American mainstream society. Chicano denunciations of U.S. institutions and talk of separatism appeared an anomaly to many who counted on making the American dream a reality for themselves and their families. Over a period of time, the activists could not sustain the fervor of the Movement—indeed, even the word "Chicano" fell into disuse by the late 1970s. In the end, the changing times made el movimiento seem anachronistic, its militant rhetoric and tactics passé. Many of the Movement's aims became institutionalized as well. In the gubernatorial election of November 1978, RUP did not garner the necessary 2 percent vote to remain viable for subsequent elections, and with that showing its hopes for evolving into a third party force died out. In 1981, Gutiérrez himself resigned his position as the Zavala County judge.[35]

THE LEGACY OF EL MOVIMIENTO

Still, el movimiento left an enduring mark. Women activists had modified old gender stereotypes and earned concessions on equality, thereby improving Mexican-American women's hopes for a better education, a path to professional careers, and a real voice in decisions regarding the size and management of the family. On the whole, Mexican Americans had come to see themselves as a cohesive ethnic group—the new attitudes and feelings the hard-won results of the Movement's emphasis on cultural pride and historical uniqueness. In addition, RUP had succeeded in wresting power from Anglos in the Democratic party, most visibly in South Texas, for as RUP declined, ex-members joined the Mexican American Democrats (MAD—founded in late 1976) and moved in to fill openings created by the void RUP left. But the new brand of politicos carried with them the ethos of the Movement; activists after the 1970s approached politics in different ways than had members of the Mexican American Generation. They held firm in the belief that their role as Mexican-descent leaders was to struggle for the needs of their communities as ethnic entities, for a special pride in being Mexican American, and for the notion that Chicanos should constitute an integral component of the body politic. Then, the Movement reinvigorated the reform organizations of the pre-Movement era such as LULAC and the G.I. Forum. Some of the veterans of these organizations joined MAD, while others participated in the Southwest Voter Registration Education Project (SVREP), founded by Willie Velásquez in 1974.[36]

The movimiento further breathed life into a burst of literary creativity that led the scholar Philip Ortego, writing during the period, to call the flowering the "Chicano Renaissance." Throughout the country, a cadre of intellectuals surfaced to articulate the nationalism of the era, using poetry, novels, short stories, theater, and the visual arts to do so. Most being products of the post–World War II process of biculturation, this crop of authors and artists profited from their public school education to deliver deftly their feelings in English or Spanish, or, as was the case with others, in a combination of the two languages. In Texas, major participants in the Chicano literary movement included internationally acclaimed authors such as Tomás Rivera, Ricardo Sánchez, and Rolando Hinojosa, as well as equally gifted writers like Abelardo Delgado, Tino Villanueva, Angela de Hoyos, Carmen Tafolla, and Evangelina Vigil Piñón, and playwrights such as Estela Portillo Trambley. Active also during the 1960s and 1970s in spreading the message of Chicanismo were theater groups, most of them consisting of volunteer actors who performed skits that sought to sensitize audiences to the richness of Mexican American life, or, on the other hand, to dramatize the struggle of la raza to ward off the corruptive influence of Anglo culture. A muralist movement also emerged as Tejano artists resurrected an old tradition traceable to pre-Columbian peoples (or the great art masters of Mexico, such as Diego Rivera) of painting murals on the walls of public buildings—such murals generally acted as another medium bolstering the political struggle then underway. At the same time of the Chicano Renaissance, Chicano scholarly studies started to find their way into professional journals, many of the articles revising the old image of Chicanos as a quaint people who were a burden to society. Old publications on Mexican Americans were re-read with a new eye, among them the works of Dr. George I. Sánchez and Dr. Américo Paredes.[37] The literary impact of the movimiento lives on today, both as an independent expression as well as an integrated component of the Texas literary tradition.

Labor Unionism in the Cities and on the Farms

Though the post–World War II decline in labor activism continued into the 1960s and 1970s, Mexican Americans still strove to improve their working conditions. During the winter of 1968 Austin became the scene of a prolonged strike of predominantly Mexican-American workers at Economy Furniture Company who wanted Local 456 of the Upholsterers International Union of North America, AFL-CIO, recognized as their bargaining agency. After more than two years of picketing, boycotting, and litigation, the union members won a favorable ruling from an appeals court, which directed management to bargain with Local 456. The strike ended in September 1971 with union recognition, increased pay, a more liberal vacation policy, and other fringe benefits. Sanitation workers in Lubbock in 1968 and 1972 launched strikes to have the city concede them an increase in hourly wages, as well as such basic needs as uniforms, drinking water while on the job, and sanitary privies at the land fill. In the first walk out, the city provided them with uniforms, water, and toilets, but no pay raise. Still pressing for better salary, the sanitation workers struck once more in 1972, this time enjoying support from the Catholic Church in Lubbock, residents of the Mexican-American community, and fellow workers in other municipal departments. Their goal of gaining better pay proved futile, as the city council after three weeks of entrenchment could only promise them their old jobs back.[38]

In 1972 in El Paso, Mexican-American women members of the Amalgamated Clothing Workers of America (ACWA) struck several Farah Manufacturing Company plants, one of the major employers in the city. The garment workers (primarily Mexican immigrants and Mexican Americans) sought protection from low wages, dangerous health and safety conditions, exposure to sexually harassing and racist supervisors, and other types of mistreatment.

The strike in El Paso intensified to the level of a national boycott of Farah products. Ultimately, the tactic forced Farah to shut down some of its plants in Texas and New Mexico and, in February 1974, to accept the ACWA as the union representing Farah workers. The strikers were not completely pleased with their new contract, but they at least felt that they had won union protection.

In the mid-1970s, Farah's fortunes continued on the downswing due to the recession of 1974–75, adverse publicity generated by the way its management had dealt with the strike, and poor executive-level decisions made in production and marketing. To continue operating, the company released several workers and intimidated union leaders. Such a tenuous situation forced workers in 1977 to make numerous concessions to management in order to keep the factory afloat and thus save their jobs.[39]

Another major strike involving Tejanos during the 1960s and 1970s was that of the aforementioned farm workers whose minimum wage march in the summer of 1966 is credited with kindling the Chicano Movement in Texas. Actually, the campesinos themselves had profited little from the famed pilgrimage: in the 1970s, they still faced lamentable working conditions. Most fields lacked any restroom facilities, and since modesty compelled women to delay their bodily functions for hours, they suffered from disproportionally high levels of kidney infections and other renal maladies. Wages remained as low as $2 or $3 for a typical day of field labor. Diseases such as typhoid, typhus, dysentery, and leprosy afflicted farm workers to a degree unknown to other Texans. Infant mortality rates among the campesinos in South Texas were among the highest in the nation at the time, and the life expectancy of field hands hovered around forty-nine years. Farm workers did not enjoy basic benefits from state laws, such as the right to collective bargaining, workman's compensation, and unemployment benefits.[40]

To assist the Texas campesinos following the March of 1966, César Chávez had sent Antonio Orendain from California to Texas to take charge of a small chapter of Chávez's own fledgling United Farm Workers' Union (UFWU). But at this time resistance to union activity in Texas was fierce, and strikes were easy to break with scabs from across the border. Fearing violence and wishing to focus his efforts on unionizing in California, Chávez recalled Orendain in 1967, and the UFWU chapter in Texas declined.[41]

Two years later, Orendain returned to the Rio Grande Valley and for a period undertook aggressive organizing efforts in behalf of the UFWU. In 1975, however, Chávez fired his UFWU lieutenant for leading strike activities at a time when Chávez was negotiating important labor contracts in California and could have done better without the added controversy. In response, Orendain formed the independent Texas Farm Workers Union (TFWU), feeling that the UFWU had forsaken the Texas campesinos. Thus, by the mid-1970s, two Texas farm workers' unions sought different strategies in efforts to improve the lot of the campesinos.[42]

Toward the Age of "Hispanics"

For a ten-year period following the Farm Workers March of 1966, a general regard for the good of la raza had held together a cause marked by differences in class, generations, and ideologies. During the era, Texas Mexicans had pursued political tactics previously shunned by activists of the Mexican-American Generation and could by the mid-1970s claim to have made real strides that had built upon their predecessors' accomplishments. When it was spent, the Chicano Movement left important statements, not the least of which was the pledge that Tejanos would no longer accede to labels of submissiveness and inferiority.

Indeed, Anglo Americans came to reject the notion that Texas Mexicans were to be kept on society's periphery, as had been the case during previous generations. Privately, some Anglos still harbored contempt for "Meskins" and worked surreptitiously to retard their progress, but many of them now accepted the fact that the majority of Tejanos could translate their numbers into economic and political clout. Businesspeople, therefore, moved away from gestures that might alienate Texas-Mexican customers. Politicians stopped discounting the Mexican-American presence and became aware of the potential of a mobilized Tejano electorate. In the 1980s, then, Texas Mexicans would find themselves living in a society more receptive to both their needs and their contributions.

CHAPTER TEN

Hispanic Texans in the Late Twentieth Century

José López illegally crossed the international border sometime in 1969. After having found steady employment in Texas, he called for the rest of his family to join him there. Like millions of other immigrants from throughout the world, he dreamed of something better for his loved ones in America, including providing them with a sound education.

But his plans for schooling his young ones abruptly went awry when the Texas legislature in 1975 barred school districts from using tax-generated funds to finance the education of immigrant children. Students unable to prove their U.S. citizenship would have to pay for schooling. López could hardly afford such tuition on the salary he made as a foundry worker in Tyler, Texas. When individuals sympathetic to the immigrants' plight approached López about possibly becoming part of a group challenging the Texas law, he agreed, albeit with doubts about himself: he conceded to being an illiterate man, knowing little of legal matters, much less about getting involved in high-stakes issues.

López thus became part of a 1977 law suit filed by MALDEF in behalf of himself and four other families against Jim Plyler, the superintendent of schools in Tyler, as well as the city's school board. The immigrants involved in the federal suit came to be listed as "Doe" in order to protect their privacy—the case consequently known as *Plyler* v. *Doe*.

In September 1977, U. S. District Judge William Wayne Justice issued an injunction directing Texas schools to refrain from closing classroom doors to immigrant children. The Tyler case ultimately made its way up to the Fifth U.S. Circuit Court of Appeals and in 1982, to the U. S. Supreme Court. In a five to four decision, the high court ruled in *Plyler* v. *Doe* that immigrants could receive a publicly financed education, a right guaranteed by the Fourteenth Amendment. In the wake of this decision, nine of the ten López children (and thousands of other immigrant students) subsequently acquired their high school diplomas.[1]

As of 1990, the Texas-Mexican population stood at just above 4 million. This figure, of course, was an undercount, for census takers have never fully succeeded in tallying those like José López who come to Texas from Mexico illegally. Of the estimate given by the 1990 census, about 75 percent were Mexican Americans—that is, they were native born.[2] According to some calculations, by 2000 this figure had dropped to 63.0 percent—out of a total Mexican (Hispanic) population of 5 million—although scholars, commentators, and demographers debated the exact total.[3]

The Middle Class and the Marginalized Masses

Significant disparities in standards of living marked the Tejano community after the late 1970s. At the bottom rung there existed the poorest of people living in makeshift homes in unincorporated subdivisions (colonias) along the border—their living conditions as poor as those that Tejanos had faced at any point in their history. The fact of the matter was that some 20 percent of Tejano families lived in impoverished circumstances in the Lone Star State, and the future did not look bright for them.[4]

At the upper extreme were more fortunate folks belonging to the old middle class, but also those tracing their well-being to the Great Society initiatives of the 1960s as well as the gains made by the Chicano Movement; these two spells of liberalism had produced increased student enrollment at the levels of higher education and newer opportunities in the business world. Overtures by government and the private sector to the formerly neglected Hispanic voter and consumer led to the further incorporation of upwardly mobile Mexican Americans into the state's government bureaucracy and corporate structure.[5] Thus, the internal fragmentation perceptible in the Tejano community since the eighteenth century remained, now in the form of a prominent middle class and a segment of the community still impoverished.

A Moderate Political Age

Following the Chicano Movement, Texas Mexicans adjusted to a political climate similar to that which prevailed during the 1940s and 1950s, when only socially sanctioned challenges to the status quo were condoned. During this post-1970s period of moderation, the designation "Hispanic" became acceptable as a label that reflected newer economic and political currents, acting as an all-embracing term for those having cultural roots in any of the Latin American nations.[6] Corporations and departments of government catering to the needs of the expanding Mexican-American middle class popularized the use of the term "Hispanic." It won acceptance among those who had disapproved of the militancy of the 1960s and 1970s and rejected such terms as "Chicano," by Tejano businesspeople who found new opportunities and sought to appeal to a wider spectrum of the buying public, by activists who found it a neutral label in formal commentary, and by politicians who recognized that the term identified a national electorate more powerful at the ballot box than did a strictly regional constituency such as "Tejanos."[7] In the opinion of historian Neil Foley, use of the term Hispanic also allowed Mexican Americans to retain the preferred racial categorization of "white," while simultaneously claiming an ethnic-group identity. The term "Latino," more popular in other parts of the United States, especially among the politically-minded and those in the scholarly community, was gradually gaining ground in Texas.[8]

In the cautious politics of the post-Movement era, the middle class maintained its role as political arbiter for the Mexican-American electorate. As indicated, the Chicano Movement had included middle-class adherents, and as the organizations of the 1960s and 1970s waned, this element moved in to seize opportunities available within the Democratic party. The middle-class reformist groups of old similarly profited from el movimiento. LULAC, for one, recaptured its place as the most-noted organization and along with MALDEF assumed a major role as an intermediary between Mexican Americans and the Establishment.[9]

In pursuit of a moderate agenda, LULAC departed from the high-profile politics espoused by LULAC national presidents of the earlier era. After the mid-1980s, LULAC leaders became more constrained and less bold in their advocacy, while the organization itself struggled to remain financially solvent. Nonetheless, they remained a political voice for Mexican Americans in Texas, lobbying for immigration reform, resisting a national "English only" movement, and contesting the manner in which Texas dispersed its university funds.[10] Similarly, MALDEF assumed a more centrist position, for as it lost its federal funding in the 1980s, it turned to the conservative corporate sector. But in the assessment of political scientist Armando Navarro, the organization nonetheless established a credible list of achievements during the last years of the twentieth century. It scored victories in behalf of immigrant rights and in favor of Mexican Americans kept from promotion and advancement by long-standing corporate habits. It tackled other issues such a racial profiling by police, affirmative action in hiring and acceptance to universities, and disparities in school funding.[11]

Also reflecting the trend toward moderation in the 1980s and 1990s was the election of postliberal Tejano leaders to office. The most visible of these political figures was Henry Cisneros (Mayor, San Antonio) who, along with others in Colorado and California, voiced Mexican-American interests and practiced a style of politics more redolent of that of the pre–World War II era than that of the Chicano Movement. Though Cisneros did not reject his Mexican American identity, he did not make ethnicity a political issue, striving to serve all people in his constituency; his critics, however, faulted him for lacking a specific agenda for Mexican Americans. During the 1990s, Cisneros served as the secretary of the U.S. Department of Housing and Urban Development under President Bill Clinton.[12]

IMPROVED POLITICAL STANDING

Thus at a time of moderate politics Tejanos witnessed numerous advances in their political representation. Actually, such gains resulted from changes generated by forces unleashed in previous periods. In the 1960s and 1970s, government had taken the lead in efforts to coerce society to change its biases against racial minorities, a public consensus built up to combat the blatant racism of the pre-1960s era, and the Chicano Movement had opened doors to the incorporation of Tejanos into the political and economic mainstream. More immediate factors that underlay these achievements included population increases, a better educated and informed Mexican-American electorate, and successful registration drives undertaken by organizations such as SVREP.[13]

But gains also resulted from self-initiatives by Mexican Americans, for the ethos of the Chicano Movement persisted into the latter decades of the century. While basically moderate, Hispanic politics of the post-1970s still demanded a commitment to group improvement by leaders who could proclaim ties to the grass roots. Ethnic pride also compelled leaders to think of Tejanos as a distinct conglomeration and to approach politics in a manner that ensured the persistence of a "Mexican American" community.

Ignacio M. García identifies the new leadership as belonging to the Mexican American/Hispanic Generation. This cohort, constituted of resilient spokespersons from the 1960s and 1970s as well as younger ones whose formative political years came in the early 1980s and after, blended aspects of the 1960s/1970s agenda with the new approaches of the 1980s/1990s. They concerned themselves with such issues as gender, school achievement, discrimination on the job, unemployment, the well-being of farm workers, and immigration. But their ranks came from the middle class, and they made no mention of separatism or of forming a third party; instead they stressed adaptation and inclusion. Hispanic politicians of the Mexican American/Hispanic Generation preferred forming coalitions with liberal Democrats as well as African-American, labor, and church groups. Their goals included integrating Tejanos into the body politic and making the Tejano vote an influential one. By acting as a unified voice representing a special interest in the legislature, for example, Tejano legislators hoped to effectively resolve problems still facing Mexican Americans as a people.[14]

In 1984, Raúl A. González was appointed to the Texas Supreme Court by the governor and went on to win election in his own right until his retirement at the end of 1998. In 1990, Dan Morales won office as the first Hispanic Attorney General of Texas and served in that office for eight years. According to the *Texas Almanac,* the number of Spanish-surnamed senators and representatives in the state legislature increased from about fifteen to thirty-one between 1976 and 2000. The number of Spanish-surnamed county commissioners and county judges rose from approximately 70 in 1976 to around 147 in 2000.[15] In San Antonio, the aforementioned Henry Cisneros, a graduate of George Washington University with a doctorate in public administration, won the mayor's seat in 1981, the first Mexican American to do so since Juan Seguín during the days of the Texas Republic. The border counties of South Texas finally yielded to the political control of the Mexican-American majority.[16] In

numerous Texas cities, including the metroplexes, there was Tejano representation in lower-level courts, the constabulary, city councils, school
boards, as well as in nonelective positions with political influence. In the
U.S. House of Representatives, six Mexican Americans were serving as
of 2000. From 1977 to 1979, Leonel Castillo of Houston became head
of the Immigration and Naturalization Service during the presidency of
Jimmy Carter. In 1988, King Ranch–born Lauro Cavazos was appointed
Secretary of Education and served until late 1990.

Increased electoral influence was evident in other ways. For example,
Mexican-American votes contributed to the election of populist Anglo
Americans at the state level. Ballot power also influenced the passage of
several bills designed to bring about school-finance reform, to improve
the lot of the campesinos, and provide health assistance to the poor.[17]

The same circumstances that produced political moderation, however, dampened possibilities for further gains. Attempts by leaders of
the Mexican American/Hispanic Generation to help the impoverished
were frustrated by the very institutions for which they worked, as their
concern over job security discouraged them from being too aggressive
in their commitment to social change. In the assessment of historian
Rodolfo Acuña, this cohort acted as brokers who served the good of ruling
interests instead of the Texas Mexican community.[18]

The Ethnic Agenda

Nonetheless, Tejano leaders from the Mexican American/Hispanic Generation (typically native-born, educated, and employed as government
bureaucrats, professionals, businesspeople, educators and academicians)
addressed ethnic policies but also other issues affecting Mexican Americans
as lower-class folks. Ethnic causes included discrimination, political powerlessness, underemployment, education, immigration, protecting the right
of people to speak Spanish in public places (the response to the so-called
"English only" movement), emphasizing the value of Mexican-American
history (in 1999, the Texas legislature directed that March 31 be hence-
forth observed as César Chávez Day), striving to improve life for migrant
and farm workers, as well as combating new challenges on affirmative
action. When in March 1996, for instance, the U.S. Fifth Circuit Court
of Appeals in *Hopwood* v. *Texas* ruled against the University of Texas Law
School's affirmative action plan, Mexican-American students protested

and Hispanic politicians and organizations condemned the decision as a retreat from fairness. To address this reversal to university admissions policy, Mexican-American legislators, academicians, and MALDEF attorneys helped devise "The Top Ten Percent Plan" and saw it steered through the Texas legislature in 1997. The new legislation required publicly financed universities to permit all students graduating in the top 10 percent of their high school class to register without restriction.[19]

Also involved in the issues of the day were members of local civic clubs, the G.I. Forum, LULAC, MALDEF, and SVREP. The latter organization was, as mentioned, founded by Willie Velásquez (one of the founders of MAYO) in San Antonio in 1974 for the purpose of registering more Mexican-American voters throughout the United States and eliminating institutional obstacles to progress as advocated by Latino officials. While SVREP sought to get out the Hispanic vote and see Mexican Americans elected to office, it joined MALDEF and other groups to overturn laws (such as those dealing with at-large elections) that deterred Mexican Americans from equal representation and weakened Tejano political influence.[20] Also committed to the goal of Mexican-American equality was Raúl Yzaguirre of Texas, who between 1974 and 2003 headed the National Council of La Raza, a Washington, D.C., public advocacy group founded in 1968.[21]

BETTER EDUCATION

Mexican Americans also carried on their crusade for better education, though after the mid-1970s, for several reasons, they deemphasized integration of schools. Anglos resisted court-mandated desegregation strenuously, and school districts usually found ways to delay it. More significant, desegregation plans usually favored Anglos instead of Mexican Americans: it was the latter, for example, who were usually bused out of their own district in order to comply with integration orders. As time passed, therefore, support for desegregation as a way to educational parity declined among Mexican Americans. According to historian Guadalupe San Miguel, parents and Mexican-American educators now turned to bilingual programs to remedy shortcomings in their children's education.[22]

Despite unremitting attempts to create an effective bilingual program, Mexican-American educators in Texas in the mid-1970s still had only a weak law mandating bilingual education from kindergarten through the third grade. In the face of this failure to enact a more effective program, bilingual education activists turned to the courts, arguing that the status quo deprived Mexican-American students of a sound education. In the legislature, Carlos Truán, whose battles for bilingual education originated in the late 1960s, continued his commitment but met little success, as public opinion opposed this compensatory program and a spate of reports from the government and private institutes argued that such approaches were expensive, ineffectual, and potentially divisive.[23]

But then in January 1981, Judge William Wayne Justice ruled that the state bilingual education plan was unacceptable to the court and ordered immediate reform. Armed with this opinion, Truán in May of that year introduced a new bill seeking to establish the bilingual program in schools through the sixth grade in districts comprising at least twenty school children with only a rudimentary command of the English language. Again, Truán faced resistance, but his argument for a bill that would help the state avoid Judge Justice's more extreme solution to the system's shortcomings swayed his adversaries. Thus had Truán and his supporters succeeded in acquiring a stronger program despite the power of the opposition. The immediate impetus had been Judge Justice's decision.[24]

On another front, Mexican Americans with the assistance of MAL-DEF questioned the institutionalized method of dispersing funds to the public school system, reasoning that it discriminated against students residing in school districts with lower property-tax bases. In 1968, parents of Mexican-American school children enrolled at the financially distressed Edgewood Independent School District in San Antonio, brought suit against the state in *Rodríguez* v. *San Antonio Independent School District.* The case went all the way to the United States Supreme Court, which ruled in 1973 for the reconsideration of the existing school finance formula. But the justices deferred to the state legislators and left it to them to resolve the matter.[25]

In 1984, MALDEF once again helped file suit, but this time in state court. In *Edgewood Independent School District* v. *Kirby,* the Texas Supreme Court ruled in October 1989 that the system of school financing violated the Texas constitution and that an equitable system of school financing be produced by the state legislature. In June 1990, after several special sessions, state lawmakers approved a $528 million school finance compromise to take effect in the fall of that year. But the plan did not satisfy the plaintiffs, who took the case back into the courts. During the next few years, the legislature offered alternative methods for funding the public school system, but these were all challenged. In January 1995, the Texas Supreme Court finally accepted a funding plan that the legislature had passed in 1993, under which wealthy school districts would share their revenue with poorer districts (this arrangement came to be dubbed the "Robin Hood System"), though the richer districts did receive five other options by which they could help ensure equal funding of the state's system of education.[26]

TEXAS-MEXICAN FICTION

The works of creative writers during the post-Chicano era resembled the movement literature of the 1960s and 1970s in conspicuous ways. Novels, short stories, autobiographies, poetry and other forms of written expression revisited many of the ugly episodes that long had characterized contact between Tejanos and Anglos (as if indelibly etched in the Tejano psyche), among them colonialism, racism, and ethnic conflict in the workplace. As had the writings of the 1960s and 1970s, this newer literature acknowledged "lo mexicano," investigating how the immigrant past shaped the Tejano character. It singled out (with considerable respect and esteem) entrenched ethnic values, customs, and celebrations that weathered the inevitable Americanization that had occurred over time.

That said, certain features of the new literature distinguished it clearly from Chicano-era works. Because most authors were native born, they wrote predominantly in English (or used "Spanglish," or code-switching)—a natural propensity since most of them had gone to college and been influenced by American literature (obviously, they had simultaneously studied the works of Latin American and Spanish authors). In addition, the new literature explored topics such as spirituality and personal identity. Women writers delved more deeply into matters such as feminism and alternate lifestyles. Gloria Anzaldúa (1942–2004) from the Rio Grande Valley, for instance, gained prominence for *Borderlands/La Frontera: The New Mestiza* (San Francisco: Aunt Lute, 1987), and other works as they validated lesbianism among Mexican Americans as a subject for open discussion. Autobiography also became a new trend during this time. Falling in this genre would be Norma E. Cantú's *Canícula: Snapshots of a Girlhood en la Frontera* (Albuquerque: University of New Mexico Press, 1995); Pat Mora's *House of Houses* (Boston: Beacon Press, 1997); and John

Phillip Santos' *Places Left Unfinished at the Time of Creation* (New York: Penguin Books, 1999).[27]

ORGANIZING ACTIVITIES: FIELDS AND FACTORIES

Another issue of priority for Texas-Mexican leaders, especially those from South Texas, was the plight of farm workers. For the decade following Tony Orendain's split with Chávez in 1975, the TFWU and the California-based United Farm Workers (by now an AFL-CIO affiliate) vied to speak for an estimated 170,000 campesinos who worked the Texas fields.[28] Facing continued failures in the Texas legislature for collective bargaining rights, Orendain's more publicity-oriented TFWU staged dramatic marches: one in 1977 from Austin to Washington, D.C.; the second in 1979 from Muleshoe in the Texas Panhandle to Austin. The most intensive efforts by Orendain and by Rebecca Flores Harrington, then the state director of the UFW, were of lobbying state legislators, for without a labor law mandating union elections, agribusiness management could easily replace strikers with scabs.[29] When the independent TFWU ended its efforts in the state in 1982, however, representation of farm workers' needs then fell to Flores Harrington, her husband James C. Harrington, attorney for the UFW, and the rank-and-file workers who constituted the many organizing committees throughout South Texas.[30]

In 1981, Mexican-American legislators from the trans-Nueces had introduced an array of bills designed to win for farm workers unemployment compensation, workers' compensation in case of injury on the job, and collective bargaining rights. Other prospective bills would prohibit work with *el cortito* (the short-handled hoe), prolonged use of which caused disabling and chronic back pain in stoop laborers, and an end to the employment of school-aged children when public schools were in session. The latter two bills were signed into law in 1981, while that same year the State Health Department directed growers to make provisions for field rest rooms, handwashing facilities, and good drinking water for their workers. Then, a favorable court ruling led to the enactment of a workers' compensation law in 1984 and an unemployment compensation act in 1985.[31] In 1987, the Texas legislature passed a law requiring that laborers be informed of any pesticides sprayed on the crops they were working, and another increasing the minimum wage from $1.40 to $3.35 an hour. During the late 1980s, Flores Harrington and UFW members also succeeded in negotiating contracts with some growers and establishing day-care centers in select South Texas colonias for the children of campesinos. Still remaining for the union to achieve was a collective bargaining law.[32]

But farm workers (some 50,000 according to some estimates) during the last years of the twentieth century faced newer problems. Dismally low pay kept most field hands—many of them first-generation immigrants—at the poverty level, although in the mid-1990s the UFW did get the state legislature to enact a provision tying the Texas minimum wage to that of the national government. Weather conditions did agricultural workers no favors: freezes in South Texas during the 1980s seriously disrupted the citrus industry—a situation that for years deprived campesinos of a livelihood during winter months—and drought spells throughout the state in the 1990s further reduced labor opportunities. The passage of the North American Free Trade Agreement (NAFTA) in 1993 gave owners of large agribusinesses the flexibility to leave South Texas farms for new lands in Mexico and Central America. Without proper skills and the essential education, many families hit the migrant trail anew or searched out city jobs rejected by those able to acquire better occupations.

During the late 1990s, the United Farmworkers Union, led by Juanita Valdez-Cox, the South Texas Regional Coordinator in San Juan, Texas, waged a campaign of holding action against growers, and a conservative political climate that she feared might try to undo the hard-won advances of farm workers. On the field, the UFW tried to protect the benefits enjoyed by union members by law and promised them by farm owners. The UFW offered the rank-and-file training programs designed to help them understand and defend their rights. In Austin, the UFW kept a close watch on the legislature to ensure that the representatives enforced the laws they passed; the union simultaneously lobbied for newer statutes beneficial to the membership, many of them Mexico-born immigrants in pursuit of the American dream.[33]

Meanwhile, the UFW became part of a political advocacy group and social service office named LUPE (*La Union del Pueblo Entero,* or The Union of all the People). LUPE activists pursued political strategies in their efforts to improve conditions for the less fortunate, but its major goal was extending social services to minimum-wage workers, farm laborers, and immigrants facing dire circumstances.[34]

Trying to help farm workers overshadowed organizing activities by Mexican Americans in industry, but by no means did attempts to improve factory conditions for urban workers cease. A good illustration of such undertakings involved the work of a labor group in El Paso named *La Mujer Obrera* (The Woman Worker). Established in 1982 following the prolonged strike against the Farah Manufacturing Company (1970s), this nonprofit agency sought to stop abuses commonly committed by management in local factory plants. Specifically, it acted to guard against violations committed by employers against women such as paying them wages lower than those mandated by law, demanding unreasonable production outputs, and keeping earnings from them under false pretenses. In 1991, *La Mujer Obrera* led (with the support of the ILGWU) a strike against several garment factories in El Paso, claiming conditions akin to those of sweat shops. After several months of talks, the organization won for women workers a slight wage hike, some vacation time, and nominal health care coverage. The walkout and a hunger strike conducted by some of the activists during the period brought so much publicity to the situation that El Paso legislators succeeded in pushing through the legislature a state law that made it a felony to withhold earned wages from employees.[35]

Working–Class Interests

Middle-class advocates for the uplifting of the masses did not always limit their attention strictly to Mexican-American concerns. To the contrary, they dealt with matters that affected Tejanos as members of the larger underprivileged class. Naturally, many such issues transcended ethnicity. For example, Communities Organized for Public Services (COPS) in San Antonio looked after the needs of the residents of the inner city (not necessarily Mexicans) who wanted better city services in the form of flood control, street maintenance, and increased attention to low-income housing issues. Parallel organizations that pursued similar objectives existed in the lower Rio Grande Valley and several Texas cities, among them El Paso where EPISO (El Paso Interreligious Sponsoring Organization) sought the political empowerment of Mexican Americans through strength at the polling booth.[36] Elsewhere, Mexican Americans entered into coalitions with other disadvantaged groups to engineer better political redistricting. In Houston in 1978, the Mexican-American leadership endorsed almost unanimously the establishment of the Metropolitan Transit Authority, a public busline planned to replace the city's outmoded mass-transit system.[37]

Epilogue

Mexican Americans in Texas have remained faithful to aspects of their Mexican past, and they have preserved that linkage through the Spanish language, familial relationships, fiestas patrias commemorations, music and other arts, and an assortment of retained cultural customs. Dimensions of *"lo Tejano"* revealed themselves to a mass audience in 1995 following the murder of the Tejano music star Selena in Corpus Christi. Slain by a trusted fan and employee at the age of twenty-three, Selena Quintanilla Pérez had since her teens symbolized by her songs, stage presence, and public demeanor the many attributes that lay at the crux of Mexican-American culture. Media attention to her life in the wake of her death created widespread exposure to those elements connecting Texas-Mexican communities to the motherland: music, religion, folklore, festivities, foods, traditional values, and as an aside, to the word "Tejano." As a consequence of this attention, millions across the United States became aware of the admiration Mexican Americans continued to hold for older traditions. Selena herself, however, represented in many ways modern-today realities. She was Texas born, English-language dominant until her teens, raised on American pop music, and at her untimely death ready to cross over into the mainstream U.S. music industry.[38]

One recent sociological study on Mexican Americans in the United States suggests that Mexican Americans, like other immigrants from all parts of the world, acculturate rapidly after about the third generation. But as Tejanos (and other Mexican Americans) become less ethnic due to Americanizing pressures, the study shows they do not necessarily forego or renounce their Mexicanness. Numerous forces, among them religion, ethnic festivities, the language they hear at home from parents or grand-parents, Mexican restaurants, the thriving Spanish-language media, as well as a conscious desire to remain "Mexican" influence their connection to "lo mexicano." Also influential in the persistence of ethnicity is exposure to unpleasant contacts with Anglo Americans, whether in the workplace, the schoolyard, or at social functions. In these and other environments, Tejanos (including professionals) often hear bigoted comments, bear racist behavior, and face constant reminders from some white Americans that a Mexican is a Mexican no matter the level of acculturation.[39]

In contrast to the classic pattern of immigrant accommodation, there-fore, Tejanos maintain a more enduring relationship with their mother culture even as they function capably in an Anglo-American milieu. Ultimately, Tejanos contribute to the Texas saga uniquely, drawing from two traditions: a Mexican and an American one. The syncretization of cultures, however, has not produced a "typical Tejano." Too many variables beget diversity, among them disparate rates of assimilation, socioeconomic standing, mastery of the English language, increased conversion to Protestantism, and geographical setting.

CHAPTER ELEVEN

The Charge Forward

Ricardo S. Sánchez accompanied the military force that marched into Iraq in March 2003 to overthrow President Saddam Hussein, whom U.S. foreign policy experts suspected of possessing weapons of mass destruction that threatened the Middle East and even American security. Born in 1953 in Rio Grande City, Starr County (one of the poorest counties in South Texas), Sánchez had struggled through his school years in that border town before enrolling in the Army ROTC program offered at Texas A&I (now Texas A&M University-Kingsville) and graduating among the top 10 percent of all U.S. ROTC cadets completing their education and training in 1973. Starting out as a second lieutenant, Sánchez earned rapid promotions, serving capably in several assignments and in various worldwide missions given him. In 1991, orders took him to the Persian Gulf, where as a Lieutenant Colonel he commanded a battalion in Operation Desert Storm, a military offensive that ousted Iraqi armed forces that had brazenly invaded and occupied neighboring Kuwait.

Twelve years later, Sánchez found himself back in the Middle East as part of the multinational force entrusted with several objectives, among them toppling Saddam Hussein and finding the deadly weapons the dictator allegedly possessed. After swiftly defeating (in three weeks) the Iraqi military, there followed the task of consolidating the victory. The military high command in June 2003 appointed Lieutenant General Sánchez as commander of the coalition ground forces. His orders were to stabilize

Iraq in order that the Iraqi people might form a representative government of their own choosing. Sánchez held that post until June 2004, when the U.S. Army reassigned him. After thirty-three years in the military, the Rio Grande City native retired in 2006.[1]

The general's career may stand as a metaphor for advances made by Tejanos over time and the place they will have in American society in upcoming years. During the first decade of the twenty-first century, the "Hispanic or Latino (of any race)"—as the 2000 U.S. census categorized those of Hispanic origin, of which the majority were of Mexican descent—population continued to climb, the results baffling even expert demographers. In the year 2003, indeed, the U.S census reported that for the first time in Texas history, Anglos no longer had the distinction of being the majority group in the state. Now they only constituted 49.5% of the total population of 21.5 million, outnumbered by a combination of racial and ethnic peoples, almost one-third of whom were Mexican Americans and Mexican immigrants.[2] By the latter years of the decade, the Hispanic-origin population in the Lone Star State approximated 10 million, almost doubling the numbers reported by the U.S. Census for 2000.[3] Mexican Americans lived throughout the state, no longer concentrated along the border counties; indeed some of the large metropolitan areas contained as many Mexican-descent people as did the old "homeland" counties. Some observers saw places like Harris County and the Dallas Metropolitan Area as indicators of the state's demographic future: a multi-ethnic (or international) land where people of Hispanic origin composed the most visible group.[4]

Political Strides

Older political approaches and ideological considerations from the post-Chicano era years lingered past 2000, carried on now by an unprecedented number of elected officials, appointed bureaucrats, and civil administrators serving mainly at the city and county levels.[5]

Indicative of the politics of this era of moderation was Tony Sánchez of Laredo, a millionaire banker selected by Democratic voters to be their candidate for governor in 2002. (Republican Rick Perry won the race that year.) Well educated and having close ties to the Democratic establishment, Sánchez ran a campaign intended to attract the wider Democratic constituency, so that his speeches dealt with issues of interest to all Texans and not solely Tejanos (though he did campaign in Spanish in certain locales, such as ones in South Texas).[6]

Perhaps an even better example of the age's political moderation within Mexican-American circles would be that of Alberto R. Gonzales. Raised amidst poverty in Houston, Gonzales's dogged determination to make something of himself eventually led to his appointment as general counselor (Law Degree from Harvard Law School) to Texas governor George W. Bush (1995–2001). Upon winning the presidency in 2000, Bush took Gonzales with him as White House counsel and by 2005, Gonzales had become the U. S. attorney general. Controversies surrounding his administration of the Justice Department, however, led Gonzales to resign his office in 2007.[7]

For the most part, Mexican-American politicians still represented ethnic districts; consequently they addressed issues having a direct impact on their constituents. In 2003, Hispanics in the state legislature joined fellow Democratic legislators in a plan to thwart Republican efforts to redistrict Texas and thereby gain an electoral advantage. The Democrats fled over the Texas border to southern Oklahoma while the legislature was in session, thereby hoping to prevent a quorum in the legislature and squelch the redistricting bill. When the Republicans ultimately succeeded in their designs, MALDEF entered the fray. Representing the G.I. Forum and LULAC, it complained that the new congressional realignments impeded fair representation for Mexican-American citizens. In June of 2006, however, the U. S. Supreme court ruled the redistricting plan to be constitutional, and its directive to the state that the lines for one of the districts be re-evaluated—as its configuration disfranchised Mexican Americans—was completed the next month.[8]

Also engaged in representing the concerns of Mexican Americans were the G.I. Forum and LULAC, though the G.I. Forum—after its many years of commitment to Tejano causes—faced difficulty recruiting members among the younger generation. LULAC, however, celebrated its seventy-fifth anniversary in 2004 and as of the first decade of the twenty-first century still held on to the prominence it had recaptured after the 1970s. Led by Texan Rosa Rosales (2006–), LULAC still acted as a watchdog for Mexican American issues, keeping an eye on matters such as racial profiling, immigration, affirmative action, education, gerrymandering, and census matters.[9]

Public Education: Setbacks and Advances

By the year 2010, authorities anticipated that Hispanics (Mexican Americans and other Latinos) would account for nearly 50 percent of all students enrolled in the state's public schools (in school districts of larger cities such as Dallas and Houston, minority groups—mostly Hispanic—they already compose 90 percent of all students). The increase was due to a number of factors, among them the aforementioned rise in the Tejano population in the state, the Supreme Court case of *Plyler* v. *Doe*, and of course, an individual desire to pursue a good education. But the high school registration figures are misleading, for the dropout rate for Hispanics approached 50 percent as of mid-decade.[10]

How to deal with a school-age population predicted to become the majority population by the year 2025—and who would then determine the state's economic well-being—distressed many, including policy makers, some of whom subscribed to the belief that the answer to preparing an intelligent Hispanic citizenry lay in totally immersing Mexican-American students in an English-speaking environment. To that the end, opponents of bilingual education (who by the 1990s were enjoying widespread public support for their plans, even among Hispanics) worked to eliminate what Mexican-American educators since the 1960s had considered a viable tool for achieving school success among the Spanish speaking. The end to bilingual instruction came with the "No Child Left Behind Act," enacted by the U.S. Congress in 2001, which dictated that instruction in the public schools be done only in English. In the words of educational historian Guadalupe San Miguel Jr. "The forces of conservatism, assimilation, and ignorance . . . [had] triumphed over pluralism and over enlightened pedagogy."[11]

Of importance to other concerned Texans was finding an adequate means by which the state's school system could be funded fairly. The Robin Hood plan (prompted by the decision of *Edgewood Independent School District* v. *Kirby,* 1989), which during the 1990s had temporarily solved the problem of unequitable financing, was overturned in 2005 when the Texas Supreme Court found the method discriminatory, as it forced wealthy districts to share their taxes with poor ones. It was not until 2006 that the state legislature found a plan agreeable to the courts (it increased taxes on businesses while cutting property taxes), but even that solution came under criticism as it failed to provide adequately for Texas schooling. Minority groups also criticized it, pointing to Anglo reluctance to contribute their taxes (property owners, and not school boards, were to vote on whether to increase their taxes to finance local schools) for the education of non-Anglos.[12]

By no means can it be said that overcrowded public schools, the demise of bilingual education, and inadequate state funding for education produced a state of widespread undereducation among Mexican Americans. Certainly, many Tejanos finished their high school commitments and the number of college educated Tejanos increased measurably. By the early years of the twenty first century, Mexican Americans throughout the state were visible in every conceivable professional capacity.[13]

What accounts for such laudable advances? One obvious explanation is the sheer commitment and sacrifice of parents who wish to see their children succeed in life. Another is the fruition of earlier efforts by Mexican-American organizations and political leaders in the last half of the twentieth century to eliminate obstacles to progress and pave an easier path to higher education. The Ten Percent Plan, for instance, had come under strong criticism since its implementation; a movement to remove it escalated when in 2003 the U.S. Supreme Court in *Grutter* v. *Bollinger* overturned the *Hopwood* decision (1996), permitting universities to use race as a criterion for admission. With race again injected into admissions consideration, opponents of the Ten Percent Plan raised this question: why preserve a policy that allowed students (many of them Hispanics and African Americans) from inferior schools to bump those who did not graduate in the top ten percent because the latter came from school districts with more rigorous curricula? When a bloc of representatives in 2007 sought to eliminate the plan, Mexican-American (assisted by MALDEF) and African-American legislators allied themselves with lawmakers from rural districts (whose students benefited from the Plan) to defeat the initiative.[14]

Also playing a very public role in opening the gateway to higher education was TACHE (Texas Association of Chicanos in Higher Education). Founded in 1975 by a cadre of Mexican-American college and university administrators and professors, it had as its mission "the commitment to improve the educational and employment opportunities for Hispanics in Higher education." To that end, TACHE held annual meetings attended by hundreds of educators, and throughout the year its president and staff worked diligently with colleges and university administrations, as well as politicians, to address problems and seek resolutions to matters that might adversely affect Hispanic performance in higher education. Periodically, TACHE published reports and position statements on matters relevant to Mexican Americans in higher education. It disseminated monthly information to its membership through its newsletter *El Noticiario*.[15]

The Immigration Question

Mexican Americans had historically been sympathetic toward Mexico-born residents who arrived in Texas desperately poor, took the most menial jobs, and sacrificed to provide for their loved ones. By the 1990s and early twenty-first century, however, Mexican-American communities divided on the question of immigration. In part, disagreement was caused by the less altruistic politics held by the Mexican American/Hispanic Generation, by a burst of illegal immigration that reached an almost unprecedented magnitude by the 1980s and 1990s, and by a nativist backlash from white America. Mexican Americans alarmed at the influx from Mexico took the position that the presence of undocumented Mexicans (much as did the G.I. Forum and LULAC during the 1950s) arrested overall development of Mexican-American communities. They further argued (much like nativists) that immigrants depressed earnings for U.S.-born workers, overcrowded the schools, and burdened the welfare system. The immigrants threatened the nation's homogeneity and imperiled national security. Those sympathizing with the immigrants countered that undocumented workers took the most undesirable jobs, helped bolster the economy as consumers and tax payers, possessed an enviable work ethic, and subscribed to the ideal of a dual heritage.[16]

Then in 2006 and thereafter, the immigrants made their own case for residence in the United States. They held huge demonstrations throughout the country to protest HB4437, an immigration reform bill then being debated in the U.S. Congress. The most stringent provisions of the bill (heavily supported by Republicans) sought to deprive immigrant children of schooling, establish high hurdles to naturalization, charge the immigrants with criminal acts for being in the country illegally, and even undertake massive deportation operations.[17]

In Texas as of 2006, some 2,339,715 of the 8,487,104 residents of Mexican heritage were foreign born.[18] Organized by (Tejano) spokespersons for the immigrants, by Spanish-language disk jockeys, and by foreign-born activists within the Mexican American community itself, a sizeable percentage of the immigrants took to the streets to demonstrate their numbers, their potential political power, and their integral importance to the economy. The marches of April 2006 involved thousands of people across the state; reports from Dallas estimated crowds of 500,000 or more coming out to demand fairness for those living almost in an underworld.[19]

When they ended, the rallies produced conflicting assessments. Pro-immigrant advocates complimented the immigrants for their comportment in showing restraint in exercising their right to demonstrate and when voicing the cause of the unrepresented. Many pointed to the patriotic signs and symbols the marchers carried as proof of their fidelity to the United States. Just as stridently, opponents of the demonstrators noted how the marchers had disrespected public property, insolently demanded equal rights, waved Mexican flags, and otherwise displayed a nationalist allegiance to Mexico that confirmed the fears of balkanization.[20]

By the summer of 2006, HB 4337 had died a slow death as support for it gradually eroded. Republicans (and Democrats) feared an Hispanic backlash at the polls should they push anti-immigrant campaigns too far. In Texas, such alarms surfaced when Republican businesspersons sought to persuade their allies in the legislature to enact anti-immigrant measures in 2007. In the end, these same business interests retreated after realizing (and encountering opposition from Hispanic representatives) that an end to illegal immigration would leave few to work construction sites, pick cantaloupes and other farm products, wash the dishes at local restaurants, or clean hotel rooms for tourists.[21] Though the immigration questioned quieted for a time, no one believed it had evaporated. Opponents of illegal immigration prepared for new battles while the immigrants and their defenders sought to keep the momentum of the 2006 marches alive. Tejano leaders and spokespersons even envisioned a resurgence of the Chicano Movement in a different guise.

After 300 Years

Beginning in the 1710s, Spanish-Mexicans trekked into Texas establishing the first outposts that served as the foundation for future Tejano communities. Over the course of three centuries, Tejanos (together with immigrants from Mexico) have—by remaining faithful to dimensions of their Mexican heritage and culture—just about transformed Texas into a bicultural land. Many are the other feats to which Tejanos can lay claim. The work of activist leaders and civic organizations long ago erased Jim Crow traditions, at least in their severest forms. The educational system, once discouraging to even the most inquisitive Mexican-American student, today opens its doors to all those eligible to receive schooling. Hispanic politicians and government bureaucrats currently serve in important and influential capacities. Middle-class status continues to grace educators, medical personnel, attorneys, accountants, corporate managers, small businesspersons, and many more. A safety net provides for the Tejano elderly and the poorest members of the community to receive basic welfare and medical assistance.

The above is, of course, the most optimistic and positive assessment of Tejano progress. There exists, at the other extreme, a negative version. For Mexican Americans, Jim Crow lives on subtly in the corporate world, in the workplace, and in the social arena. Intolerance manifests itself in the sometimes venomous condemnation of affirmative action programs, porous borders, Spanish language usage, and of bilingual education approaches and English as a Second Language (ESL) instruction that opponents perceive as exclusively for the benefit of Spanish-speaking students. While middle-class life has become a reality for many Texans, the fact of the matter remains that poverty continues to plague many established Mexican-American communities as well as first-generation immigrants. Certainly, Mexican Americans have greater political representation than ever, but Tejano politicos (as is the case with all politicians) at times find themselves having to favor the interests of campaign donors and lobby-ists over those of their constituents. The educational standing of Tejanos can in no way be proclaimed a success: too many students drop out, a higher number of them do not perform up to expectations in the Texas Assessment of Knowledge and Skills (TAKS), and the average number of school years attended by Mexican Americans remains the lowest among all racial/ethnic groups in the state.

What implications does this mixed record have for the future? For some it augurs continued struggles against entrenched racial feelings, an economic system that thrives on the existence of an underclass, unforeseen issues that will get in the way of ethnic progress, and the cultural priorities that sometimes clash with those of the mainstream society. It bodes well for those who believe the American dream has no bounds; that Tejanos no longer have to hurdle as many barriers as stood in the way of earlier generations. Optimists can take to heart the achievements of twentieth-century Tejanos including Jovita González, Emma Tenayuca, Hector P. Garcia, Américo Paredes, Henry B. González, Raúl A. Gonzalez, Henry Cisneros, Lydia Mendoza, and, recently, General Ricardo Sánchez and the actor Eva Longoria.

Glossary

adobes Homes constructed of bricks made from mud mixed with straw.

agringado Literally, to become gringo; actually to be too acculturated.

altarcitos Home altars.

arrieros Freighters, cart drivers.

barrios Texas-Mexican neighborhoods or enclaves.

Béxar The shortened name for San Antonio (de Béxar), Texas, during the colonial era.

Bexareño A resident of Béxar.

botas Name of a political club in South Texas during the late nineteenth and early twentieth centuries. Literal meaning is boots.

braceros Men from Mexico contracted to work in the United States during World War II and through 1964. Literal meaning: those who work with their arms.

cabrito A delectable dish made from goat meat (usually that of a kid).

campesino A farm worker.

cantina A saloon or barroom.

caudillo In Latin America, a political chieftain, who rules through force.

causa (la) The cause. Reference to the cause of Mexican Americans during the Chicano Movement of the 1960s and 1970s.

Chicanismo The philosophical/political position advanced by Chicanos.

Chicano An in-group label used among Mexican Americans. Employed politically during the 1960s and 1970s.

Cinco de Mayo May 5. Reference to a Battle in Puebla, Mexico, on May 5, 1862, in which the native Mexican army repelled a superior French force.

colonia Until about the 1950s, a reference to a Mexican neighborhood (or neighborhoods) in a city. Presently applied to unincorporated, poverty stricken areas of towns in the Texas border region.

compadre The relationship assumed by an individual with the parents of a person whom she/he sponsors at baptism or confirmation.

congreso congress.

conjunto A musical ensemble which features the accordion as its lead instrument.

conquistadores Spaniards who reconquered Spain from the Moors or who conquered Latin America for Spain in the sixteenth century.

corridos Folk ballads.

cortito (el) The short-handled hoe used for working in onion, lettuce, and carrot fields.

cuida la honra Protect your honor, your chastity.

curanderismo The art of folk healing.

curandero One who practices curanderismo; a folk healer.

Diez y Seis de Septiembre   Sixteenth of September. Reference to the date in 1810 when Father Miguel Hidalgo y Costilla issued the Grito de Dolores calling for Mexico's independence from Spain.

Escuadrón Volante   "Flying Squadron" composed of LULACers who visited Texas communities during the 1930s in the effort to organize more councils and spread the LULAC message.

fandango   A festive occasion during which the revelers engaged in dancing or social carousing. Also refers to a specific dance.

fiestas patrias   The festive commemoration of the Mexican national holidays of *Cinco de Mayo* and *Diez y Seis de Septiembre.*

gente decente   Decent people; people of high culture.

gente jaitona   Pretentious folks.

gringo   Spanish slang for Anglo American.

Grito de Dolores   The cry for independence issued by Father Miguel Hidalgo y Costilla on September 16, 1810, in Dolores, Guanajuato.

guaraches   Name of a political club in South Texas during the late nineteenth and early twentieth centuries. Literal meaning is sandals.

hacienda   A rural estate in Mexico worked by peons.

honra   Honor, chastity.

Iglesia   The Catholic Church.

jacales   Makeshift homes built by Tejanos. Usually constructed of mesquite posts, with walls daubed with mud. Thatched coverings served as roofs.

leñadores   Woodmen; the Woodmen of the World (WOW).

ley de fuga   A form of execution applied on the frontier. Assumes that prisoners were killed while trying to escape.

los del otra lado   The people from the other side of the Rio Grande; the people from Mexico.

machismo A male personality trait emphasizing prowess and virility.

mesteños Wild herds of livestock in the colonial Texas frontier.

mestizaje A process of racial congress that took place from the sixteenth through the eighteenth centuries among Spaniards, the indigenous tribes of Latin America, and Africans.

mestizo A person who descends from the union of a Spaniard and a Native American.

México de afuera Reference by people of Mexico to their compatriots living in the United States. Literal meaning is Mexico of the outside.

mojados "Wetbacks." Persons from Mexico who reside in the United States illegally.

movimiento (el) The Chicano Movement of the 1960s to 1970s.

mutualistas Mutual aid societies; benefit associations.

noche triste (la) The night on June 30, 1520, when the Aztecs inflicted devasting casualties on Spanish occupiers of Tenochtitlán as the Iberians sought to escape the Aztec capital.

nopalitos A delectable dish made from cactus leaves.

obreros Laborers.

"pal wes" *Para el west,* or going to West Texas to pick farm crops.

partera A midwife.

pastores Sheep herders.

patria The country, or the motherland (Mexico).

patrón A political boss or a ranch/farm owner.

peones Members of the peasantry; commoners.

plan A political platform (or plan) proposed by an opposition group in a movement to overthrow an existing government. If the rebellion succeeds, the new platform will be implemented.

pobladores Settlers, those who populate.

pocho A term used by people from Mexico to label Mexican Americans who have lost elements of their Mexican culture.

presidio A Spanish military garrison.

rancho A ranch.

raza (la) The people. Reference to Mexican Americans as a community.

reconquista The reconquest of Spain from the Moors, circa eighth to fifteenth centuries.

ricos The rich, or the wealthier class.

rinches Spanish for Texas Rangers.

Tejana A woman of Spanish-Mexican descent who lives in Texas. Feminine version of Tejano.

Tejanito A school-age Mexican American who lives in Texas.

Tejano A male of Spanish-Mexican descent who lives in Texas.

traque The rail, a reference to the railroad tracks.

troquero Trucker who transported migrant workers to fields throughout Texas, circa 1920s to 1950s.

vaquero One who works with cattle. A cowhand.

vendidos Sellouts; those not allied with the cause of Chicanismo.

wes (el) West Texas.

Notes

PREFACE

[1]Carlos Muñoz, Jr., *Youth, Identity, Power: The Chicano Movement* (New York: Verso, 1989), pp. 64, 70, 71, 78, 134–35, 145.

[2]David J. Weber, "John Francis Bannon and the Historiography of the Spanish Borderlands: Retrospect and Prospect," in David J. Weber, ed., *Myth and the History of the Hispanic Southwest* (Albuquerque: University of New Mexico Press, 1988), pp. 69–71.

[3]Gilbert G. Gonzalez and Raul A. Fernandez, *A Century of Chicano History: Empire, Nations, and Migration* (New York: Routledge 2003), pp. 11–14, 32–45.

[4]Gerald E. Poyo and Gilberto M. Hinojosa, eds., *Tejano Origins in Eighteenth-Century San Antonio* (Austin: University of Texas Press, 1991), pp. xiv–xix; Arnoldo De León, "Texas-Mexicans: Twentieth Century Interpretations," in Walter L. Buenger and Robert A. Calvert, eds., *Texas Through Time: Evolving Interpretations* (College Station: Texas A&M University Press, 1991), pp. 20–49.

[5]Arnoldo De León, "Whither Tejano History: Origins, Development, and Status," *Southwestern Historical Quarterly* 106 (January 2003): 349–64.

CHAPTER ONE

[1]Quoted in Jesús F. de la Teja, *San Antonio de Béxar: A Community on New Spain's Northern Frontier* (Albuquerque: University of New Mexico Press, 1995), p. 45.

[2]Gilbert R. Cruz, *Let There be Towns: Spanish Municipal Origins in the American Southwest, 1610–1810* (College Station: Texas A&M University Press, 1988), pp. 63–65, 68, 70.

[3]*Ibid.*, pp. 5–6.

[4]Robert Ryal Miller, *Mexico: A History* (Norman: University of Oklahoma Press, 1985), Chapter 3.

[5]John Francis Bannon, et al., *Latin America* 4th ed. (Encino, Calif.: Glencoe Press, 1977), p. 89.

[6]*Ibid.*, pp. 90–91.

[7]Carlos Eduardo Castañeda, *The Mission Era: The Winning of Texas, 1693–1751*, vol. 2 of *Our Catholic Heritage in Texas, 1519–1936* (7 vols; Austin: Von

Boeckmann-Jones Co., 1936–1958; reprinted by New York: Arno Press, 1976), pp. 46 (n22), 47, 59–60; Donald Chipman, *Spanish Texas, 1519–1821* (Austin: University of Texas Press, 1992), p. 112.

[8]Cruz, *Let There Be Towns*, p. 90; Jack Jackson, *Los Mesteños: Spanish Ranching in Texas* (College Station: Texas A&M University Press, 1986), pp. 13–14.

[9]Cruz, *Let There Be Towns*, pp. 82, 86–87; Chipman, *Spanish Texas*, pp. 166–69.

[10]Oakah L. Jones, Jr., *Los Paisanos: Spanish Settlers on the Northern Frontier of New Spain* (Norman: University of Oklahoma Press, 1979), p. 47.

[11]Cruz, *Let There Be Towns*, pp. 94–95, 128–29; Jones, *Los Paisanos*, p. 70.

[12]Jesús F. de la Teja, "Forgotten Founders: The Military Settlers of Eighteenth-Century San Antonio de Béxar," in Poyo and Hinojosa, eds., *Tejano Origins in Eighteenth-Century San Antonio*, pp. 29–30, 38; and Gerald E. Poyo, "Immigrants and Integration in Late Eighteenth-Century Béxar," in *ibid.*, p. 85.

[13]Juan Gómez Quiñones, *Making of the Mexican Working Class North of the Rio Bravo* (Los Angeles: Aztlán Publications, 1977), pp. 5–6; Poyo, "Immigrants and Integration in Late Eighteenth-Century Béxar," p. 86; Cruz, *Let There Be Towns*, p. 127.

[14]Gerald E. Poyo and Gilberto M. Hinojosa, "Spanish Texas and Borderlands Historiography in Transition: Implications for United States History," *Journal of American History* 75 (September 1988): 408, 409, 410; John R. Chávez, *The Lost Land: The Chicano Image of the Southwest* (Albuquerque: University of New Mexico Press, 1984), p. 31.

[15]Gómez-Quiñones, *Making of the Mexican Working Class*, p. 7.

[16]Herbert E. Bolton, "The Mission As A Frontier Institution in the Spanish American Colonies," in David J. Weber,

ed., *New Spain's Far Northern Frontier: Essays on Spain in the American West, 1540–1821* (Albuquerque: University of New Mexico Press, 1979), pp. 49–65; Gilberto M. Hinojosa, "The Enduring Hispanic Faith Communities: Spanish and Texas Church Historiography," *The Journal of Texas Catholic History and Culture* 1 (March 1990): 22, 27–28; and Robert E. Wright, "The Hispanic Church in Texas under Spain and Mexico," *U.S. Catholic Historian* 20 (Fall 2002): 19–22.

[17]Max L. Moorhead, *The Presidio: Bastion of the Spanish Borderlands* (Norman: University of Oklahoma Press, 1975), pp. 3–4; Gilberto M. Hinojosa, "The Religious-Indian Communities: The Goals of the Friars," in Poyo and Hinojosa, eds., *Tejano Origins in Eighteenth-Century San Antonio*, p. 79.

[18]de la Teja, "Forgotten Founders," pp. 30, 33; de la Teja, *San Antonio de Béxar*, pp. 159, 105, 112–14.

[19]de la Teja, *San Antonio de Béxar*, pp. 105, 112–14.

[20]Jackson, *Los Mesteños*, pp. 11, 12–13, 30; Sandra L. Myers, *The Ranch in Spanish Texas, 1691–1800* (El Paso: Texas Western Press, 1969), pp. 12–13.

[21]Jackson, *Los Mesteños*, p. 52.

[22]de la Teja, *San Antonio de Béxar*, p. 110; Myers, *Ranching in Spanish Texas*, pp. 15, 16.

[23]Poyo and Hinojosa, "Spanish Texas and Borderlands Historiography in Transition," p. 406.

[24]*Ibid.*, p. 407; Jackson, *Los Mesteños*, pp. 130, 131; de la Teja, *San Antonio de Béxar*, p. 105; and Jesús F. de la Teja, "The Saltillo Fair and Its San Antonio Connections," in Arnoldo De León. ed., *Tejano Epic: Essays in Honor of Félix D. Almaráz, Jr.* (Austin: Texas State Historical Association, 2005), pp. 15–27.

[25]Poyo and Hinojosa, "Spanish Texas and Borderlands Historiography," p. 408; and C. Allan Jones, *Texas Roots: Agriculture*

and Rural Life Before the Civil War (College Station: Texas A&M University Press, 2005), p. 43.

[26]Jones, *Los Paisanos*, pp. 54; Poyo and Hinojosa, eds., *Tejano Origins in Eighteenth Century San Antonio*, p. 138; Chipman, *Spanish Texas*, p. 205; and Jones, *Texas Roots*, pp. 37–38.

[27]Poyo, "Immigrants and Integration in Eighteenth-Century Béxar," pp. 90–96; Cruz, *Let There Be Towns*, p. 128.

[28]James Michael McReynolds, "Family Life in a Borderlands Community: Nacogdoches, Texas, 1779–1861" (Ph. D. Dissertation, Texas Tech University, 1978), Chapter 2.

[29]Jones, *Los Paisanos*, pp. 60–61.

[30]Jesús F. de la Teja, "Indians, Soldiers, and Canary Islanders: The Making of a Texas Frontier Community," *Locus* 3 (Fall 1990): 82, 85, 89. Also see, Poyo and Hinojosa, eds., *Tejano Origins in Eighteenth Century San Antonio*, pp. xx–xxi, 137.

[31]Cruz, *Let There Be Towns*, p. 170.

[32]de la Teja, *San Antonio de Béxar*, p. 149.

[33]Jackson, *Los Mesteños*, p. 130.

[34]Poyo and Hinojosa, eds., *Tejano Origins in Eighteenth Century San Antonio*, p. 140.

[35]Odie B. Faulk, *A Successful Failure* (Austin: Steck-Vaughn, 1965), pp. 176–78; Odie B. Faulk, *The Last Years of Spanish Texas* (London: The Hague Paris Press, 1964), pp. 50, 109–12.

[36]de la Teja, "Indians, Soldiers, and Canary Islanders," pp. 88, 95.

[37]*Ibid.*, p. 95; Gómez-Quiñones, *Making of Mexican Working Class*, p. 12.

[38]Jones, *Los Paisanos*, p. 60; Poyo, "Immigrants and Integration in Eighteenth-Century Béxar," pp. 85–86; Cruz, *Let There Be Towns*, p. 129.

[39]de la Teja, *San Antonio de Béxar*, pp. 25–26; Gerald E. Poyo, "The Canary Islands Immigrants of San Antonio: From Ethnic Exclusivity to Community in Eighteenth-Century Béxar," in Poyo

and Hinojosa, eds., *Tejano Origins in Eighteenth Century San Antonio*, p. 47; de la Teja, "Forgotten Founders," in *ibid.*, pp. 32–33; Poyo, "Immigrants and Integration in Late Eighteenth Century Béxar," in *ibid.*, pp. 96–97; Gilberto M. Hinojosa and Anne E. Fox, "Indians and Their Culture in San Fernando de Béxar," in *ibid.*, pp. 106–07; and Alicia V. Tjarks, "Comparative Demographic Analysis of Texas, 1777–1793," *Southwestern Historical Quarterly* 78 (January 1974): 322–38.

[40]Tjarks, "Comparative Demographic Analysis," p. 294; de la Teja, *San Antonio de Béxar*, pp. 24–26, 28–29; Poyo, "Immigrants and Integration in Late Eighteenth-Century Béxar," pp. 86–87.

[41]David J. Weber, *The Mexican Frontier, 1821–1848: The American Southwest Under Mexico* (Albuquerque: University of New Mexico Press, 1982), pp. 215–216; Jean A. Stuntz, *Hers, His, and Theirs: Community Property Law in Spain and Early Texas* (Lubbock: Texas Tech University Press, 2005), Chapter 6; Teresa Palomo Acosta and Ruthe Winegarten, *Las Tejanas: 300 Years of History* (Austin: University of Texas Press, 2003), pp. 15–18; and Nora Ríos McMillan, "'Siendo Mi Derecho . . .': The Hispanic Woman's Legal Identity in the Spanish Southwest," *South Texas Studies* 10 (1999): 102–42.

[42]Colin M. MacLachlan and Jaime E. Rodríguez-O, *The Forging of the Cosmic Race: A Reinterpretation of Colonial Mexico* (Berkeley: University of California Press, 1980), pp. 296–297.

[43]Jackson, *Los Mesteños*, pp. 294–95.

[44]Poyo and Hinojosa, "Spanish Texas and Borderlands Historiography," p. 414; de la Teja, *San Antonio de Béxar*, p. 111.

[45]Poyo and Hinojosa, "Spanish Texas and Borderlands Historiography," pp. 415, 412.

[46]Poyo, "The Canary Islands Immigrants of San Antonio," pp. 57–58.

CHAPTER TWO
[1]Timothy M. Matovina, *The Alamo Remembered: Tejano Accounts and Perspectives* (Austin: University of Texas Press, 1995), documents 23, 24, and 26; Stephen L. Hardin, *Texian Iliad: A Military History of the Texas Revolution, 1835–1836* (Austin: University of Texas Press, 1994), Chapter 7.
[2]Seymour V. Connor, *Texas: A History* (Wheeling, Ill.: Harlan Davidson, Inc., 1971), p. 57; Gilberto M. Hinojosa, *A Borderlands Town in Transition: Laredo, Texas 1755–1870* (College Station: Texas A&M University Press, 1983), p. 32.
[3]Weber, *The Mexican Frontier*, p. 280.
[4]*Ibid.*, p. 284; Miguel León-Portilla, "The Norteño Variety of Mexican Culture: An Ethnohistorical Approach," in Edward H. Spicer and Raymond H. Thompson, eds., *Plural Society in the Southwest* (Albuquerque: University of New Mexico Press, 1972), pp. 109–14.
[5]Poyo and Hinojosa, eds., *Tejano Origins in Eighteenth-Century San Antonio*, pp. 140, 141.
[6]Poyo and Hinojosa, "Spanish Texas and Borderlands Historiography in Transition," pp. 411–12, 413; Jesús F. de la Teja, "Rebellion on the Frontier," in Gerald E. Poyo, ed., *Tejano Journey, 1770–1850* (Austin: University of Texas Press, 1996).
[7]Weber, *The Mexican Frontier*, pp. 9–10; Jackson, *Los Mesteños*, p. 526; Félix D. Almaráz, *Tragic Cavalier: Manuel Salcedo of Texas* (Austin: University of Texas Press, 1970), p. 119.
[8]Jackson, *Los Mesteños*, p. 527.
[9]Weber, *The Mexican Frontier*, p. 9.
[10]Jackson, *Los Mesteños*, pp. 528, 530–33; and David E. Narrett, "José Bernardo Gutiérrez de Lara: *Caudillo* in the Mexican Republic in Texas," *Southwestern Historical Quarterly* 106 (October 2002): 195–228.
[11]Almaráz, *Tragic Cavalier*, pp. 118–24;

Weber, *The Mexican Frontier*, p. 10.
[12]Jackson, *Los Mesteños*, pp. 537, 555.
[13]*Ibid.*, pp. 526, 546–47.
[14]Weber, *The Mexican Frontier*, p. 10.
[15]Carey McWilliams, *North From Mexico: The Spanish Speaking People of the United States* (New York: Greenwood Press, 1968), pp. 146, 153, 154, 155, 156.
[16]Donald E. Worcester, "The Significance of the Spanish Borderlands in the United States," in Weber, ed., *New Spain's Far Northern Frontier*, pp. 4–10; Pauline Kibbe, *Latin Americans in Texas* (Albuquerque: University of New Mexico Press, 1946), p. 34; McWilliams, *North From Mexico*, pp. 153–54; Paul H. Carlson, *Texas Woollybacks: The Texas Sheep and Goat Industry* (College Station: Texas A&M University Press, 1982), p. 17; Chipman, *Spanish Texas*, Chapter 12.
[17]Weber, *The Mexican Frontier*, p. 160.
[18]Juan N. Almonte, "Statistical Report on Texas," translated by C. E. Castañeda, *Southwestern Historical Quarterly* 28 (January 1925): 186, 206. Also see *The Handbook of Victoria County* (Austin: The Texas State Historical Association, 1990), p. 113; and Hinojosa, *A Borderlands Town in Transition*, p. 45.
[19]Jesús F. de la Teja and John Wheat, "Béxar: Profile of a Tejano Community, 1820–1832," *Southwestern Historical Quarterly* 89 (July 1985): 28.
[20]*Ibid.*, pp. 19–20; Timothy M. Matovina, *Tejano Religion and Ethnicity: San Antonio, 1821–1860* (Austin: University of Texas Press, 1995), pp. 17–19; Félix D. Almaráz, Jr., "The Warp and the Weft: An Overview of the Social Fabric of Mexican Texas," *East Texas Historical Journal* 27, No. 2 (1989): 18; and, Acosta and Winegarten, *Las Tejanas*, p. 33.
[21]Wright, "The Hispanic Church in Texas Under Spain and Mexico," pp. 23–29.
[22]Jackson, *Los Mesteños*, pp. 596–597; de la Teja and Wheat, "Béxar," pp. 26, 28.
[23]de la Teja and Wheat, "Béxar," pp. 26, 28.

[24]Jackson, *Los Mesteños*, p. 592; Paul S. Taylor, *An American Mexican Frontier: Nueces County, Texas* (Chapel Hill: University of North Carolina Press, 1934), pp. 10–13; Hinojosa, *A Borderlands Town in Transition*, p. 42.
[25]de la Teja and Wheat, "Béxar," p. 26; Weber, *The Mexican Frontier*, pp. 140–41.
[26]Andreas V. Reichstein, *Rise of the Lone Star: The Making of Texas* (College Station: Texas A&M University Press, 1989), pp. 87–88; Weber, *The Mexican Frontier*, p. 208.
[27]Reichstein, *Rise of the Lone Star*, pp. 87–88; de la Teja and Wheat, "Béxar," pp. 10, 23; Matovina, *Tejano Religion and Ethnicity*, pp. 20–22.
[28]Weber, *The Mexican Frontier*, pp. 215–16; Richard Griswold del Castillo, *La Familia: Chicano Families in the Urban Southwest, 1840 to the Present* (Notre Dame: University of Notre Dame Press, 1984), pp. 30, 28–29.
[29]Fane Downs, "'Tryels and Trubbles': Women in Early Nineteenth Century Texas," *Southwestern Historical Quarterly* 90 (July 1986): 45, 55–56; Acosta and Winegarten, *Las Tejanas*, pp. 20–24, 26, 31-33; and Ana Carolina Castillo Crimm, *De León: A Tejano Family History* (Austin: University of Texas Press, 2003), pp. 83, 103–06, 125–28.
[30]Nora Ríos McMillan, "A Woman of Worth: Ana María del Carmen Calvillo," in De León, ed., *Tejano Epic*, pp. 30, 33, 35, 41–42.
[31]Weber, *The Mexican Frontier*, pp. 158–61, 164.
[32]de la Teja and Wheat, "Béxar," pp. 30–31; Jesús F. de la Teja, *A Revolution Remembered: The Memoirs and Selected Correspondence of Juan N. Seguín* (Austin: Texas State Historical Association, 2004), pp. 7, 10, 15; Weber, *Myth and the History of the Hispanic Southwest* pp. 145–46; and Andrés Reséndez, *Changing National Identities at the Frontier: Texas and New Mexico, 1800–1850* (Cambridge: Cambridge University Press, 2005), pp. 4–6, 99–100, 160.
[33]Reichstein, *Rise of Lone Star*, p. 55; Weber, *Myth and the History of the Hispanic Southwest*, pp. 147–48; and Almonte, "Statistical Report on Texas," p. 207.
[34]Randolph B. Campbell, *An Empire For Slavery: The Peculiar Institution in Texas, 1821–1865* (Baton Rouge: Louisiana State University Press, 1989), pp. 25–27.
[35]Weber, *The Mexican Frontier*, p. 177.
[36]Weber, *Myth and the History of the Hispanic Southwest*, p. 144; Jackson, *Los Mesteños*, p. 599; Alwyn Barr, *Texans in Revolt: The Battle for San Antonio, 1835* (Austin: University of Texas Press, 1990), p. 12; and Crimm, *De León*, pp. 144–51.
[37]Rodolfo Acuña, *Occupied America: A History of Chicanos*, 5th ed. (New York: Pearson Longman, 2004), p. 48; Rodolfo F. Acuña, "Inside the Alamo: A Dispatch From Bexar County," *Texas Observer*, January 26, 1990, p. 23; Tom Glaser, "Victory or Death," in Susan P. Schoelwer, *Alamo Images: Changing Perceptions of a Texas Experience* (Dallas: DeGolyer Library and SMU Press, 1985), p. 76; and William C. Davies, *Lone Star Rising: The Revolutionary Birth of the Republic of Texas* (New York: Free Press, 2004), pp. 200-01, 203.
[38]Richard Santos, *Santa Anna's Campaign Against Texas* (Waco: Texian Press, 1970), pp. 17, 34, 63; Glaser, "Victory or Death," pp. 85–86.
[39]Santos, *Santa Anna's Campaign Against Texas*, pp. 74–76; Glaser, "Victory or Death," pp. 83, 85, 92, 94; Hardin, *Texian Iliad, 1835–1836* (Austin: The University of Texas Press, 1994), pp. 138–49; Acosta and Winegarten, *Las Tejanas*, pp. 42–43; Davies, *Lone Star Rising*, pp. 221, 222, 223, 224; Richard Bruce Winders, *Sacrificed at the Alamo: Tragedy and Triumph in the Texas Revolution* (Abilene:

State House Press, 2004), p. 122; and Stephen L. Hardin, *The Alamo 1836: Santa Anna's Texas Campaign* (Westport, Conn.: Praeger, 2004), pp. 40–41, 45, and 49. Hardin reports that Santa Anna's army may have suffered as many as 600 deaths.

⁴⁰Thomas Lloyd Miller, "Mexican Texans at the Alamo," *Journal of Mexican American History* 2 (Fall 1971): 33; Raúl Casso IV, "Damacio Jiménez: The Lost and Found Alamo Defender," *Southwestern Historical Quarterly* 96 (July 1992): 87, 91.

⁴¹David J. Weber, *Foreigners in Their Native Land: Historical Roots of the Mexican Americans*, 30th Anniversary Edition (Albuquerque: University of New Mexico Press, 2003), p. 92. Chapters 6 and 7 of Margaret Swett Henson's *Lorenzo de Zavala: The Pragmatic Idealist* (Fort Worth: Texas Christian University Press, 1996), cover de Zavala's involvement in the Texas war for independence.

⁴²H. M. Henderson, "A Critical Analysis of the San Jacinto Campaign," *Southwestern Historical Quarterly* 59 (January 1956): 344–62; Reichstein, *Rise of the Lone Star*, pp. 145–46; Hardin, *Texian Illiad*, pp. 209–10; Conner, *Texas: A History*, p. 118; Davies, *Lone Star Rising*, pp. 270-71; and Winders, *Sacrificed at the Alamo*, p. 132.

⁴³Weber, *The Mexican Frontier*, p. 251.

⁴⁴Paul D. Lack, *The Texas Revolutionary Experience: A Social and Political History* (College Station: Texas A&M University Press, 1992), pp. 183–207; Weber, *Foreigners in Their Native Land*, p. 93.

⁴⁵Fernando V. Padilla, "Early Chicano Legal Recognition, 1846–1897," *Journal of Popular Culture* 13 (Spring 1980): 564–65.

CHAPTER THREE

¹Abel G. Rubio, *Stolen Heritage: A Mexican-American's Rediscovery of His Family's Lost Land Grant* (Austin: Eakin Press, 1986), pp. x, 5, and Chapter 10.

²Oscar J. Martínez, "On the Size of the Chicano Population: New Estimates, 1850–1900," *Aztlán: International Journal of Chicano Studies Research* 6 (Spring 1975): 54; Emilio Zamora, *The World of the Mexican Worker in Texas* (College Station: Texas A&M University Press, 1993), p. 211; Arnoldo De León and Kenneth L. Stewart, *Tejanos and the Numbers Game: A Socio-Historical Interpretation from the Federal Censuses, 1850–1900* (Albuquerque: University of New Mexico Press, 1989), p. 24.

³Neil Foley, "Mexican Migrant and Tenant Labor in Central Texas Cotton Counties, 1880–1930," *Wooster Review*, No. 9 (Spring, 1989), 90–91; Arnoldo De León, *The Tejano Community, 1836–1900* (Albuquerque: University of New Mexico Press, 1982), pp. 63–65; Arnoldo De León and Kenneth L. Stewart, "Tejano Demographic Patterns and Socio-economic Development," *The Borderlands Journal* 7 (Fall 1983): 3–4. The small Tejano population of East Texas (in the Nacogdoches area) during the late 1830s and early 1840s receives attention in Paul D. Lack, "The Cordova Revolt," in Poyo, ed., *Tejano Journey*.

⁴De León and Stewart, "Tejano Demographic Patterns," p. 2.

⁵W. H. Timmons, "The El Paso Area in the Mexican Period," *Southwestern Historical Quarterly* 84 (July 1980): 26–28; C. L. Sonnichsen, *Pass of the North* (El Paso: Texas Western Press, 1968), p. 442, n2; De León and Stewart, "Tejano Demographic Patterns," pp. 1–3.

⁶Lack, *The Texas Revolutionary Experience*, pp. 183–207; Arnoldo De León, *They Called Them Greasers: Anglo Attitudes*

Toward Mexicans in Texas (Austin: University of Texas Press, 1983), p. 77; Lack, "The Cordova Revolt," pp. 99–100.
⁷De León, *They Called Them Greasers*, p. 78.
⁸De León, *The Tejano Community*, pp. 15–16; Ellen Schneider and Paul H. Carlson, "Gunnysackers, *Carreteros*, and Teamsters: The South Texas Cart War of 1857," *The Journal of South Texas* 1 (Spring 1988): 1–9.
⁹Jerry Thompson, *Cortina: Defending the Mexican Name in Texas* (College Station: Texas A&M University Press, 2007), Chapters 1–3; "Juan N. Cortina," in Pedro Castillo and Albert Camarillo, eds., *Furia y Muerte: Los Bandidos Chicanos* (Los Angeles: Aztlán Publications, 1973), pp. 84–112; Acuña, *Occupied America*, 5th ed., pp. 71–72.
¹⁰Thompson, *Cortina*, pp. 222–27; William D. Carrigan and Clive Webb, "*Muertos Por Unos Desconocidos* (Killed by Persons Unknown): Mob Violence Against Blacks and Mexicans," in Stephanie Cole and Alison M. Parker, eds., *Beyond Black and White: Race, Ethnicity, and Gender in the U.S. South and Southwest* (College Station: Texas A&M University Press, 2004): 43–44.
¹¹De León, *The Tejano Community*, pp. 20–21; Paul Cool, *Salt Warriors: Insurgency on the Rio Grande* (College Station: Texas A&M University Press, 2008), pp. 2, 3, 192–96, 262–64, and Chapters 10, 11, 12, 14, 15, and 19. See further, Manuel Callahan, "Mexican Border Troubles: Social War, Settler Colonialism and the Production of Frontier Discourses, 1848-1880" (Ph. D. Dissertation, University of Texas at Austin, 2003), Chapters 5 and 6.
¹²Jackson, *Los Mesteños*, pp. 613–15.
¹³David Montejano, *Anglos and Mexicans in the Making of Texas, 1836–1986* (Austin: University of Texas Press,

1987), pp. 34–37; Jane Dysart, "Mexican Women in San Antonio, 1850–1860: The Assimilation Process," *Western Historical Quarterly* 7 (October 1976): 370, 371.
¹⁴Walter Prescott Webb, *The Texas Rangers: A Century of Frontier Defense* (New York: Houghton Mifflin Co., 1935), p. 175; De León, *The Tejano Community*, p. 46.
¹⁵Montejano, *Anglos and Mexicans in the Making of Texas*, p. 40.
¹⁶*Ibid.*, pp. 37–38, 41.
¹⁷De León, *They Called Them Greasers*, p. 88; David E. Screws, "Hispanic Texas Rangers Contribute to Peace on the Texas Frontier, 1838–1880," *Journal of Big Bend Studies* 13 (2001).
¹⁸Jackson, *Los Mesteños*, pp. 615–16.
¹⁹Montejano, *Anglos and Mexicans in the Making of Texas*, pp. 50–51, 56–58, 59, 60, 63, 68–70; Armando C. Alonzo, *Tejano Legacy: Ranchers and Settlers in South Texas, 1734–1900* (Albuquerque: University of New Mexico Press, 1998), pp. 171–81, 235–38.
²⁰De León, *The Tejano Community*, pp. 67–68.
²¹Jackson, *Los Mesteños*, p. 610.
²²De León, *The Tejano Community*, pp. 50, 52, 57–58.
²³Montejano, *Anglos and Mexicans in the Making of Texas*, pp. 79–84; Alonzo, *Tejano Legacy*, pp. 281–282.
²⁴De León and Stewart, *Tejanos and the Numbers Game*, p. 68.
²⁵*Ibid.*, p. 92.
²⁶De León, *The Tejano Community*, p. 104; Matovina, *Tejano Religion and Ethnicity*, pp. 59–68; Timothy Matovina, *Guadalupe and Her Faithful: Latino Catholics in San Antonio, from Colonial Origins to the Present* (Baltimore: the Johns Hopkins University Press, 2005), pp. 73–94.
²⁷De León, *The Tejano Community*, pp. 114–18, 172–77, 195–201 passim; Matovina, *Tejano Religion and Ethnicity*,

188   Mexican Americans in Texas

[28]De León, *The Tejano Community*, pp. 158, 176–77, 204–06; Guadalupe San Miguel, Jr., *"Let All of them Take Heed": Mexican Americans and the Campaign for Educational Equality in Texas, 1910–1981* (Austin: University of Texas Press, 1987), p. 9; Timothy M. Matovina, "Our Lady of Guadalupe Celebrations in San Antonio, Texas, 1840–1841," *Journal of Hispanic/Latino Theology* 1 (November 1993): 92–94; Alonzo, *Tejano Legacy*, pp. 121–24; Guadalupe San Miguel, Jr., and Richard R. Valencia, "From the Treaty of Guadalupe Hidalgo to *Hopwood*: The Educational Plight and Struggle of Mexican Americans in the Southwest," *Harvard Educational Review* 68 (Fall 1998): 357–63.

[29]Montejano, *Anglos and Mexicans in the Making of Texas*, pp. 34, 51; Ana Carolina Castillo Crimm, "Success in Adversity: The Mexican Americans of Victoria County, Texas, 1800–1880" (Ph. D. Dissertation, University of Texas at Austin, 1994) pp. 8–9, 187–89, 191–96, 226–36; Alonzo, *Tejano Legacy*, pp. 106–10, 146–48, 152–58, 171–81.

[30]Crimm, *De León: A Tejano Family History*, pp. 165–84, 187–94; Mary Margaret McAllen Amberson, et al., *I Would Rather Sleep in Texas: A History of the Lower Rio Grande Valley & the People of the Santa Anita Land Grant* (Austin: Texas State Historical Association, 2003), pp. 5, 175–77, 201; Jane Clements Monday & Frances Brannen Vick, *Petra's Legacy: The South Texas Ranching Empire of Petra Vela and Mifflin Kenedy* (College Station: Texas A&M University Press, 2007), pp. 45, 267–68, 347, 349; and Acosta and Winegarten, *Las Tejanas*, p. 62.

[31]De León, *The Tejano Community*, pp. 79–81; Alonzo, *Tejano Legacy*, pp. 190–93, 210–14.

[32]Montejano, *Anglos and Mexicans in the Making of Texas*, p. 47.

[33]De León, *The Tejano Community*, pp. 96–97, 98–100.

[34]*Ibid.*, pp. 118, 134, 174, 185; Matovina, "Our Lady of Guadalupe Celebrations," pp. 93–94.

[35]Kenneth L. Stewart and Arnoldo De León, *Not Room Enough: Mexicans, Anglos, and Socio-Economic Change in Texas, 1850–1900* (Albuquerque: University of New Mexico Press, 1993), pp. 55–60.

[36]de la Teja, ed., *A Revolution Remembered*, 2nd ed., pp. 40–50; Matovina, *Tejano Religion and Ethnicity*, pp. 34–36.

[37]Walter Buenger, *Secession and the Union in Texas* (Austin: University of Texas Press, 1984), pp. 90, 91, 94, 95.

[38]Jerry D. Thompson, *Mexican Texans in the Union Army* (El Paso: Texas Western Press, 1986), pp. vii–ix; Jerry Don Thompson, *Vaqueros in Blue and Gray* (Austin: State House Press, 2000), pp. 5, 25, 81.

[39]See for example, Jerry Thompson, *Warm Weather and Bad Whiskey: The 1886 Laredo Election Riot* (El Paso: Texas Western Press, 1991); Carlysle Graham Raht, *Romance of Davis Mountains and Big Bend Country* (El Paso: The Raht Books Co., 1919), p. 216; Arnoldo De León, *San Angeleños: Mexican Americans in San Angelo, Texas* (San Angelo: Fort Concho Museum Press, 1985).

[40]James Ernest Crisp, "Anglo-Texan Attitudes Toward the Mexicans, 1821–1845" (Ph.D. Dissertation, Yale Univeristy, 1976), pp. 399–403, 408–50; Buenger, *Secession and the Union in Texas*, pp. 85, 90–91, 95, 104; David R. McDonald and Timothy M. Matovina, eds., *Defending Mexican Valor in Texas: José Antonio Navarro's Historical Writings, 1853–1857* (Austin: State House Press, 1995), pp. 11–12, 19–26; Stewart and De

León, *Not Room Enough*, pp. 46–47.
⁴¹John Denny Riley, "Santos Benavides:
His Influence on the Lower Rio Grande,
1823–1891" (Ph.D. Dissertation, Texas
Christian University, 1976), pp. 256–57,
263–64; Stewart and De León, *Not Room
Enough*, pp. 47–48.
⁴²Buenger, *Secession and the Union in
Texas*, pp. 90–91; Stewart and De León,
Not Room Enough, pp. 45–46; Thompson,
Cortina, pp. 46–47, 67–68, 96, 97, and
Chapters 7 and 8.

CHAPTER FOUR
¹Teresa Palomo Acosta, "Sara Estela
Ramírez," in *New Handbook of Texas*,
6 vols. (Austin: Texas State Historical
Association, 1996), 5, p. 424; and
Montejano, *Anglos and Mexicans in the
Making of Texas*, pp. 94–95.
²De León, *They Called Them Greasers*,
pp. 92–94, 104–05; José E. Limón,
"Healing the Wounds: Folk Symbols
and Historical Crisis," *The Texas
Humanist* 6 (March–April 1984): 22–23;
Carrigan and Webb, "*Muertos Por Unos
Desconocidos*," pp. 35, 57.
³Arnoldo De León, "In Re Ricardo
Rodríguez: An Attempt at Chicano
Disfranchisement in San Antonio,
1896–1897," in Manuel G. Gonzales
and Cynthia M. Gonzales, eds., *En Aquel
Entonces: Readings in Mexican American
History* (Bloomington: Indiana University
Press, 2000), pp. 57–63.
⁴Montejano, *Anglos and Mexicans in the
Making of Texas*, p. 110.
⁵*Ibid.*, pp. 91, 104, 109; Alonzo, *Tejano
Legacy*, pp. 235–38.
⁶Robert A. Calvert, Arnoldo De León,
and Gregg Cantrell, *The History of
Texas*, 4th ed., (Wheeling, Ill.: Harlan
Davidson, Inc., 2007), pp. 191, 205–06,
210, 212, 240–41.
⁷Mario T. García, *Desert Immigrants: The
Mexicans of El Paso, 1880–1920* (New

Haven: Yale University Press, 1981), pp.
9–32.
⁸Montejano, *Anglos and Mexicans in the
Making of Texas*, p. 107; Calvert, De
León, and Cantrell, *The History of Texas*,
4th ed., pp. 191–92.
⁹Montejano, *Anglos and Mexicans in the
Making of Texas*, p. 130; Calvert, De
León, and Cantrell, *The History of Texas*,
4th ed., p. 280.
¹⁰Zamora, *The World of the Mexican
Worker in Texas*, p. 211; Emily Skop,
Brian Gratton, and Myron P. Guttman,
"*La Frontera* and Beyond: Geography
and Demography in Mexican American
History," *The Professional Geographer:
The Journal of the Association of
American Geographers* 58 (February
2006): 91.
¹¹De León and Stewart, "Tejano
Demographic Patterns and Socio-
Economic Development," p. 6.
¹²Foley, "Mexican Migrant and Tenant
Labor in Central Texas Cotton
Counties," p. 91.
¹³Stuart Jamieson, *Labor Unionism in
American Agriculture* (New York: Arno
Press, 1976), p. 260.
¹⁴De León and Stewart, *Tejanos and the
Numbers Game*, p. 33 (Table 3.2), 37–38.
¹⁵De León, *The Tejano Community*, pp.
97, 96.
¹⁶Montejano, *Anglos and Mexicans in the
Making of Texas*, p. 72; Alonzo, *Tejano
Legacy*, p. 252.
¹⁷De Leon, *The Tejano Community*, pp.
80, 81–82, 84; Alonzo, *Tejano Legacy*, pp.
254–56.
¹⁸Elliott Young, "Deconstructing La
Raza: Identifying the *Gente Decente*
of Laredo, 1904–1911," *Southwestern
Historical Quarterly* 98 (October 1994).
¹⁹De León, *The Tejano Community*, pp.
35–42; Montejano, *Anglos and Mexicans
in the Making of Texas*, pp. 95, 129; Elliott
Young, *Catarino Garza's Revolution on*

the Texas-Mexico Border (Durham, N. C.: Duke University Press, 2004), pp. 157, 172.

[20]De León, *The Tejano Community*, pp. 42–44.

[21]*Ibid.*, pp. 33–34; Ana Luisa R. Martínez, "The Voice of the People: Pablo Cruz, *El Regidor*, and Mexican American Identity in San Antonio, Texas, 1888–1910" (Ph. D. Dissertation, Texas Tech University, 2003), pp. 90–92, 98–99, 154, 161–63, 173–92.

[22]De León, *The Tejano Community*, pp. 46–47.

[23]Evan Anders, *Boss Rule in South Texas: The Progressive Era* (Austin: University of Texas Press, 1982), p. 89.

[24]*Ibid.*, Chapter 3.

[25]Zamora, *World of the Mexican Worker in Texas*, pp. 56–57.

[26]*Ibid.*, p. 56.

[27]Mario T. García, "Racial Dualism in the El Paso Labor Market, 1880–1920," *Aztlán: International Journal of Chicano Studies Research* 6 (Summer 1975): 213.

[28]Zamora, *World of the Mexican Worker in Texas*, pp. 57, 69–70; Acuña, *Occupied America*, 5th ed., p. 156.

[29]Zamora, *World of the Mexican Worker in Texas*, Chapter 5.

[30]Roberto R. Calderón, *Mexican Coal Mining Labor in Texas and Coahuila, 1880–1930* (College Station: Texas A&M University Press, 2000), pp. 176–96.

[31]Lawrence A. Cardoso, *Mexican Emigration to the United States, 1897–1931* (Tucson: University of Arizona Press, 1980), pp. 27–29.

[32]Zamora, *World of the Mexican Worker in Texas*, p. 211.; De León and Stewart, *Tejanos and the Numbers Game*, pp. 28–29; Terry G. Jordan, "A Century and a Half of Ethnic Change in Texas, 1836–1986," *Southwestern Historical Quarterly* 89 (April 1986): 394.

[33]De León and Stewart, *Tejanos and the*

Numbers Game, pp. 85, 86–88.

[34]Jovita González, "America Invades the Border Towns," *Southwest Review* 15 (Summer 1930): 469.

[35]De León and Stewart, *Tejanos and the Numbers Game*, pp. 67–68.

[36]Montejano, *Anglos and Mexicans in the Making of Texas*, p. 91; David Montejano, *Race, Labor Repression, and Capitalist Agriculture: Notes from South Texas, 1920–1930* (Berkeley: Institute for the Study of Social Change, 1977), p. 7.

[37]Carlson, *Texas Woollybacks*, pp. 86, 87, 88–92, 95, 97, 99, 100.

[38]De León and Stewart, *Tejanos and the Numbers Game*, pp. 33, 34–35.

[39]Guadalupe San Miguel, Jr., "Social and Educational Influences Shaping the Mexican American Mind," *Journal of Midwest History of Education Society* 14 (1986): 62; González, "America Invades the Border Towns," p. 474; Roberto R. Calderón, "Mexican Politics in the American Era, 1846–1900: Laredo, Texas" (Ph.D. Dissertation, University of California at Los Angeles, 1993), pp. 642–50. For more on schooling and Mexican Americans during this era, see San Miguel and Valencia, "From the Treaty of Guadalupe Hidalgo to *Hopwood*," p. 364; and Carlos Kevin Blanton, *The Strange Career of Bilingual Education in Texas, 1836–1981* (College Station: Texas A&M University Press, 2004), pp. 25–31.

[40]Young, "Deconstructing La Raza," pp. 240–242; Ben Procter and Archie P. McDonald, eds., *The Texas Heritage* (Wheeling, Ill.: Forum Press, 1980), p. 173.

[41]De León and Stewart, *Tejanos and the Numbers Game*, pp. 45–46.

[42]*Ibid.*, p. 45.

[43]De León, *The Tejano Community*, pp. 150–51.

[44]Limón, "Healing the Wounds," pp. 22–23.

[45]Américo Paredes, "José Mosqueda and

the Folklorization of Actual Events,"
*Aztlán: Chicano Journal of the Social
Sciences and the Arts,* 4 (Spring 1973):
5–6, 14.
[46]Rodolfo Rocha, "The Sting and Power
of Rebellion," *The Texas Humanist* 6
(March–April 1984): 20; Américo
Paredes, *A Texas-Mexican Cancionero*
(Urbana: University of Illinois Press,
1976), p. 32.
See further the series of articles published
on Jacinto Treviño in *The Valley Morning
Star,* Harlingen, Texas, October 2, 2005,
pp. 1C, 5C, 6C; and October 23, 2005,
pp. 1C, 3C, 8C.
[47]Limón, "Healing the Wounds," pp.
22–23.
[48]Gilbert M. Cuthbertson, "Catarino
Garza and the Garza War," *Texana*
12 (No. 4): 337; Elliott Young,
"Remembering Catarino Garza's
1891 Revolution: An Aborted Border
Insurrection," *Estudios Mexicanos/Mexican
Studies,* 12 (Summer 1996): 242–50.
[49]De León, *They Called Them Greasers,* pp.
60–61; Cuthbertson, "Catarino Garza,"
p. 345; Young, "Remembering Catarino
Garza," pp. 250–70; Young, *Catarino
Garza's Revolution on the Texas-Mexico
Border,* pp. 102–08, 117–22, 126–30,
169–72, 189–90, 290–300.

CHAPTER FIVE

[1]Luis G. Gómez, *Crossing the Rio Grande:
An Immigrant's Life in the 1880s* (College
Station: Texas A&M University Press,
2006), pp. 9, 11, 13, 25–26, 42–48, 52,
68–69, 70–75, 99.
[2]McWilliams, *North From Mexico,* p.
163; Ricardo Romo, "The Urbanization
of Southwestern Chicanos," in Ricardo
Romo and Raymund Paredes,eds., *New
Directions in Chicano Scholarship* (La Jolla:
University of California at San Diego,
1978), p. 194.
[3]Mario T. García, "La Frontera: The Border
as Symbol and Reality," *Estudios Mexicanos/*

Mexican Studies 1 (Summer 1985): 197.
[4]Cardoso, *Mexican Emigration to the
United States,* pp. 2, 6–7, 9–10.
[5]Arthur Corwin, *Immigrants—and
Immigrants* (Westport, Conn.:
Greenwood Press, 1978), pp. 46, 52.
[6]Gonzalez and Fernandez, *A Century of
Chicano History,* pp. xii, 34–38, 43–45,
123–29.
[7]Quoted in Mark Reisler, *By the Sweat
of Their Brow* (Westport, Conn.:
Greenwood Press, 1976), p. 40.
[8]Cardoso, *Mexican Emigration to the
United States,* pp. 28–29, 46; Manuel
Bernardo Ramírez, "El Pasoans: Life
and Society in Mexican El Paso,
1920–1945" (Ph.D. Dissertation,
University of Mississippi, 2000), pp.
51–55.
[9]Cardoso, *Mexican Emigration to the
United States,* pp. 83, 129–30; Wayne A.
Cornelius, "Mexican Immigration to the
United States: Causes, Consequences,
and United States Responses"
(Cambridge: MIT, 1978), pp. 3, 7.
[10]R. Reynolds McKay, "Texas Mexican
Repatriation During the Great
Depression" (Ph.D. Dissertation,
University of Oklahoma, 1982), p. 66.
[11]Montejano, *Anglos and Mexicans in the
Making of Texas,* pp. 180, 186–88.
[12]*Ibid.,* pp. 183, 188; Clare Sheridan,
"Contested Citizenship: National
Identity and the Mexican Immigration
Debates of the 1920s," *Journal of
American Ethnic History* 21 (Spring
2002): 22–24.
[13]Montejano, *Anglos and Mexicans in
the Making of Texas,* pp. 183, 189, 179,
190; Neil Foley, *The White Scourge:
Mexicans, Blacks, and Poor Whites in Texas
Cotton Culture* (Berkeley: University
of California Press, 1997) pp. 52–55;
Sheridan, "Contested Citizenship," pp.
6-8, 12–19.
[14]Montejano, *Anglos and Mexicans in the
Making of Texas,* pp. 182, 190; Corwin,

Immigrants—and Immigrants, p. 146.
[15]Corwin, *Immigrants—and Immigrants*, p. 45.
[16]Hubert J. Miller, "Mexican Migrations to the United States, 1900–1920," *The Borderlands Journal* 7 (Spring 1984): 180; Corwin, *Immigrants—and Immigrants*, p. 47.
[17]García, *Desert Immigrants*, p. 2; George Coalson, *The Development of Migrant Farm Labor System in Texas, 1900–1954* (San Francisco: R&E Research Associates, 1977), p. 2; Romo, "Urbanization of Southwestern Chicanos," p. 185; Ramírez, "El Pasoans," Chapter 2.
[18]De León, *San Angeleños*, p. 35.
[19]Richard A. García, *Rise of the Mexican American Middle Class, San Antonio, 1929–1941* (College Station: Texas A&M University Press, 1991), pp. 28–29.
[20]Foley, "Mexican Migrant and Tenant Labor in Central Texas Cotton Counties," p. 99; McWilliams, *North From Mexico*, p. 170; McKay, "Texas Mexican Repatriation," p. 84; Neil Foley, *White Scourge*, pp. 35–37, 44–45.
[21]Arnoldo De León, *Ethnicity in the Sunbelt: A History of Mexican Americans in Houston* (Houston: Mexican American Studies Program, 1989), pp. xv, 7, 23, 10; "A Report on Illiteracy in Texas" (Austin: U. T. Bulletin No. 2328, 1923), p. 12. On Mexicans in Northeast Texas along the Arkansas, Oklahoma, and Louisiana border, see Walter L. Buenger, *The Path to a Modern South: Northeast Texas between Reconstruction and the Great Depression* (Austin: University of Texas Press, 2001), pp. 64, 171–72.
[22]*Dallas Morning News*, September 13, 1987, p. 22A, June 29, 1988, p. 2C; Romo, "The Urbanization of Southwestern Chicanos," p. 185; Flora Lowrey, "Night School in Little Mexico," *Southwest Review* 16 (October 1930): 37; Nina L. Nixon-Méndez, "*Los Fundadores*

Urbanos (Urban Pioneers): The Hispanics of Dallas, 1850–1940," *Journal of the West* 32 (October 1993); Gwendolyn Rice, "Little Mexico and the Barrios of Dallas," in Michael V. Hazel, ed., *Dallas Reconsidered: Essays in Local History* (Dallas: Three Forks Press, 1995), pp. 159–60.
[23]Reisler, *Sweat of Their Brow*, p. 51; Romo, "Urbanization of Southwestern Chicanos," p. 185; Carlos E. Cuéllar, *Stories from the Barrio: A History of Mexican Fort Worth* (Fort Worth: Texas Christian University Press, 2003), pp. 7–16; Kenneth N. Hopkins, "The Early Development of the Hispanic Community in Fort Worth and Tarrant County, 1849–1949," *East Texas Historical Journal* 38 (Fall 2000): 54–62.
[24]Jordan, "A Century and a Half of Ethnic Change in Texas, 1836–1986," p. 399; "A Report on Illiteracy in Texas," p. 11; William D. Carrigan, *The Making of Lynching Culture: Violence and Vigilantism in Central Texas, 1836–1916* (Urbana: University of Illinois Press, 2004), pp. 175–76.
[25]Miller, "Mexican Migration to the U.S.," p. 180; García, *Rise of the Mexican American Middle Class*, p. 35.
[26]García, *Rise of the Mexican American Middle Class*, pp. 240–41, 234, 103, 104; Richard A. García, "The Mexican American Mind: A Product of the 1930s," in Mario T. García, *History, Culture, and Society* (Ypsilanti: Bilingual Press/Editorial Bilingue, 1983), pp. 76, 78.
[27]Emory Bogardus, "The Mexican Immigrant and Segregation," *American Journal of Sociology* 36 (July 1930): 76–77.
[28]Lyle Saunders, *Wetbacks in the Lower Rio Grande Valley* (New York: Arno Press, 1976), p. 61.
[29]Mario T. García, *Mexican Americans: Leadership and Ideology* (New Haven: Yale University Press, 1989), pp. 14–15.
[30]García, *Rise of the Mexican American*

Middle Class, pp. 44, 77, 81–83.
[31]Mario García, *Desert Immigrants*, pp. 74, 75, 76; Mario T. García, "The Chicana in American History: Mexican Women in El Paso," *Pacific Historical Review* 49 (May 1980): 321; Acosta and Winegarten, *Las Tejanas*, pp. 100, 128–33. On the morality that immigrant society expected of women, see Juanita Luna Lawhn, "*El Regidor* and *La Prensa*: Impediments to Women's Self-Definition," *Third Woman Press* 4 (1989): 134–42.
[32]Julie Leininger Pycior, "La Raza Organizes: Mexican American Life in San Antonio, 1915–1930, as Reflected in Mutualista Activities" (Ph. D. Dissertation, University of Notre Dame, 1979), pp. 189, 198; Acosta and Winegarten, *Las Tejanas*, pp. 78–79; Emma Pérez, *The Decolonial Imaginary: Writing Chicanas Into History* (Bloomington: Indiana University Press, 1999), pp. 68–69.
[33]Yolanda G. Romero, "From Rebels to Immigrants to Chicanas: Hispanic Women in Lubbock County" (M.A. Thesis, Texas Tech University, 1987), pp. 8, 9, 10.
[34]De León, *Ethnicity in the Sunbelt*, pp. 33–34, 37, 38; Lowrey, "Night School in Little Mexico," p. 39.
[35]Nick Kanellos, "Two Centuries of Hispanic Theatre in the Southwest," *Revista Chicano-Riqueña* 11 (Spring 1983): 24–25, 35; Nick Kanellos, *A History of Hispanic Theatre in the United States* (Austin: University of Texas Press, 1990), pp. 180–81, 198, 199–200; Manuel Peña, *The Texas Mexican Conjunto: History of a Working Class Music* (Austin: University of Texas Press, 1985), pp. 29, 35–36, 38.
[36]Manuel Gamio, *Mexican Immigration to the United States* (New York: Arno Press, 1969), p. 129.
[37]De León, *Ethnicity in the Sunbelt*, pp. 31,

75; Pycior, "La Raza Organizes," pp. 94–95; Martínez, "The Voice of the People," p. 113–14; Nora Ríos McMillan, "A Biography of a Man and His Newspaper," *The Americas Review* 17 (Nos. 3-4 (Fall/Winter 1989): 113–14.
[38]Acosta and Winegarten, *Las Tejanas*, pp. 75–78; De León, *Ethnicity in the Sunbelt*, p. 14.
[39]Zamora, "Mexican Labor Activity," pp. 76–77; Zamora, *World of the Mexican Worker in Texas* (College Station: Texas A&M University Press, 1993), p. 140; Gómez-Quiñones, *Sembradores*, p. 29.
[40]Gómez-Quiñones, *Sembradores*, pp. 29, 35–36.
[41]Zamora, *World of the Mexican Worker in Texas*, p. 147.
[42]García, *Mexican Americans*, p. 175.
[43]Marta Cotera, *Diosa y Hembra: The History and Heritage of Chicanas in the United States* (Austin: Information Systems Development, 1976), pp. 65–66; Gómez-Quiñones, *Sembradores*, p. 36; Acuña, *Occupied America*, 5th ed., p. 156.
[44]Zamora, *World of the Mexican Worker in Texas*, p. 74.
[45]Lowrey, "Night School in Little Mexico," pp. 39–40; John Ernest Gregg, "The History of Presidio County" (M.A. Thesis, University of Texas, 1933), pp. 201–202; De León, *Ethnicity in the Sunbelt*, p. 33; Zamora, *World of the Mexican Worker in Texas*, p. 93; Calderón, "Mexican Politics in the America Era," Chapter 10.
[46]Zamora, *World of the Mexican Worker in Texas*, pp. 99–100.
[47]García, *Mexican Americans*, p. 28.
[48]Pycior, "La Raza Organizes," pp. 126–27, 128, 130, 132, 134, 136; Rodolfo F. Acuña, *Occupied America: A History of Chicanos*, 3rd ed. (New York: Harper and Row, 1988), p. 170.
[49]Cotera, *Diosa y Hembra*, p. 73; Pycior, "La Raza Organizes," pp. 76–81.
[50]Pycior, "La Raza Organizes," p. 76.

51 Gamio, *The Mexican Immigrant*, pp. 136–37. See further Nicolás Kanellos with Helvetia Martell, *Hispanic Periodicals in the United States, Origins to 1960: A Brief History and Comprehensive Bibliography* (Houston: Arte Publico Press, 2000), pp. 28–32, 39–43.

52 Roberto R. Treviño, "Prensa y Patria: The Spanish Language Press and the Biculturation of the Tejano Middle Class, 1920–1940," *Western Historical Quarterly* 22 (November 1991): 451–72. On the efforts made by one immigrant newspaper to further literary creativity, see Blanca Rodríguez, "Fronteras y Literatura: El Periódico La Patria (El Paso, Texas, 1919–1925)," *Mexican Studies/Estudios Mexicanos* 19 (Winter 2003): 107–25.

53 García, "La Frontera: The Border as Symbol and Reality," p. 198; García, *Rise of the Mexican American Middle Class*, p. 35; Ríos McMillan, "A Biography of a Man and His Newspaper," pp. 136–42.

54 Treviño, "Prensa y Patria," p. 454.

55 García, "The Mexican American Mind," p. 69.

CHAPTER SIX

1 This story is recounted masterfully and engrossingly in Beatriz de la Garza, *A Law for the Lion: A Tale of Crime and Injustice in the Borderlands* (Austin: University of Texas Press, 2003), pp. 5, 9, 11–15, 25–26, 39–41, 49–51, 56–57, 91, 101, 116–19.

2 Nelson Cisneros, "*La Clase Trabajadora en Tejas*," p. 240.

3 Montejano, *Anglos and Mexicans in the Making of Texas*, pp. 103, 104, 109; Jordan, "A Century and a Half of Ethnic Change in Texas, 1836–1986," p. 398.

4 García, *Desert Immigrants*, pp. 30–31; Ramírez, "El Pasoans," pp. 20–21, 32–33; Coalson, "The Development of Migrant Farm Labor System in Texas, 1900–

1954," p. 2; Foley, "Mexican Migrant and Tenant Labor in Central Texas Cotton Counties," pp. 95–99.

5 Montejano, *Anglos and Mexicans in the Making of Texas*, pp. 113, 149, 151; Alonzo, *Tejano Legacy*, pp. 257–58; Benjamin Heber Johnson, *Revolution in Texas: How a Forgotten Rebellion and Its Bloody Suppression Turned Mexicans into Americans* (New Haven: Yale University Press, 2003), pp. 31–34.

6 Montejano, *Race, Labor Repression, and Capitalist Agriculture*, pp. 11, 12; Montejano, *Anglos and Mexicans in the Making of Texas*, p. 173.

7 Nelson Cisneros, "*La Clase Trabajadora*," pp. 241, 244; Johnson, *Revolution in Texas*, pp. 34–36.

8 Montejano, *Anglos and Mexicans in the Making of Texas*, pp. 129–130, 143, 148, 253; Anders, *Boss Rule in South Texas*, pp. 90–91; Johnson, *Revolution in Texas*, pp. 35, 166–69.

9 García, *Rise of the Mexican American Middle Class*, pp. 38–39; De León, *Ethnicity in the Sunbelt*, pp. 11–12; Ramírez, "El Pasoans," pp. 76–85.

10 Montejano, *Anglos and Mexicans in the Making of Texas*, pp. 114, 162–63, 168, 232.

11 *Ibid.*, pp. 191–92; San Miguel, "*Let All of Them Take Heed,*" p. 24; Ramirez, "El Pasoans," pp. 106–25.

12 Zamora, *The World of the Mexican Worker in Texas*, pp. 21–24; Carole E. Christian, "Joining the American Mainstream: Texas' Mexican Americans During World War I," *Southwestern Historical Quarterly* 93 (April 1989).

13 Acosta and Winegarten, *Las Tejanas*, pp. 119, 121; De León, *Ethnicity in the Sunbelt*, p. 25.

14 González, "America Invades the Border Towns," pp. 476–77.

15 Cynthia E. Orozco, "The Origins of the League of United Latin American

Citizens (LULAC) and the Mexican American Civil Rights Movement in Texas With an Analysis of Women's Political Participation in a Gendered Context, 1910–1929" (Ph.D. Dissertation, University of California at Los Angeles, 1992), pp. 15, 92, 95; Peña, *The Texas Mexican Conjunto*, p. 116.

[16]Ramírez, "El Pasoans," pp. 205–09; García, *Desert Immigrants*, pp. 211, 213–14, 217–19; Guadalupe San Miguel, Jr., "Social and Educational Influences Shaping the Mexican American Mind," *Journal of Midwest History of Education Society* 14 (1986): 58; De León, *Ethnicity in the Sunbelt*, p. 13.

[17]García, *Desert Immigrants*, pp. 117–122; Ramirez, "El Pasoans," pp. 110–11; San Miguel, "Social and Educational Influences," pp. 58–59; Gene B. Preuss, "Cotulla Revisited: A Reassessment of Lyndon Johnson's Year as a Public School Teacher," *The Journal of South Texas* 10 (1997): 26–28; Blanton, *Strange Career of Bilingual Education*, pp. 59–69.

[18]San Miguel, "Let All of Them Take Heed," pp. 25, 19.

[19]González, "America Invades the Border Towns," p. 477. See further, Orozco, "Origins of LULAC," pp. 249–52.

[20]Christian, "Joining the American Mainstream," pp. 559, 569, 577. Quote is from José A. Ramírez, "'To the Line of Fire, Mexican-Texans!': The Tejano Community and World War I" (Ph. D. Dissertation, Southern Methodist University, 2007), p. 49–50.

[21]Christian, "Joining the American Mainstream," pp. 574, 584, 586. See further, Ramírez, "'To the Line of Fire!'," pp. 49-50, 65-66, 111–13, 116–19, 126–33.

[22]Ramírez, "'To the Line of Fire!'," pp. 43–44, 47–48, 55–58, 61–64, 70–71. On Tejanos in the war front, see *ibid.*, Chapter 6, titled "Over There."

[23]Christian, "Joining the American Mainstream," pp. 582–83; Orozco, "Origins of LULAC," p. 124; Ramírez, "'To the Line of Fire!'," pp. 177–79, 223–24.

[24]Ramírez, "'To the Line of Fire!'," pp. 1-2, 8, 184–85, 209–10, 231–32.

[25]Christian, "Joining the American Mainstream," pp. 559–60.

[26]Zamora, *World of the Mexican Worker in Texas*, pp. 86.

[27]Zamora, "Mexican Labor Activity," pp. 104–05, 112; Zamora, *World of the Mexican Worker in Texas*, pp. 149, 186.

[28]Zamora, *World of the Mexican Worker in Texas*, pp. 133, 145, 157, 159, 160–61, 195; Foley, *The White Scourge*, pp. 107–14.

[29]Zamora, "Mexican Labor Activity," p. 186.

[30]Zamora, *World of the Mexican Worker in Texas*, p. 168; García, *Desert Immigrants*, p. 99.

[31]García, *Desert Immigrants*, pp. 107–08; Irene Ledesma, "Unlikely Strikers: Mexican American Women in Strike Activity in Texas, 1919–1974" (Ph. D. Dissertation, The Ohio State University, 1992), pp. 83–92.

[32]Pycior, "La Raza Organizes," pp. 137–38; Acuña, *Occupied America*, 3rd ed., pp. 164–65, 170.

[33]Zamora, "Mexican Labor Activity," pp. 200–01; Zamora, *World of the Mexican Worker in Texas*, pp. 168–69.

[34]McWilliams, *North From Mexico*, p. 113; Reisler, *By the Sweat of Their Brow*, p. 142.

[35]Arnoldo De León, "Blowout 1910 Style: A Chicano School Boycott in West Texas," *Texana* 12 (1974). In 1929, Mexican American parents in South El Paso launched their own effort to bring better education to their children. They did not demand integration, only getting a new school that would accommodate the growing number of Mexican-

196   *Mexican Americans in Texas*

American students. Their effort still did not bring success. Ramírez, "El Pasoans," pp. 125–28.

[36]Zamora, *World of the Mexican Worker in Texas*, pp. 80–81.; Montejano, *Anglos and Mexicans in the Making of Texas*, pp. 116–17; José A. Hernández, *Mutual Aid for Survival: The Case of the Mexican American* (Malabar, Fla.: Robert E. Krieger Publishing Co., 1983), p. 72; Sylvia Alicia Gonzales, *Hispanic American Voluntary Associations* (Westport, Conn.: Greenwood Press, 1985), p. 120.

[37]Anders, *Boss Rule in South Texas*, p. 220; Montejano, *Anglos and Mexicans in the Making of Texas*, p. 117; Don M. Coerver and Linda B. Hall, *Texas and the Mexican Revolution: A Study in State and National Border Policy* (San Antonio: Trinity University Press, 1984), pp. 85–108; James A. Sandos, *Rebellion in the Borderlands: Anarchism and the Plan de San Diego, 1904–1923* (Norman: University of Oklahoma Press, 1992).

[38]Montejano, *Anglos and Mexicans in the Making of Texas*, pp. 117–18, 125; Rodolfo Rocha, "The Influence of the Mexican Revolution on the Mexico-Texas Border, 1910–1916" (Ph.D. Dissertation, Texas Tech Univerity, 1981), Chapter 6; Coerver and Hall, *Texas and the Mexican Revolution*, pp. 85–108; Sandos, *Rebellion in the Borderlands*, pp. xv–xvi, 72–74, 127, 174; Johnson, *Revolution in Texas*, pp. 113–20; Charles H. Harris III and Louis R. Sadler, *The Texas Rangers and the Mexican Revolution: The Bloodiest Decade, 1910–1920* (Albuquerque: University of New Mexico Press, 2004), pp. 210–15, 252–53, 268, 295–96.

[39]Edgar Shelton, *Political Conditions Among Texas Mexicans Along the Rio Grande* (San Francisco: R&E Research Associates, 1974), pp. 17–18, 34–36, 40–47, 60–66, 73–74, 74–76, 76–77, 79, 81–82, 84–86.

[40]Lewis Gould, *Progressives and Prohibitionists* (Austin: University of Texas Press, 1973), p. 287; Montejano, *Anglos and Mexicans in the Making of Texas*, p. 292; Ignacio García, *United We Win: The Rise and Fall of the Raza Unida Party* (Tucson: MASRC, University of Arizona Press, 1989), p. 7; Johnson, *Revolution in Texas*, p. 3.

[41]García, *Rise of the Mexican American Middle Class*, p. 206; Shelton, *Political Conditions*, pp. 74–76.

[42]Anders, *Boss Rule in South Texas*, pp. 15, 266; Garcia, *Desert Immigrants*, pp. 170–71.

[43]Anders, *Boss Rule in South Texas*, pp. 63, 221, 236, 192.

[44]*Ibid.*, pp. 152, 227, 246–47, 250, 266–73; *New Handbook of Texas*, I, 953–54; Richard Henry Ribb, "José Tomás Canales and the Texas Rangers: Myth, Identity, and Power in South Texas, 1900–1920" (Ph. D. Dissertation, University of Texas, 2001); Harris and Sadler, *The Texas Rangers*, pp. 460–61; Frank L. Madla, "The Political Impact of Latin Americans and Negroes in Texas Politics" (M.A. Thesis, St. Mary's University, 1964), p. 72.

[45]Christian, "Joining the American Mainstream," p. 594; Ramírez, "El Pasoans," pp. 227–28.

[46]Johnson, *Revolution in Texas*, pp. 5, 42–52, 126–28.

[47]Orozco, "Origins of LULAC," pp. 127–29; Douglas O. Weeks, "The Texas Mexican and the Politics of South Texas," *American Political Review* 24 (August 1930): 622.

[48]Julie Leininger Pycior, "Tejanas Navigating the 1920s," in De León, ed., *Tejano Epic*, Chapter 6.

[49]Christian, "Joining the American Mainstream," p. 589, 590; Hernández, *Mutual Aid for Survival*, p. 73.

[50]Christian, "Joining the American

Mainstream," pp. 589–90.
[51]*Ibid.*, pp. 589–91.
[52]Treviño, "Prensa y Patria," pp. 461, 463–64.

CHAPTER SEVEN
[1]Zaragosa Vargas, "Tejana Radical: Emma Tenayuca and the San Antonio Labor Movement During the Great Depression," *Pacific Historical Review* 66 (November 1997): 556, 559, 561, 565–74, 579, and 580 n57.
[2]R. Reynolds McKay, "Texas Mexican Repatriation During the Great Depression" (Ph.D. Dissertation, University of Oklahoma at Norman, 1982), pp. 101–07, 270, 566–71; Nora E. Ríos McMillan, "The Repatriation of Mexicans During the Great Depression," *Journal of South Texas* 11, No. 1 (1998): 44–73; Ramírez, "El Pasoans," Chapter 6.
[3]Peña, *The Texas-Mexican Conjunto*, p. 126.
[4]Montejano, *Anglos and Mexicans in the Making of Texas*, pp. 168, 227, 232, 265.
[5]*Ibid.*, p. 227; Kibbe, *Latin Americans in Texas*, p. 125.
[6]Montejano, *Anglos and Mexicans in the Making of Texas*, pp. 174, 176; Foley, *The White Scourge*, pp. 162–67, 175–78, 205.
[7]Coalson, *The Development of the Migrant Farm Labor System in Texas*, pp. 23, 25.
[8]Carey McWilliams, *Ill Fares the Land* (Boston: Little, Brown and Co., 1942), p. 238; Zaragosa Vargas, *Labor Rights are Civil Rights: Mexican American Workers in Twentieth-Century America* (Princeton: Princeton University Press, 2005), pp. 17–22, and Yolanda G. Romero, "The Mexican American Frontier Experience in Twentieth Century Northwest Texas," (Ph.D. dissertation, Texas Tech University, 1993), Chapter 3.
[9]McWilliams, *Ill Fares the Land*, pp. 238–39; Kibbe, *Latin Americans in Texas*, pp. 159, 177; Coalson, *The Development of*

the *Migrant Farm Labor System*, p. 23.
[10]García, *Rise of the Mexican American Middle Class*, p. 39; Kibbe, *Latin Americans in Texas*, pp. 123, 126, 128; De León, *Ethnicity in the Sunbelt*, pp. 51–52; Rice, "Little Mexico and the *Barrios* of Dallas," pp. 100–04; Vargas, *Labor Rights are Civil Rights*, pp. 22–27.
[11]Peña, *The Texas Mexican Conjunto*, pp. 115, 127.
[12]Acuña, *Occupied America*, 5th ed., p. 234; De León, *Ethnicity in the Sunbelt*, p. 62.
[13]García, *Rise of the Mexican American Middle Class*, p. 250.
[14]Kanellos, *A History of Hispanic Theatre in the United States*, pp. 86, 100, 199; De León, *Ethnicity in the Sunbelt*, p. 65; Ramírez, "El Pasoans," pp. 169–70.
[15]Mario Barrera, "The Historical Evolution of Chicano Ethnic Goals," *Sage Race Relations Abstracts* 10 (February 1985): 6–7; Pycior, "La Raza Organizes," p. 226.
[16]García, *Rise of the Mexican American Middle Class*, pp. 86–87; Julie Leininger Pycior, *LBJ and Mexican Americans: The Paradox of Power* (Austin: University of Texas Press, 1997), pp. 31–35.
[17]Roberto R. Treviño, *The Church in the Barrio: Mexican American Ethno-Catholicism in Houston* (Chapel Hill: The University of North Carolina Press, 2006), pp. 121, 70; Paul Barton, *Hispanic Methodists, Presbyterians, and Baptists in Texas* (Austin: University of Texas Press, 2006), pp. 2, 4–5, 57, 60–61.
[18]Treviño, "Prensa y Patria," pp. 463–71.
[19]*New Handbook of Texas*, IV, pp. 1013–14, 1176–77; Cotera, *Diosa y Hembra*, pp. 82–84. See further, Bryce Milligan, "Ever Radical: A Survey of Tejana Writers," in Sylvia Ann Grider and Lou Halsell Rodenberger, eds., *Texas Women Writers: A Tradition of Their Own* (College Station: Texas A&M University Press, 1997), pp. 210–17.

[20]Christian, "Joining the American Mainstream," pp. 591–92; De León, *Ethnicity in the Sunbelt*, p. 80; Benjamin Márquez, *LULAC: The Evolution of a Mexican American Political Organization* (Austin: University of Texas Press, 1993), pp. 17–27; Johnson, *Revolution in Texas*, pp. 185–87, 189–90.

[21]García, *Rise of the Mexican American Middle Class*, p. 275.

[22]De León, *Ethnicity in the Sunbelt*, pp. 81, 86, 87–89; Montejano, *Anglos and Mexicans in the Making of Texas*, p. 232.

[23]García, *Rise of the Mexican American Middle Class*, pp. 301–02; San Miguel, *"Let All of Them Take Heed,"* p. 76.

[24]Mario T. García, "Mexican Americans and the Politics of Citizenship," *New Mexico Historical Review* 59 (April 1984): 188, 198–99, 200–01.

[25]San Miguel and Valencia, "From the Treaty of Guadalupe Hidalgo to *Hopwood*," pp. 368–77.

[26]Everett Ross Clinchy, "Equality of Opportunity for Latin Americans in Texas" (Ph.D. Dissertation, Columbia University, 1954), pp. 188–89; Neil Foley, "Over the Rainbow: *Hernández v. Texas, Brown v. Board of Education,* and *Black v. Brown*," in Michael A. Olivas, ed., *"Colored Men" and "Hombres Aquí": Hernández v. Texas and the Emergence of Mexican-American Lawyering* (Houston: Arte Público Press, 2006), pp. 113–14.

[27]García, *Rise of the Mexican American Middle Class*, p. 272; San Miguel, *"Let All of Them Take Heed,"* p. 81; Márquez, *LULAC*, pp. 28–29.

[28]5San Miguel, *"Let All of Them Take Heed,"* pp. 85–86; García, *Mexican Americans*, pp. 62, 72, 73.

[29]De León, *Ethnicity in the Sunbelt*, pp. 71–76; García, "Mexican Americans and the Politics of Citizenship," 95–98.

[30]Juan Gómez-Quiñones, *Chicano Politics: Reality and Promise, 1940–1990*

(Albuquerque: University of New Mexico Press, 1990), p. 48; Madla, "The Political Impact of Latin Americans and Negroes in Texas Politics," p. 72.

[31]García, *Rise of the Mexican American Middle Class*, pp. 261, 266; Kibbe, *Latin Americans in Texas*, p. 220.

[32]García, *Rise of the Mexican American Middle Class*, pp. 261, 272, 281.

[33]*Ibid.*, pp. 271–72; García, *Mexican Americans*, p. 42; De León, *Ethnicity in the Sunbelt*, p. 90; Benjamin Márquez, "The Politics of Race and Assimilation: The League of United Latin American Citizens, 1929–1940," *The Western Political Quarterly* 42 (June 1989): 360.

[34]García, *Mexican Americans*, pp. 38–40.

[35]Cynthia E. Orozco, "Alice Dickerson Montemayor: Feminism and Mexican American Politics in the 1930s," in Elizabeth Jameson and Susan Armitage, eds., *Writing the Range: Race, Class, and Culture in the Women's West* (Norman: University of Oklahoma Press, 1997), pp. 435–56.

[36]Acuña, *Occupied America*, 3rd ed., p. 198; Nelson Cisneros, *"La Clase Trabajadora en Tejas,"* p. 247.

[37]Vargas, *Labor Rights are Civil Rights*, pp. 68–70; Arnoldo De León, *"Los Tasinques* and the Sheep Shearers' Union of North America: A Strike in West Texas, 1934," *West Texas Historical Association Yearbook* 55 (1979).

[38]Victor Nelson Cisneros, "UCAPAWA Organizing Activities in Texas, 1935–1950," *Aztlán: International Journal of Chicano Studies Research* 9 (Spring and Summer 1978): 73–74; Vargas, *Labor Rights are Civil Rights*, pp. 117–22.

[39]Nelson Cisneros, "UCAPAWA Organizing Activities in Texas," pp. 74, 75, 77.

[40]García, *Mexican Americans*, Chapter 7; Vargas, *Labor Rights are Civil Rights*, pp. 162–75.

[41]Cisneros, "UCAPAWA," pp. 80–81; Kenneth P. Walker, "The Pecan Shellers of San Antonio and Mechanization," *Southwestern Historical Quarterly* 69 (July 1965): 44–58; Ledesma, "Unlikely Strikers," pp. 92–103, 114–26; Vargas, "Tejana Radical," 561, 565–74; Vargas, *Labor Rights are Civil Rights*, pp. 123–47.
[42]Julia Kirk Blackwelder, *Women of the Depression* (College Station: Texas A&M University Press, 1984), p. 132.
[43]Acuña, *Occupied America*, 3rd ed., pp. 223–24; Melissa Hield, "Union Minded: Women in Texas ILGWU, 1937–1950," in Richard Croxdale, *Women in the Texas Workforce Yesterday and Today* (Austin: People's History in Texas, Inc., 1979), pp. 8–11, 13; Ledesma, "Unlikely Strikers," pp. 103–14.
[44]Blackwelder, *Women of the Depression*, p. 151.
[45]Montejano, *Anglos and Mexicans in the Making of Texas*, p. 269; Vargas, *Labor Rights are Civil Rights*, pp. 206–11.
[46]Matt Meier and Feliciano Rivera, *Los Chicanos: A History of Mexican Americans* (New York: Hill and Wang, 1972), p. 186; Vargas, *Labor Rights are Civil Rights*, pp. 208–10.
[47]Kibbe, *Latin Americans in Texas*, pp. 283–86; Ramírez, "El Pasoans," p. 240. Accounts of Mexican American participation in World War II are contained in Maggie Rivas Rodríguez, et al., *A Legacy Greater than Words: Stories of US Latinos & Latinas of the World War II Generation* (Austin: U.S. Latino and Latina WWII Oral History Project, 2006).
[48]Thomas A. Guglielmo, "Fighting for Caucasian Rights: Mexicans, Mexican Americans, and the Transnational Struggle for Civil Rights in World War II Texas," *The Journal of American History* 92 (March 2006): 1212–13, 1216–33, 1235–36.

CHAPTER EIGHT
[1]Patrick J. Carroll, *Felix Longoria's Wake: Bereavement, Racism, and the Rise of Mexican American Activism* (Austin: University of Texas Press, 2003), pp. 1–2, 11, 53, 55–57, 63, 69–76, 87, 138–39.
[2]Montejano, *Anglos and Mexicans in the Making of Texas*, pp. 276, 286.
[3]Robert A. Calvert, Arnoldo De León, and Gregg Cantrell, *The History of Texas*, 4th ed. (Wheeling, Ill.: Harlan Davidson, Inc., 2007), p. 368.
[4]Montejano, *Anglos and Mexicans in the Making of Texas*, pp. 263, 271–72; Calvert, De León, and Cantrell, *The History of Texas*, 4th ed., p. 368.
[5]Leo Grebler, Joan W. Moore, and Ralph Guzmán, *The Mexican American People: The Nation's Second Largest Minority* (New York: Free Press, 1970), p. 106; *U.S. Census of Population: 1960*. Final Report PC(2)—1B, "Persons of Spanish Surname," Table 1, p.2.
[6]San Miguel, *"Let All of Them Take Heed,"* p. 113; Montejano, *Anglos and Mexicans in the Making of Texas*, pp. 272, 273.
[7]Peña, *The Texas Mexican Conjunto*, p. 128.
[8]Dallas *Morning News*, September 13, 1987, pp. 22A–23A; De León, *Ethnicity in the Sunbelt*, p. 98; Acuña, *Occupied America*, 3rd ed., p. 282; Oscar J. Martínez, *The Chicanos of El Paso: An Assessment of Progress* (El Paso: Texas Western Press, 1980), p. 6.
[9]Peña, *The Texas Mexican Conjunto*, pp. 128, 130; Carl Allsup, *The American G.I. Forum: Origins and Evolution* (Austin: Center for Mexican American Studies and the University of Texas Press, 1982), p. 21.
[10]Allsup, *The American G.I. Forum*, p. 21; Robert H. Talbert, *Spanish-Name People of the Southwest and West* (Fort Worth: Texas Christian University Press, 1955), p. 79.
[11]Talbert, *Spanish-Name People of the Southwest and West*, p. 62 (Table 28); and

Allsup, *The American G.I. Forum*, p. 21.
[12]Coalson, *The Development of the Migrant Farm Labor System in Texas*, pp. 107, 115.
[13]Allsup, *The American G.I. Forum*, p. 21; Acuña, *Occupied America*, 3rd ed., p. 276; Kibbe, *Latin Americans in Texas*, pp. 174, 177, 179, 180–81.
[14]Peña, *The Texas Mexican Conjunto*, pp. 126–28, 130–31.
[15]See Thomas H. Kreneck, *Mexican American Odyssey: Felix Tijerina, Entrepreneur and Civic Leader, 1905–1965* (College Station: Texas A&M University Press, 2001).
[16]Manuel Peña, *The Mexican American Orquesta* (Austin: University of Texas Press, 1999), pp. 100–01, 103–04, and Chapter 4.
[17]Treviño, *The Church in the Barrio*, pp. 5–7, 13, 43–47, 49–50, 55, 62, 67–70.
[18]Quote is from Ríos McMillan, "A Biography of a Man and His Newspaper," *Americas Review*, p. 147; Peña, *The Mexican American Orquesta*, pp. 113–20.
[19]Acuña, *Occupied America*, 3rd ed., p. 277.
[20]Allsup, *The American G.I. Forum*, p. 104.
[21]George N. Green, "The ILGWU in Texas, 1930–1970," *Journal of Mexican American History* 1 (Spring 1971): 150–51.
[22]Ledesma, "Unlikely Strikers," pp. 138–42.
[23]Acuña, *Occupied America*, 3rd ed., pp. 277–78; Ledesma, "Unlikely Strikers," pp. 157–79.
[24]Montejano, *Anglos and Mexicans in the Making of Texas*, p. 270.
[25]Allsup, *The American G.I. Forum*, p. 25.
[26]Montejano, *Anglos and Mexicans in the Making of Texas*, p. 270.
[27]George N. Green, "The Good Neighbor Commission and Texas Mexicans," in Jerrell H. Shofner and Linda V. Ellsworth, eds., *Ethnic Minorities in Gulf Coast Society* (Pensacola, Florida: Gulf Coast History and Humanities

Conference, 1979), pp. 112–13, 124–25.
[28]Allsup, *The American G.I. Forum*, p. 65; Ozzie Simmons, *Anglo-Americans and Mexican Americans in South Texas* (New York: Arno Press, 1974), pp. 296–315. A work portraying bossism in a different light than do most general studies (as corrupt opportunists) is J. Gilberto Quezada, *Border Boss: Manuel B. Bravo and Zapata County* (College Station: Texas A&M University Press, 1999).
[29]Montejano, *Anglos and Mexicans in the Making of Texas*, pp. 280–81; Ignacio García, *United We Win: The Rise and Fall of the Raza Unida Party* (Tucson: MASRC, University of Arizona Press, 1989), pp. 7–8.
[30]Montejano, *Anglos and Mexicans in the Making of Texas*, p. 281; Matt Meier, *Mexican American Biographies* (New York: Greenwood Press, 1988), p. 217. See further, Mario T. García, *The Making of a Mexican American Mayor: Raymond L. Telles of El Paso* (El Paso: The University of Texas at El Paso and Texas Western Press, 1998).
[31]Madla, "The Political Impact of Latin Americans and Negroes in Texas Politics," pp. 73–74; James R. Soukup, et al., *Party and Factional Divisions in Texas* (Austin: University of Texas Press, 1964), pp. 133–34.
[32]García, *Mexican Americans*, pp. 74, 75–76, 77, 78, 79, 82–83; San Miguel, "*Let All of Them Take Heed*," p. 114; Montejano, *Anglos and Mexicans in the Making of Texas*, p. 279.
[33]Sister Frances Jerome Woods, *Mexican Ethnic Leadership in San Antonio* (Washington D.C.: Catholic University of America Press, 1949), pp. 109–10; Eugene Rodríguez, *Henry B. González: A Political Profile* (New York: Arno Press, 1976), p. 47.
[34]Allsup, *The American G.I. Forum*, pp. 33, 40–49; Montejano, *Anglos and Mexicans*

in the Making of Texas, p. 279. The definitive study on the Felix Longoria episode is Carroll, *Felix Longoria's Wake*. See further, Ignacio García, *Hector P. Garcia: In Relentless Pursuit of Justice* (Houston: Arte Público Press, 2002), pp. 104–39. This latter work is presently the best biography of Dr. Héctor P. García.
[35]De León, *Ethnicity in the Sunbelt*, p. 129; Henry A. J. Ramos, *The American G.I. Forum: In Pursuit of the Dream 1948–1983* (Houston: Arte Público Press, 1998), pp. 27–30.
[36]San Miguel, "*Let All of Them Take Heed*," p. 117; Guadalupe San Miguel, Jr., "The Struggle Against Separate and Unequal Schools: Middle Class Mexican Americans in the Desegregation Campaign in Texas, 1929–1957," *History of Education Quarterly* 32 (Fall, 1983): 348. For a good discussion of the dismal facilities in which Mexican American children in South Texas studied, see Patrick J. Carroll, "Tejano Living and Educational Conditions in World War II South Texas," *South Texas Studies* 5 (Victoria: The Victoria College Press, 1994).
[37]Allsup, *The American G.I. Forum*, pp. 79–80.
[38]San Miguel, "*Let All of Them Take Heed*," pp. 118–19.
[39]*Ibid.*, pp. 123–24.
[40]*Ibid.*, pp. 125–26, 133–34; Jorge Rangel and Carlos Alcalá, "Project Report: De Jure Segregation of Chicanos in Texas Schools," *Harvard Civil Rights–Civil Liberties Law Review* 7 (March 1972): 326.
[41]San Miguel, "*Let All of Them Take Heed*," pp. 142–43; De León, *Ethnicity in the Sunbelt*, pp. 135–36.
[42]Allsup, *The American G.I. Forum*, pp. 73–77. Michael A. Olivas, "*Hernández v. Texas*: A Litigation History," in Olivas, ed., "*Colored Men*" and "*Hombres Aquí*,"

pp. 209–22; and Ian Haney López, "Race and Colorblindness after *Hernández* and *Brown*," in *ibid.*, p. 41–52.
[43]Ricardo Romo, "George I. Sánchez and the Civil Rights Movement," *La Raza Law Journal* 1 (1986): 342, 343, 353, 354, 357, 360, 361.
[44]Green, "The Good Neighbor Commission," p. 114; Clinchy, "Equality of Opportunity for Latin Americans," pp. 77, 87, 96; De León, *Ethnicity in the Sunbelt*, p. 132; Allsup, *The American G.I. Forum*, pp. 104–105. On the position that LULAC took against the Bracero Program, see Craig A. Kaplowitz, *LULAC, Mexican Americans, and National Policy* (College Station: Texas A&M University Press, 2005), pp. 40–43.
[45]Allsup, *The American G.I. Forum*, pp. 103, 107–08; Kaplowitz, *LULAC*, pp. 46–51.
[46]Allsup, The American G.I. Forum, pp. 109, 110; Kaplowitz, *LULAC*, pp. 54–57.
[47]Félix D. Almaráz, Jr., *Knight Without Armor: Carlos E. Castañeda, 1896–1958* (College Station: Texas A&M University Press, 1999), p. xiii; García, *Mexican Americans*, p. 250.
[48]García, *Desert Immigrants*, pp. 287–88.
[49]*New Handbook of Texas* IV, 770–71.
[50]Américo Paredes, *Humanidad: Essays in Honor of George I. Sánchez* (Los Angeles: Chicano Studies Center Publications, 1977), pp. 121–22.
[51]*New Handbook of Texas*, IV, 953–54.
[52]Meier, *Mexican American Biographies*, pp. 174–75.
[53]Montejano, *Anglos and Mexicans in the Making of Texas*, p. 281.
[54]San Miguel, "*Let All of Them Take Heed*," pp. 114–15; Montejano, *Anglos and Mexicans in the Making of Texas*, p. 280; Grebler, et. al., *The Mexican American People*, pp. 150–51.
[55]Montejano, *Anglos and Mexicans in the Making of Texas*, pp. 275–77.

CHAPTER NINE

[1]Ignacio M. García, *Chicanismo: The Forging of a Militant Ethos Among Mexican Americans* (Tucson: The University of Arizona Press, 1997), pp. 120–21, 123–24, 126, 128–30.

[2]Calvert, De León, and Cantrell, *The History of Texas*, 4th ed., p. 417.

[3]Peña, *The Texas Mexican Conjunto*, p. 131; and Mario Barrera, *Race and Class in the Southwest: A Theory of Racial Inequality* (Notre Dame: University of Notre Dame Press, 1979), p. 132.

[4]Montejano, *Anglos and Mexicans in the Making of Texas*, pp. 276–78; Calvert, De León, and Cantrell, *A History of Texas*, 4th ed., pp. 403–04.

[5]De León, *Ethnicity in the Sunbelt*, p. 167.

[6]David R. Johnson, et al., eds., *Politics of San Antonio: Community, Progress, and Power* (Lincoln: University of Nebraska Press, 1983), p. 196. In 1961, President John F. Kennedy appointed Reynaldo Garza of Brownsville as the first Tejano Federal District Judge. Louise Ann Fisch, *All Rise: Reynaldo G. Garza: The First Mexican American Federal Judge* (College Station: Texas A&M University Press, 1996).

[7]De León, *Ethnicity in the Sunbelt*, pp. 167–68; García, *Chicanismo*, p. 23; Ignacio M. García, *Viva Kennedy: Mexican Americans in Search of Camelot* (College Station: Texas A&M University Press, 2000), pp. 172–73.

[8]De León, *Ethnicity in the Sunbelt*, pp. 168–69. See further Armando Navarro, *Mexicano Political Experience in Occupied Aztlán: Struggles and Change* (Walnut Creek, Calif.: AltaMira Press, 2005), pp. 305–13.

[9]Marilyn Rhinehart and Thomas H. Kreneck, "The Minimum Wage March of 1966: A Case Study in Mexican American Politics, Labor, and Identity," *The Houston Review* 11 (1989).

[10]García, *Chicanismo*, pp. 3, 4, 7–11, 16, 143; Navarro, *Mexicano Political Experience in Occupied Aztlán*, pp. 313–20.

[11]San Miguel, "*Let All of Them Take Heed,*" pp. 167–68.

[12]Acuña, *Occupied America*, 5th ed., p. 359; Navarro, *Mexicano Political Experience in Occupied Aztlán*, pp. 357–58; Kaplowitz, *LULAC*, pp. 87–88.

[13]Ignacio García, *United We Win: The Rise and Fall of the Raza Unida Party* (Tucson: MASRC, University of Arizona Press, 1989), pp. 10–11; De León, *Ethnicity in the Sunbelt*, p. 174; Márquez, *LULAC*, pp. 68–70.

[14]San Miguel, "*Let All of Them Take Heed,*" pp. 169–177; García, *Chicanismo*, p. 11.

[15]San Miguel, "*Let All of Them Take Heed,*" pp. 177–181. Guadalupe San Miguel, Jr., "Mexican American Organizations and the Changing Politics of School Desegregation in Texas, 1945–1980," *Social Science Quarterly* 63 (December 1982): 710.

[16]San Miguel, "*Let All of Them Take Heed,*" pp. 192–94, 195–96.

[17]García, *United We Win*, pp. 11, 17; Muñoz, *Youth, Identity, Power*, p. 51. See especially Armando Navarro, *Mexican American Youth Organization: Avant-Garde of the Chicano Movement in Texas* (Austin: University of Texas Press, 1995). The Chicano movement in Lubbock is discussed in Romero, "The Mexican American Frontier Experience in Twentieth Century Northwest Texas," pp. 144–52.

[18]De León, *Ethnicity in the Sunbelt*, pp. 175, 176, 177; Navarro, *Mexicano Political Experience in Occupied Aztlán*, pp. 357–58.

[19]García, *United We Win*, pp. 24–26, 29.

[20]*Ibid.*, pp. 37, 41; John Staples Shockley, *Chicano Revolt in a Texas Town* (Notre Dame: University of Notre Dame Press, 1974), pp. 120–24. For more on the politics of Crystal City during

the 1970s as well as those of the Raza Unida Party during the same decade, see José Angel Gutiérrez, *The Making of a Chicano Militant: Lessons from Cristal* (Madison: University of Wisconsin Press, 1998); Armando Navarro, *The Cristal Experiment: A Chicano Struggle for Community Control* (Madison: University of Wisconsin Press, 1998); and Armando Navarro, *La Raza Unida Party: A Chicano Challenge to the U.S. Two-Party Dictatorship* (Philadelphia: Temple University Press, 2000).

[21]García, *United We Win*, pp. 29, 45, 46–47, 49; Shockley, *Chicano Revolt*, pp. 127–38. Regarding the movement for educational equality in a large metropolis during the same period, see Guadalupe San Miguel, Jr., *Brown, Not White: School Integration and the Chicano Movement in Houston* (College Station: Texas A&M University Press, 2001).

[22]García, *United We Win*, pp. 47, 50; Shockley, *Chicano Revolt*, pp. 133, 181–83.

[23]García, *United We Win*, pp. 19, 20, 50, 53, 56–57; Muñoz, *Youth, Identity, Power*, p. 101.

[24]García, *United We Win*, pp. 59–60, 62–63; Shockley, *Chicano Revolt*, pp. 183–89.

[25]García, *United We Win*, pp. 72–73.

[26]*Ibid*, pp. 84, 128.

[27]*Ibid.*, pp. 61–62, 152, 156, 157–61, 164–65, 166–68.

[28]Cotera, *Diosa y Hembra*, pp. 107–08; García, *United We Win*, p. 230; *New Handbook of Texas*, III, 472–73.

[29]García, *United We Win*, pp. 33, 229–30; Acosta and Winegarten, *Las Tejanas*, pp. 236-38.

[30]De León, *Ethnicity in the Sunbelt*, pp. 196–98; Acosta and Winegarten, *Las Tejanas*, pp. 230–49.

[31]García, *Chicanismo*, pp. 136, 137.

[32]Treviño, *The Church in the Barrio*, Chapter 7.

[33]García, *United We Win*, pp. 180–81, 189, 190, 191, 205–06.

[34]*Ibid.*, pp. 208–09, 210, 213; Montejano, *Anglos and Mexicans in the Making of Texas*, p. 289.

[35]García, *United We Win*, pp. 202, 227, 219; García, *Chicanismo*, pp. 141–42; Gutiérrez, *Making of a Chicano Militant*, p. 275.

[36]Montejano, *Anglos and Mexicans in the Making of Texas*, pp. 289, 290–92; De León, *Ethnicity in the Sunbelt*, p. 198; García, *Chicanismo*, pp. 3, 9.

[37]García, *United We Win*, pp. 229, 231. See Further, Navarro, *Mexicano Political Experience in Occupied Aztlán*, pp. 320–26; Peña, *The Mexican American Orquesta*, pp. 114–20, 211–20; "Chicano Literary Renaissance," *New Handbook of Texas*, II, 71–72; "Mexican American Theater," *Ibid.*, IV, 679–80; and "Chicano Mural Movement," *Ibid.*, II, 72–73.

[38]*New Handbook of Texas*, II, 780; Anthony Quiroz, "'We Are Not Wetbacks, Meskins, or Slaves, but Human Beings': The Economy Furniture Strike of 1968–1971," in De León, ed., *Tejano Epic*, Chapter 9; Yolanda G. Romero, "Adelante Compañeros: The Sanitation Workers' Struggle in Lubbock, Texas, 1968–1972," West Texas Historical Association *Yearbook* 69 (1993).

[39]Laurie Coyle, Gail Hershatter, and Emily Honig, "Women at Farrah: An Unfinished Story," in Magdalena Mora and Adelaida R. del Castillo, eds., *Mexican Women in the United States: Struggles Past and Present* (Los Angeles: Chicano Studies Research Center, 1980), pp. 117–44; Ledesma, "Unlikely Strikers," pp. 179–201.

[40]*Nuestro*, November 1979, p. 25; *Texas Observer*, Austin, Texas, February 3, 1978, p. 10.

[41]*Nuestro*, January 1979, pp. 27–28. Excellent coverage of the Texas farm

workers movement during this era is provided in Timothy Paul Bowman, "What About Texas?: The Forgotten Cause of Antonio Orendain and the Rio Grande Valley Farm Workers, 1966–1982" (M.A. Thesis: University of Texas at Arlington, 2005).
[42]*Texas Observer*, April 17, 1981, pp. 4–5.

CHAPTER TEN
[1]Katherine Leal Unmuth, "Tyler Case Opened Schools to Illegal Migrants," *Dallas Morning News*, June 14, 2007, www.dallasnews.com/shared-content/dws/news/dmn/stories/061107dnmetplyler.3a34, accessed April 11, 2008.
[2]Census of Population, 1990, *General Social and Economic Characteristics, Texas*, CP-2-45, Table 12, p. 124.
[3]Betsy Guzmán, *The Hispanic Population: Census 2000 Brief* (Washington D.C.: U.S. Census Bureau, 2001), p. 4, Table 2: "Hispanic Population by Type for Regions, States, and Puerto Rico: 1990 and 2000," places the figure for Mexicans (of Hispanic-type) at 5,071,963. According to census figures for Texas for the year 2000, the total foreign-born population was 2,899,640, of which 64.8% was Mexico-born. If the Mexico-born population was 1,878,967 and the total Mexican (of Hispanic-type) population in the state was 5,071,963, then the percent of native-born population amounts to 63.0%. Nolan Malone, et al., *The Foreign-Born Population: Census 2000 Brief* (Washington D.C.: U.S. Census Bureau, 2003), p. 7 (Table 4: "Percent Distribution of the Foreign-Born Population by World Regions of Birth for the United States, Regions, States, and Puerto Rico: 2000").
[4]*Newsweek*, June 8, 1987, pp. 27–28; San Angelo *Standard-Times*, San Angelo,

Texas, December 16, 1989, p. 12A; December 17, 1989, p. 1A.
[5]Montejano, *Anglos and Mexicans in the Making of Texas*, pp. 299, 285; Acuña, *Occupied America*, 5th ed., p. 357; García, *Chicanismo*, p. 142.
[6]Muñoz, *Youth, Identity, Power*, pp. 175, 184.
[7]Acuña, *Occupied America*, 5th ed., pp. 357–58; Ignacio M. García, "Backwards From Aztlán: Politics in the Age of Hispanics," in Roberto M. De Anda, *Chicanas and Chicanos in Contemporary Society* (Boston: Allyn and Bacon, 1996), p. 198.
[8]Neil Foley, "Becoming Hispanic: Mexican Americans and the Faustian Pact with Whiteness," in Neil Foley, ed., *Reflexiones 1997: New Directions in Mexican American Studies* (Austin: CMAS Books, University of Texas at Austin, 1998), pp. 53–70. On the word "Latino," see José Cuello, *Latinos and Hispanics: A Primer on Terminology* (Detroit, Mich.: Wayne State University Press, 1996), and Suzanne Oboler and Deena J. González, compilers, *The Oxford Encyclopedia of Latino and Latinas in the United States*, 4 vols. (Oxford: Oxford University Press, 2005), vol. 2, "Latino Identities and Ethnicities," pp. 512–13.
[9]Montejano, *Anglos and Mexicans in the Making of Texas*, p. 287; Muñoz, *Youth, Identity, Power*, pp. 175, 176; García, *Chicanismo*, p. 143.
[10]Navarro, *Mexicano Political Experience in Occupied Aztlán*, pp. 521–22.
[11]Márquez, *LULAC*, pp. 94–95; Acuña, *Occupied America*, 5th ed., p. 359; Muñoz, *Youth, Identity, Power*, pp. 178, 181; Navarro, *Mexicano Political Experience in Occupied Aztlán*, pp. 529–32.
[12]Muñoz, *Youth, Identity, Power*, p. 175; Acuña, *Occupied America*, 5th ed., p. 385; García, *Chicanismo*, pp. 143, 144.
[13]De León, *Ethnicity in the Sunbelt*, p. 203;

Navarro, *Mexicano Political Experience in Occupied Aztlán*, pp. 474, 483.

[14]García, *Chicanismo*, pp. 8, 9, 15–16, 144; García, "Backwards from Aztlán," pp. 191, 192, 193, 197–201; Navarro, *Mexicano Political Experience in Occupied Aztlán*, pp. 410–11; García, *Viva Kennedy*, pp. 176–78.

[15]*Texas Almanac and State Industrial Guide, 1976–1977* (Dallas: A. H. Bello, 1975), pp. 612–13, 566–71, 572–79; *Texas Almanac, 2002–2003* (Dallas: Dallas Morning News, 2001), pp. 429–30, 467–77.

[16]Montejano, *Anglos and Mexicans in the Making of Texas*, pp. 293, 294.

[17]*Ibid.*, p. 291.

[18]Acuña, *Occupied America*, 5th ed., p. 357; De León, *Ethnicity in the Sunbelt*, p. 206.

[19]García, "Backwards from Aztlán," pp. 193, 198, 199; Montejano, *Anglos and Mexicans in the Making* of Texas, pp. 306–07; Muñoz, *Youth Identity, Power*, p. 182; David Montejano, "On Hopwood: The Continuing Challenge," in Foley, ed., *Reflexiones 1997*, pp. 133–56; Navarro, *Mexicano Political Experience in Occupied Aztlán*, p. 458.

[20]Acuña, Occupied America, 3rd ed., p. 417; *Texas Observer*, July 29, 1988, p. 6; Juan A. Sepúlveda Jr., *The Life and Times of Willie Velásquez: Su Voto es su Voz* (Houston: Arte Público Press, 2003); Navarro, *Mexicano Political Experience in Occupied Aztlán*, pp. 539–42.

[21]Meier, *Mexican American Biographies*, pp. 245–46; Gonzales, *Hispanic American Voluntary Organizations*, pp. 157–60.

[22]San Miguel, *"Let All of Them Take Heed,"* pp. 185–86.

[23]*Ibid.*, pp. 197, 198–200.

[24]*Ibid.*, pp. 201, 208, 209, 210.

[25]*Ibid.*, pp. 173–74.

[26]*New Handbook of Texas*, II, 784–85; Paul A. Sracic, *San Antonio v. Rodríguez and the Pursuit of Equal Education: The Debate over Discrimination and School Funding* (Lawrence: University Press of Kansas, 2006), p. 131.

[27]Acosta and Winegarten, *Las Tejanas*, pp. 287–88; Bert Almon, *This Stubborn Self: Texas Autobiographies* (Fort Worth: TCU Press, 2002), Chapters 11 and 13; and Nicholas Kanellos, ed., *Herencia: The Anthology of Hispanic Literature of the United States* (Oxford: Oxford University Press, 2002), pp. 15–16.

[28]*Texas Observer*, April 17, 1981, p. 5.

[29]*Ibid.*, February 2, 1979, pp. 18, 19; April 17, 1981, p. 6.

[30]Letter of Rebecca Flores Harrington to author, December 19, 1990, in author's files.

[31]*Texas Observer*, April 17, 1981, pp. 6, 7; September 11, 1981, p. 8; May 17, 1985, pp. 6–7.

[32]Letter of Rebecca Flores Harrington to author, December 19, 1990, in author's files; *Texas Observer*, May 17, 1985, p. 7.

[33]*Texas Observer*, March 21, 1986, p. 11; Letters of Juanita Valdez-Cox, November 2, 1998, and Rebecca Flores Harrington, August 3, 1998, to Arnoldo De León, in author's files.

[34]www.lupenet.org/

[35]Benjamin Marquez, "Organizing Mexican-American Women in the Garment Industry: *La Mujer Obrera*," *Women and Politics* 15 No. 1 (1995): 65–87.

[36]Montejano, *Anglos and Mexicans in the Making of Texas*, pp. 299–300; Johnson, et al., eds., *Politics of San Antonio*, Chapter 9; Roberto E. Villarreal, "EPISO and Political Empowerment: Organizational Politics in a Border City," *Journal of Borderlands Studies* 3 (Fall 1988): 85.

[37]De León, *Ethnicity in the Sunbelt*, pp. 214, 215.

[38]*New Handbook of Texas*, V, 392–93.

[39]Thomas Macías, *Mestizo in America: Generations of Mexican Ethnicity in*

the Suburban Southwest (Tucson: The University of Arizona Press, 2006), especially Chapters 2 and 3.

CHAPTER ELEVEN

[1]www.hispaniconline.com/magazine/2003/dec/CoverStory/index.html; accessed April 3, 2008; http://en.wikipedia.org/wiki/Ricardo_Sanchez

[2]San Antonio *Express-News*, San Antonio, Texas, August 27, 2004, p.1A; August 11, 2005, p. 1A.

[3]Texas State Data Center, www.txsdc.utsa.edu/tpepp/2006ASREstimates//alldata.pdf, accessed April 1, 2008.

[4]Houston *Chronicle*, Houston, Texas, August 9, 2007, p. 1A; Anne Marie Weiss-Armush, *North Texas Immigration 2005: Dallas . . . A Blueprint for the Future. and the Future is now!* www.dfwinternational.org/resource_center/Study_of_north_TexasImmigrant_communities_2005.pdf, accessed April 3, 2008.

[5]For Latina officials serving (or having served) in various elected positions and appointed posts, *see* Sonia R. García, et al., *Políticas: Latina Public Officials in Texas* (Austin: University of Texas Press, 2008).

[6]The Houston *Chronicle*, November 6, 2002, p. 1A.

[7]The Houston *Chronicle*, September 15, 2007, 6A; Bill Minutaglio, *The President's Counselor: The Rise to Power of Alberto Gonzales* (Scranton: HarperCollins, Publisher, 2006).

[8]www.texasobserver.org/article.php?aid=2254, accessed April 8, 2008; The Houston *Chronicle*, August 5, 2006, p. 1A.

[9]www.LULAC.org/about/president.html, accessed April 10, 2008; Navarro, *Mexicano Political Experience in Occupied Aztlán*, pp. 635–36.

[10]Houston *Chronicle*, September 3, 2006, p. 1B.

[11]Guadalupe San Miguel, Jr., *Contested Policy: The Rise and Fall of Federal Bilingual Education in the United States, 1960–2001* (Denton: University of North Texas Press, 2004), Chapter 4.

[12]http://www.interversity.org/lists/arnl/archives/Jun2003/msg00201.html, accessed April 13, 2008; Houston *Chronicle*, September 3, 2006, p. 1B; Calvert, De León, and Cantrell, *The History of Texas*, 4th ed, pp. 454–55.

[13]San Angelo *Standard Times*, San Angelo, Texas, January 28, 2006, p. 1A.

[14]Olivas, ed., *"Colored Men" and "Hombres Aquí,"* p. xix; Austin *American-Statesman*, May 5, 2007, p. 17A; May 31, 2007, p. 1B.

[15]www.tache.org/

[16]Navarro, *Mexicano Political Experience in Occupied Aztlán*, p. 411; www.floc.com/documents/IRContributons.pdf, accessed April 14, 2008.

[17]Houston *Chronicle*, April 9, 2006, p. 1B; April 12, 2006, p. 1A.

[18]www.txsdc.utsa.edu/tpepp/2006ASREstimates//alldata.pdf, and http://factfinder.census.gov/servlet/STTable?_bm=y&-state=st&-context=st&-qr_name=ACS_2006_EST_G00_S0506&-ds_name=ACS_2006_EST_G00_&-tree_id=306&-_caller=geoselect&-geo_id=04000US48&-format=&-_lang=en, accessed April 8, 2008.

[19]www.truthout.org/docs_2006/041106F.shtml, accessed April 8, 2008.

[20]www.floc.com/documents/IRContributions.pdf, accessed April 14, 2008.

[21]www.texasobserver.org/article.php?aid=2453, accessed April 8, 2008.

Index

96, 114–116, 124, 125, 138, 150–152,
162–163; in ranches, 27, 29, 46, 50, 60,
64, 90; skilled, 30, 136, 154; unskilled,
50, 60, 90, 122, 136, 154; women, 67,
82. *See also* businesspeople, middle class,
professionals, and labor unions
labor unions, 63–64, 94–96, 114, 134,
150–152
La Crónica, 97
La Cruz Blanca, 81
Ladies Council (LULAC), 114, 128
Ladies G.I. Forum Auxiliaries, 128
La Grán Liga Mexicana, 82
La Grán Liga Mexicanista, 97
La Grulla, Texas, 70
Laguna Seca Ranch, 50
Lake Texcoco, 9
La Liga Femenil Mexicanista, 97
Lamesa, Texas, 87
La Mujer Obrera, 164
Lancastrian, 28
land grants, 45–46, 49
Land League of America, 95
la noche triste, 9
La Prensa, 84, 93, 99, 103, 108, 124
La Raza Unida party. *See* Raza Unida party
Laredo, Texas: 29, 55, 67, 69, 81, 85, 93,
94, 97, 113, 115, 168; *gente decente* in,
61; growth in, 60; immigration to, 75,
78; labor activity in, 64, 68, 97, 115,
116; middle class in, 78, 90, 93, 113;
origins of, 11, 16; politics in, 51, 52, 61;
population of, 23, 28
Larrazolo, Octaviano, 62
Las Hermanas, 147
La Salle County, 145
Latin American Health Week, 113
Latin Americans, 112, 119, 131
Latin Sons of Texas, 114

Latino, 4, 155, 168
La Unión del Pueblo Entero (LUPE), 163
La Volanta, 85
Law of April 6, 1830, 33
law enforcement, 45
League of Latin American Citizens, 102
League of Loyal Americans, 113
League of United Latin American Citizens
(LULAC), 105, 111–112, 113–114, 118,
128, 129, 130, 131, 133, 136–139 *passim,*
140, 141, 146, 149, 155, 159, 169, 172
ley de fuga, 45
Liga Pro-Defensa Escolar, 112, 117, 127
Littlefield, Texas, 87
Little Mexico, 77
Little School of the 400, 129–130
Limón, José E., 68, 69
Lockhart, Texas, 145
longhorns, 46
Longoria, Beatriz, 120
Longoria, Eva, 175
Longoria, Félix, 120, 121, 128
López, José, 153, 154
López, José M., 117
Los Ojuelos Ranch, 50
Los Olmos, Texas, 68
Louisiana, 15, 21, 24, 25, 26, 29, 41, 50
Loyal American Democrats, 127
Lozano, Ignacio E., 84
Lozano, Juan Elias, 39
Lozano, Paula, 39
Lubbock, Texas, 87, 136, 150
LULAC News, 114
lynching, 56, 91, 96, 98, 101

machismo, 67
Machuca, J. C., 114
Magón, Ricardo Flores, 55, 81, 98
Martínez, Ana Luisa, 62

Mexican Americans in Texas: A Brief History, Third Edition
Developmental Editor and Copy Editor: Andrew J. Davidson
Production Editor: Linda Gaio
Typesetter: Bruce Leckie
Proofreader: Claudia Siler
Cartographer: James Bier
Cover Design: Linda Gaio

CPSIA information can be obtained
at www.ICGtesting.com
Printed in the USA
BVHW082245110820
585987BV00024B/355